CHOOSING Glory

©2009 Lili DeHoyos Anderson, Ph. D.

All Rights Reserved. No part of this book may be reproduced in any form or by any means without permission from the author. Requests for permission may be made by contacting the author at lilianderson.com. The views expressed herein are the responsibility of the author, and do not necessarily represent the position of the Church of Jesus Christ of Latter-day Saints.

Cover and Book Design by Nate and Maren Ingles

These Are Great Days Publishing Company, LLC

"Do not let us speak of darker days; let us speak rather of sterner days. These are not dark days: these are great days--the greatest days our country has ever lived; and we must all thank God that we have been allowed, each of us according to our stations, to play a part in making these days memorable in the history of our race."

—Winston Churchill, In an address at Harrow School, 29 October 1941

ISBN 978-0-615-29979-2

Printed in the United States of America

10 9 8 7 6 5 4 3 2 1

Table of Contents

Acknowledgments vii
Preface xi
  1. More Than Future Glory 1
  2. The "Can't Skip" Principle 21
  3. Telestial Counterfeits 29
  4. Safe Dating and Marriage Choices 49
  5. From Victim to Non-Victim 61
  6. Moving Toward Celestial Marriage 77
  7. Better Parenting 97
  8. Worst Things First 119
  9. How to Be Anxiously Engaged
      Without Being Anxious 135
 10. A Stepping Stone, Not a Stopping Place 163
 11. Choosing Our Glory 175
Appendix A - Selected References 197
Appendix B - Judgement Without Condemnation 227
Index 233
Scripture Index 239

Acknowledgments

There are many, many people I wish to thank for their help in the completion of this book:

My husband, Chris, for his unfailing, and evidently inexhaustible, love and support in this and every other part of my life. He listens; he adds understanding and insight; he absorbs the overflow of my intensity; he gets me to the places I've committed to be; he uses his many skills, and acquires more, to advance my projects. I can neither conceive of nor do I desire to know how I would survive without him.

My children and their spouses have also demonstrated tremendous support, provided helpful feedback, and shown great patience during this process: Adam and Sara Anderson, Nate and Bethany Callister, Rob and Caitlin Justiniano, Dominic and Jen Anderson, Eden Anderson, Spencer and Faith Cotterell, Graydon Anderson, and Harper Anderson. I especially thank Faith for acting as my scheduling assistant, saving me a great deal of time and often protecting me from my tendency to over schedule. Caitlin accepted the essential job of checking all my sources and citations for accuracy.

Graydon continually volunteered for and completed random but necessary tasks. And Sara contributed countless hours (for which she refused compensation) to reading the developing manuscript: first, to reassure me that what I was writing in 15 and 20 minute increments was coherent, and then to offer intelligent and insightful feedback at literally every step of the process. I owe Sara a great deal.

Many others contributed in a variety of ways:

Chris Schoebinger, of Deseret Book, who suggested that I write this book.

Many clients who have encouraged, even prodded, me to complete this project. Many friends who have shown great interest and offered generous support along the way. I hesitate to name any knowing I cannot name all, but I must make particular mention of the following—

Emma Marroquin who generously contributes her time and business expertise to allow me more time for writing.

Mel and Joan Young and Scott and Cindy Higginson, who have encouraged me and offered their considerable talents and good ideas in a number of ways.

Julie Blasini, who came up with a title I love.

With perfect timing, David Brake, Founder and CEO of Content Connections, showed interest in the book and generously provided the professional services of his company. He introduced me to his associate, Holly McAllister, who is Project Director of Content Connections' AuthorBound Division. Holly set up their Content Assessment Portal (CAP) to carry out an online review process that was of great value in the final stages of manuscript revision. Thanks also to Becky Wilcken and Haley Birkeland of Content Connections. Becky administered the CAP, and Haley set up the community

ACKNOWLEDGMENTS

page for *Choosing Glory*. David and Holly continued to offer their professional expertise throughout the completion of the project.

Thanks to the following individuals who took the time to read and give feedback on the entire manuscript:

Celeste Ensign
Laurie Hildebrandt
Candy Hunt
Nance Kohlert
John Livingstone

Diana Merrill
Kristen Nelson
Laura Riggs
Kevin Theriot

And to the following individuals who read a selection of chapters, also offering thoughtful and valuable feedback:

Annette Ashton
Tami Benson
Alison Beytien
Julie Blasini
Julie Brannelly
Lisa Busch
Emily Call
Jaidi Clayton
Lisa Collett
Kay Collins
Connie Eddington
Marion Elton
Doug Forsha
Caroline Gappmeier
Claudene Gordon
Linda Hanks
McKenzi Harro
Cindy Higginson
Randalin Hilton
Ingrid Jones
Rebecca Jorgensen
Doug LeCheminant
Mary Louise LeCheminant
Chris Luders
Carrie Mannes
Carolyn Mildenhall

Tom Mildenhall
Shelly Moore
Calleen Morris
Annette Moss
Jennifer Neal
Christine Nelson
Evelyn Nelson
Elise Noorda
Debra O'Neil
Emily Orton
Judy Phan
Juli Rees
Carla Riggs
Elizabeth Riggs
Steve Rogers
Julie Schenk
Bonnie Schroeder
Stephen Sorensen
Verla Sorensen
Kammy Thompson
Emilee Tikalsky
Karen Truscott
Tami Ure
Kathryn DeSantis Walker
Mona White
Jennilyn Young

Many thanks to Amy Kendall, my wonderfully patient copyeditor, and to the talented Nate and Maren Ingles for cover design and layout, as well as for help with my website and a number of other marketing ideas and designs. Nate, Maren, and Amy logged many "extra miles" and late nights to bring this book to press.

Special thanks, also, to my sister, Sylvia Coates, a highly sought-after professional back-of-the-book indexer, who insisted on fitting into her extraordinarily busy schedule the time to do the index.

Preface

Many years ago, as a young wife and mother, I was reading through the Doctrine and Covenants as a part of my scripture study and saw again these verses:

> For he who is not able to abide the law of a celestial kingdom cannot abide a celestial glory.
>
> And he who cannot abide the law of a terrestrial kingdom cannot abide a terrestrial glory.
>
> And he who cannot abide the law of a telestial kingdom cannot abide a telestial glory . . . (D&C 88:22-24).

Although I had read these verses many times before, on this occasion I felt some concern. I wasn't sure what celestial law was. Or terrestrial, or telestial law, for that matter. What if I desired to qualify for celestial glory, but was in reality living only a terrestrial law? Judgment day might be a horribly rude awakening. Of course, such concerns didn't last for long, as I knew that "God granteth unto men according to their desires" (Alma 29:4) and He would not let an honest seeker of the celestial kingdom continue in ignorance forever without sending sufficient guidance, direction, and course correction, as needed. Nevertheless, I still desired to better understand the different laws of each of the three kingdoms. Further reading in section 88 of the Doctrine and Covenants emphasized:

> All kingdoms have a law given;
>
> And unto every kingdom is given a law; and unto every law there are certain bounds also and conditions.
>
> All beings who abide not in those conditions are not justified.
>
> And again, verily I say unto you, he hath given a law unto all things (D&C 88:36, 38-39, 42).

It became increasingly clear to me that the law of each kingdom constituted the bounds and conditions by which we must live on earth in order to inherit that kingdom hereafter. As I continued to read the scriptures and to apply their teachings to my life and in my roles as wife and mother, I started to see clearer and clearer distinctions between the laws of each kingdom. I learned that in the choices we make every day, each of us is choosing which level of law we will obey—telestial, terrestrial, or celestial. I saw that the law we choose to live does more than determine which kingdom we will ultimately inherit in the hereafter. The law we choose to obey brings a corresponding level of light, truth, intelligence, and glory into our lives (see D&C 93:36). I began to see how choosing to live a celestial law would impact life and relationships, and how living a terrestrial or telestial law would have a different and predictable impact. I learned that on a daily basis, the law we live affects the quality of life we live, the strength of our relationships, and our access to the Spirit, from which comes courage, conviction, and sanctification.

Years later, after my children were older and I had gone back to graduate school for a master's degree and later a doctorate, I saw that explaining the distinctions between levels of law was a useful tool in the individual, marriage, and family counseling work I did. Understanding the laws and their associated outcomes gave me tools as a clinical diagnostician and gave my clients tools to apply as individuals trying to live safer, happier lives; as partners trying to improve their marriages; and as parents trying to rear healthy, successful, and righteous children.

Let me explain a bit about how this book is organized. The concept of the three realms of law is explained in Chapter One. The three realms perspective is further elaborated in Chapters Two and Three. Then, with the framework somewhat fleshed out, the remainder of the book applies the concept to individual life, dating, choosing a spouse, marriage, parenting, stress, and life-long progression. The foundation of the three realms perspective gained in the first three chapters will make the concrete applications understandable and useful to the reader. The illustrations and applications should be more clear and satisfying because of the up-front investment. Finally, the book includes two appendices. Appendix A contains a selection of scriptural and prophetic statements, out of which the three realms perspective grew. Appendix B addresses the need for "righteous judgment" (JST, Matthew 7:1; John 7:24)—a necessary tool in applying the three realms perspective—and explains how correct judgment of good and evil is not intolerance. This is of particular importance in our politically correct society that regularly challenges the individual's right to determine right from wrong. This appendix also discusses the dangers of moral relativism and the difference between limiting freedoms, which is necessary in any society, and limiting agency, which is impossible. I hope some readers—especially those who are uncomfortable with the idea of making judgments—will take the time to at least glance through these appendices.

My purpose in writing this book is to make available an idea that has seemed to be of benefit and use to many students, clients, and others with whom I have shared it. I hope it is useful to you, as well.

—Lili De Hoyos Anderson, July 2009

CHAPTER ONE

More Than Future Glory

Safety from Danger, Safety from Complacency—Through a Three Realms Perspective

We are born for glory. Children of a glorious deity Who authored a plan for our progression. We, His offspring, choose how much of our Father's glory we will inherit. In the pre-earth life, our first estate, we chose the path of glory as evidenced by our presence on this planet. And in this mortal sphere—our second estate—we are deciding how much glory we will receive hereafter. Right here, right now, we are choosing our glory.

> And they who keep their first estate shall be added upon; and they who keep not their first estate shall not have glory in the same kingdom with those who keep their first estate; and they who keep their second estate shall have glory added upon their heads for ever and ever (Abraham 3:26).

But our choices in this life do not only determine our future glory. The principles we allow to govern our behavior every day determine how much light, truth, and intelligence—a measure of glory (see D&C 93:36)—we experience now. Some of us make choices that trap us in a telestial realm with telestial troubles, relationships, and outcomes. Some of us make choices that lift us to a more terrestrial realm of greater peace and safety, even in the midst of telestial troubles around us. And some of us make choices that lift us higher, refining us and preparing us for even greater glory.

While all of us are, of course, subject to the telestial world we live in, the principles of the gospel invite us to higher levels of light, *if we choose to embrace them.* Individually, all people who live on this planet choose how much light they want in their mortal lives. Occasionally, whole societies have embraced a certain level of light. Those in the City of Enoch, in Melchizedek's Salem, and those living on the American continent after the personal ministry of Jesus Christ were all able to achieve, through their choices, Zion societies. The world was still telestial, but those societies lived according to higher, celestial principles that lifted them to a better life.

So, how do we choose glory? The ideas in this book are intended to answer that question by first presenting a summary of telestial, terrestrial, and celestial laws, then discussing the implications of this perspective, and finally, by applying that framework to a number of life's concerns and challenges in ways that illustrate how we can find safety in our increasingly telestial world while avoiding the trap of settling for a decent terrestrial life.

Safety in a Dangerous World

The gospel of Jesus Christ gives us the light we need to find safety in our dangerous world. And the world *is* getting more dangerous. The scriptures have prophesied that it would happen, and prophets have told us it is happening *now*. We even know it will get worse before the Savior comes. In 2004,

More Than Future Glory

President Gordon B. Hinckley spoke of our world as "a world that is marching toward self-destruction," saying,

> . . . the family appears to be falling apart. The traditional family is under heavy attack. I do not know that things were worse in the times of Sodom and Gomorrah.[1]

Just a few weeks later, President Boyd K. Packer also spoke plainly:

> These are days of great spiritual danger for this people. The world is spiraling downward at an ever-quickening pace. I am sorry to tell you that it will not get better.
>
> I know of nothing in the history of the Church or in the history of the world to compare with our present circumstances. Nothing happened in Sodom and Gomorrah which exceeds the wickedness and depravity which surrounds us now.[2]

But there *is* safety. There *is* peace. God has not left us without comfort, without answers, or without tools. He does not desire that His people feel vulnerable and helpless in a deteriorating world. The Lord and His gospel are "the same yesterday, today, and forever." (2 Nephi 27:23, Mormon 9:9), and, in the Church of Jesus Christ of Latter-day Saints, we believe that the gospel has the answers to life's problems today and in every day, but sometimes we may struggle to understand how gospel principles translate into the concrete tools needed to fight back the tide of evil around us. The ideas in this book are intended

---

1. Gordon B. Hinckley, (address, worldwide leadership training satellite broadcast, January 10, 2004).

2. Boyd K. Packer, "On the Shoulders of Giants," (J. Reuben Clark Law Society devotional address, Brigham Young University, Provo, UT, Feb 28, 2004).

to help translate principles into tools for finding safety from telestial elements in our world.

Safety from Complacency

Of course, in spite of living in an increasingly telestial world, some of us may actually feel that, for the most part, our life and our relationships are comfortable and satisfying. Not only are we active in the Church and worthy of our temple recommend, but we also live gospel principles with a fair amount of consistency. Significantly, *those around us* may also live pretty much the same way. Our good lives and the good lives of those close to us can provide a level of safety and peace. So although we know the world is going down in flames, we may not feel much of the heat personally. Ironically, the blessings and comfort of a good life may put us at risk for complacency, for settling for "good enough" when the plan of salvation invites us to go much further—in reality, all the way to celestial life and glory. The ideas in this book are also intended to help us avoid the trap of settling for good, terrestrial lives.

The basic gospel doctrine of three realms of law, light, and glory can help us find safety from both danger and complacency.

Looking at Life Through a Three Realms Perspective

The plan of salvation teaches clearly that after this life the inhabitants of this earth, save for a few sons of perdition, will eventually inhabit one of three kingdoms of glory—telestial, terrestrial, or celestial. The scriptures explain:

> For he who is not able to abide the law of a celestial kingdom cannot abide a celestial glory.

> And he who cannot abide the law of a terrestrial kingdom cannot abide a terrestrial glory.
>
> And he who cannot abide the law of a telestial kingdom cannot abide a telestial glory . . . All kingdoms have a law given;
>
> And unto every kingdom is given a law; and unto every law there are certain bounds also and conditions.
>
> All beings who abide not in those conditions are not justified (D&C 88:22-24, 36, 38-39).

Each kingdom is governed by its own law, and with the choices we make every day, each of us is choosing which level of law we will obey—telestial, terrestrial, or celestial. But the law we live now does more than determine which kingdom we will ultimately inherit in the hereafter. On a daily basis, the law we live affects our quality of life, including the earthly consequences we deal with in mortality; the nature of our relationships; and our ability to heal from what has injured us, to forgive others, and to find peace.

The world has been through many cycles of righteousness and unrighteousness. In recent history, however, we have seen society drop from the somewhat terrestrial level of post-World War II, middle-class, American society to the more telestial society we see today. Understanding the differences between the telestial and terrestrial realms can give us ways to better protect ourselves and provide us with tools to deal more effectively with the telestial trouble all around us. Further, understanding the differences between the terrestrial and celestial realms can help us better evaluate our progress toward truly and completely coming to Christ.

How, then, do we recognize the differences between a telestial and a terrestrial world? How does it help us be safer and better equipped to deal with the troubles around us? And how do we distinguish between a good terrestrial life and the valiant life of one preparing for the celestial kingdom? We'll begin by reviewing the laws that govern each kingdom and recognizing the outcomes of living the laws of the different realms. Then we will discuss how those outcomes impact us individually and in our relationships.

Please understand—the intent of this book is not to designate rigid, inflexible labels for specific behaviors or for the individuals who behave in those ways. References to a "telestial roommate" or "terrestrial partner" are intended to describe individuals who *mostly* choose behaviors consistent with that level of law. Of course, human beings are complex, layered, and consistently inconsistent. Nevertheless, the doctrine of the three realms should remind and warn us that, ultimately, our choices do make of us telestial, terrestrial, or celestial beings.

WHEREVER WE ARE, WE CAN MOVE FORWARD.

Readers are likewise encouraged to avoid using the ideas presented here to make rigid determinations or to condemn their neighbors. The purpose of this information is to help each of us better understand the kind of life we are choosing and the kind of people we are becoming that we may more effectively avoid the dangers of the telestial and the complacency of the terrestrial. As we examine our own levels of behavior throughout the course of this book, we may be surprised to find that we are sometimes choosing telestial law, which may explain some of the difficulties of our lives. We may see how the telestial behavior of those around us affects us and find ways to protect ourselves from their actions. Perhaps we will find that we are in a terrestrial rut, satisfied with being pretty good, and determine that we need to more actively seek the next level—celestial law and celestial life. *The good news is that wherever we are, we can move forward.*

Telestial Law

Living telestial law can be described as immediate gratification and appetite satisfaction.[3] The natural man is in charge. People in a telestial realm focus on themselves and their own desires, often without concern for the needs or rights of others. They do what they want, when they want, largely governed by their appetites.

Appetites are not always evil. It is not evil to feel hunger or fatigue or sexual desire. Letting appetites govern us, however, is evil. Eating without restraint; indulging sexual appetites outside of legal and lawful marriage; being selfish, rude, or unkind; and lashing out in anger when hurt or offended are all behaviors that are offensive to God.

Pain, violence, and destruction are the outcomes of living telestially. Those close to the offender are usually the first to feel the pain, violence, and destruction. For instance, an abuser is living telestial law, but those he abuses will be first to experience the pain. Eventually, as the Old Testament prophet Hosea warned, the offender "shall reap the whirlwind" for he has "sown the wind" (Hosea 8:7), but this may take some time, justice being promised at the final harvest, not necessarily along life's paths.

Even in non-abusive relationships, living with telestial behaviors is painful. A roommate who is largely governed by his appetites and urges may consider your possessions to be fair game, borrow money he never returns, consider it his right to make noise even if you need to sleep, and expect you to put up with his temper, his moods, and his mess. Telestial friends, neighbors, or co-workers are similarly challenging, and a telestial spouse brings destructive behaviors into marriage

---

3. See Appendix A for scriptural foundation of telestial law.

and parenting relationships, sometimes including addictions, dishonesty, and infidelity.

While it may seem obvious that telestial living is undesirable and painful, this basic truth remains a mystery to some. Telestial lifestyles are so often advocated as the ultimate success in life. Television, movies, talk shows, billboards, and other media advertise how good life can be when you eat, drink, and make merry. They issue a not-so-subtle call to "grab all the gusto you can get," as an old beer commercial once invited. Not surprisingly, this all seems to attract a great deal of interest and envy, in spite of the constant evidence before us that money, status, fame, possessions, and beauty cannot buy happiness, no matter where you shop.

Terrestrial Law

Living terrestrial law is characterized by self-control and deferred or delayed gratification.[4] Learning to control the natural man brings us out of the telestial realm and into the terrestrial. Living in the terrestrial makes us safer and puts an end to our enmity with God (see Mosiah 3:19).

Obedience to the commandments of God, and even compliance with the basic rules of society, requires that we control our desires, appetites, and passions, and living with and around those who do the same makes for basically peaceful and safe lives. Terrestrial partners in marriage, while not perfect, are not painful or destructive to live with. They control their tempers; they tell the truth; they handle money responsibly and cooperatively, and they are not abusive, selfish, or addicted to substances or other destructive behaviors. They are faithful to their spouses, they keep their promises, and they are willing to work. Terrestrial neighbors are respectful of

---

4. See Appendix A for scriptural foundation of terrestrial law.

property and privacy, control their tempers, return borrowed items in good condition, don't disturb the peace, care for their residences, and so on. Terrestrial co-workers and roommates are likewise respectful of property, cooperative, honest, non-invasive of others' space or privacy, and maintain a pleasant temperament.

Exercising self-control and harnessing the natural man does not mean that one must live an ascetic life, denying oneself any and every pleasure. Rather, the person who lives terrestrial law often defers or delays pleasure for the right time and place. It is not that the terrestrial individual never eats, spends money, or has a good time, but that he enjoys these things in the appropriate context. Many of us were taught this kind of restraint as children: eat your vegetables before having ice cream, save your money and pay cash, get your homework done before you go out to play. Some of us learned these basic terrestrial patterns quite early and, whether we recognize it or not, we have enjoyed the benefits of terrestrial living ever since.

In the 1960s, Walter Mischel, a researcher at Stanford University, conducted studies with preschoolers to see if these young children had developed any ability to delay gratification. In what has come to be known as "The Marshmallow Experiment," several four-year-olds were seated in a room with a table and an adult interviewer. The adult told each child that he or she could eat one marshmallow now or wait twenty minutes until the adult returned to the room and receive two marshmallows. Some ate the marshmallow before the adult had even left the room. About one-third of the children waited to get the extra prize. Following these preschoolers into adolescence, researchers found that those who had demonstrated delayed gratification and waited for the extra marshmallow were better adjusted and more socially competent, self-assertive, trustworthy, dependable, and academically successful. These follow-up measures, taken ten years later, showed that the students who had successfully waited to get two marshmallows scored, on average, 210 points higher on the Scholastic Aptitude Test (a perfect score on the SAT was 1600) than students who had eaten one marshmallow right away. "The Marshmallow Test" was twice as accurate a predictor of SAT scores as IQ tests. It has been suggested that high levels of delayed gratification—which can be equated with terrestrial living—constitute the best predictor of success in every area of life.[5]

Individuals who are willing to delay gratification don't do so out of some bizarre streak of self-denial. They do so because there is a reason, and the reason is always along the same lines: I can satisfy my appetite right now, but if I deny myself this immediate pleasure, I will end up with something better. Reason supersedes appetites to convince us that it is worth a measure of immediate self-denial or discomfort to obtain something of greater value.

So a terrestrial student skips a party to study for an important test because she realizes good grades will be of greater benefit to her future life than one night of recreation. The terrestrial dieter gives up a second serving of a high-calorie dessert because he knows a healthy body is more satisfying in the long run than the quick-passing pleasure of eating the treat. The terrestrial wage-earner sets up a savings plan for retirement because she sees that future security will be more valuable than extra spending money right now. Our feelings might lean strongly toward the party, the dessert, or the extra spending money, but rationally, logically, sacrificing now for important future benefits makes more sense.

---

5. Yuichi Shoda, Walter Mischel, and Philip K. Peake, "Predicting adolescent cognitive and self-regulatory competencies from preschool delay of gratification: Identifying diagnostic conditions," *Developmental Psychology* 26, no. 6, (1990): 978-986.

Celestial Law

Christ makes the celestial standard clear: "Be ye therefore perfect, even as your Father which is in heaven is perfect" (Matthew 5:48). Celestial law might be summarized, then, as Christlike *being*.[6] *Being* like Jesus Christ is distinct from exhibiting Christlike behavior, which can be found at the terrestrial level. If we have self-control and we can delay gratification, we can *behave* like Christ, but we still are not *as He is*. In order to truly become as the Savior is, our hearts and behavior must be integrated; so not only do we *do* the right things, but we *feel* the right things. We are not only innocent of adulterous behavior; we are free of lustful thoughts. We are not only kind because we should be or because it works better; we see people as God does, and it is no longer in us to be *un*kind. We don't just tell the truth because it's right or because we have learned it works better in the long run; we live truthfully, and lying violates who we are. As we become more celestial, the laws of God are not merely observed, they are written in our hearts (see Jeremiah 31:33). At this level, we do the right things for the right reasons. We seek "the kingdom of God and his righteousness," and give Him the glory (Matthew 6:33, 3 Nephi 13:33).[7] We have not only clean hands but also a pure heart (see Psalms 24:4).

The outcomes of living celestial law are inner peace, the peace that passeth all understanding (see Philippians 4:7), and creation or rebirth. This kind of creation is not only a reference to the future, when celestialized individuals will be able to participate in the same kind of creative work that the Father does, but a reference to the birth of the *new creature* in each of us (see 2 Corinthians 5:17, Mosiah 27:26) as we are born of the Holy Ghost and sanctified (see Alma 13:12, 3 Nephi 27:20). At this level, we experience "the mighty change of

---

6. See Appendix A for scriptural foundation of celestial law.

7. See also Dallin H. Oaks, "Why Do We Serve?," *Ensign*, Nov 1984, 12.

heart" that Alma wrote of (Alma 5:14), and, like the people of King Benjamin, we have "no more disposition to do evil, but to do good continually" (Mosiah 5:2).

While it may be hard to visualize exactly what celestial life on this planet might be, it would include some specific qualities. An individual approaching the celestial lives with integrity, beginning with scrupulous honesty and including the consistency of an integrated life. In such individuals, "What you see is what you get." They don't have hidden vices, hypocrisies, or double standards. They are clean in body and in mind. They don't hurt others through intention or neglect. They walk "a peaceable walk" (Moroni 7:4). They don't get offended, and they are not offensive.[8] They are free of self-righteousness and condescension, and they struggle successfully against pride. Although they are "strict in the plain road" (2 Nephi 4:32) and they "obey . . . with exactness" (Alma 57:21), they are not stiff or haughty because of their commitment—they don't seek personal recognition. They judge righteous judgments (see JST, Matthew 7:1), and, while having charity for the sinner, they abhor sin. They are no "respecter[s] of persons" (Alma 1:30), and they don't consider themselves above others. They are not tied to the rewards of the world, and they are not covetous, even of their own possessions, but are prudent and wise in their stewardships. They let their light shine (see Matthew 5:16) so others are inspired and uplifted by coming in contact with them. Their spouses and children are also inspired and uplifted by them and receive the full benefit of their kindness, honesty, and service. They seek and receive guidance from the Spirit, "taking the Holy Spirit for their guide" (D&C 45:57) and receiving "many revelations daily" (Helaman 11:23).

---

8. This doesn't mean others might not sometimes be offended by honest, integrated living, which may be a reproach to the wicked (see 1 Nephi 16:2). Marion G. Romney once warned: "Now there are those among us who are trying to serve the Lord without offending the devil." (Marion G. Romney, "The Price of Peace," (devotional address, Brigham Young University, Provo, UT, March 1, 1955).

When around such individuals, we feel their genuine care and concern; they truly love other people (see Alma 26:31), and that love is a reflection of "the pure love of Christ" (Moroni 7:47), which seeks not just the temporal but the eternal welfare of others. The celestially striving individual lives as an agent, neither victim nor victimizer; not acting inappropriately toward others, neither suffering himself to be chronically victimized. He is at peace, living for the most part without agitation or worry. This individual is free of grudges and has found a healthy way to forgive those who have offended him. Finally:

> . . . he who doeth the works of righteousness shall receive his reward, even peace in this world, and eternal life in the world to come (D&C 59:23).

THE LAWS OF THE KINGDOMS

We can generalize and summarize the characteristics of the three realms in the following way:

CELESTIAL REALM—*The heart and the behavior are integrated.*

LAW	OUTCOMES
Christlike Being	Inner Peace
	Creation, New Birth

The celestial realm is built on a terrestrial foundation.

TERRESTRIAL REALM— *The natural man is harnessed.*

LAWS	OUTCOMES
Self-Control	External Peace
Deferred/Delayed Gratification	Safety, Prosperity

Those living terrestrially are not offensive to God.

TELESTIAL REALM— *The rule of the natural man.*

LAWS	OUTCOMES
Appetite Satisfaction	Pain
Immediate Gratification	Violence, Destruction

Those living telestially are a "law unto themselves" (Romans 2:14).

Making Judgments

We hear frequent reminders of the Savior's admonition in Matthew 7:1, "Judge not, that ye be not judged." Given such reminders, some readers may feel concern that the ideas in this book promote making judgments. They do. In fact, the three realm perspective is of no use unless we make some judgments. Remember, however, the Joseph Smith translation of this verse: "Judge not *unrighteously*, that ye be not judged: *but judge righteous judgment.*"[9] It is not judgment that the Lord prohibits, it is unrighteous judgment.[10]

Elder Dallin H. Oaks spoke on the subject of righteous judgment, saying that we must make intermediate, not final judgments.[11] As we consider in the upcoming chapters how to use the three realm perspective as a tool, it is intermediate judgments that are needed. God will be the final judge, presiding with perfect justice and mercy as each of His children receives his or her measure of glory. God knows our hearts and will take into perfect consideration many factors that combine to determine our choices and our accountability, including how much truth we have access to, what we have been taught, our level of understanding and experience, injuries we may have sustained, the traditions we have been reared with, and our desires and motivations. While we know that mercy cannot rob justice (see Alma 42:25), we must also recognize that our Heavenly Father's plan for us is referred to as "the plan of mercy" (Alma 42:15) and "the merciful plan of the great Creator" (2 Nephi 9:6). If we consider the repeated messages of God's love for His children in the scriptures, it should be undeniable that

---

9. Emphasis in original (or at least as it appears in the New Testament footnotes of the LDS scriptures).

10. See Appendix B, "Judgment Without Condemnation," for further discussion of this topic.

11. See Dallin H. Oaks, "Judge Not and Judging" (devotional address, Brigham Young University, Provo, UT, March 1, 1998).

God is looking for ways to bring us *in*to His kingdom, not for ways to keep us out. The Prophet Joseph Smith taught:

> Our heavenly Father is more liberal in His views, and boundless in His mercies and blessings, than we are ready to believe or receive.[12]

The scriptures teach that God cannot look upon sin with the least degree of allowance (see Alma 45:16, D&C 1:31), but that does not make Him a harsh, rejecting deity. He loves us. And because He loves us, He sent the Savior.

> For God so loved the world, that he gave his only begotten Son, that whosoever believeth in him should not perish, but have everlasting life.
>
> For God sent not his Son into the world to condemn the world; but that the world through him might be saved (John 3:16-17).

The Savior came to earth to show us the path by which we could rise above a telestial sphere, learn the safety of the terrestrial, and then fulfill the measure of our creation in becoming more like Him—more celestial. After marking that path, He completed His divine mission, offering His perfect life for our sake. And His "grace is sufficient" (Ether 12:26-27, 2 Corinthians 12:9, Moroni 10:32, D&C 17:8, D&C 18:31) to save us, if we do "all we can do" (2 Nephi 25:23).

We start from so many different places. Some learn the gospel in their youth, others much later. Some have kind and loving parents, others deal with the pain of abuse and neglect. Our strengths and weaknesses, and our trials and challenges differ greatly. God will take all of it into perfect account.

---

12. Joseph Smith, *Teachings of the Prophet Joseph Smith*, comp. Joseph Fielding Smith (Salt Lake City: Shadow Mountain, 1977), 257. See also Jeffrey R. Holland, "The Grandeur of God," *Ensign*, Nov 2003, 70.

As we pursue our earthly journeys, it should be obvious to all of us that, as complex human beings, we do not always fit neatly into one of the three discreet categories suggested by the three realms perspective. We may have consistent control over our natural man in many areas of life (terrestrial and potentially moving toward the celestial),[13] but still struggle with a bad temper (telestial)[14] or some other uncontrolled appetite or passion. Most of us, from time to time, have danced in more than one realm of law and light. The purpose here is not to become obsessive about categorizing behaviors or to be sidetracked into labeling everything and everyone around us, but to increase our awareness that the choices we make do lead us in a path that will culminate in either telestial, terrestrial, or celestial glory. *The gospel, and in fact the Savior Himself, invites us—no matter where we currently stand—to move forward in faith and to more consistently choose His path, leading to the kingdom of God.*

Safety in Our Time

If you read only this far in the book, I hope you will remember this: our society has deteriorated from a rather terrestrial society to an increasingly telestial society. Of course, this is not the first time the world has gone through the cycle of righteousness and iniquity, but prophecy makes it clear that, this time, the deterioration is going to continue until the second coming of the Savior, Jesus Christ. As things worsen, the ways we lived, got along with others, fell in love, conducted relationships, married, and reared children in a more terrestrial world won't work very well in the increasingly telestial environment. If we learn how to identify the destructive, telestial elements around

---

13. Alma 38:12 "See that ye bridle all your passions, that ye may be filled with love."

14. 3 Nephi 12:22 "Whosoever is angry with his brother shall be in danger of his judgment. And whosoever shall say to his brother, Raca, shall be in danger of the council; and whosoever shall say, Thou fool, shall be in danger of hell fire."

us and then learn to use good, solid terrestrial principles and behaviors, we can protect ourselves and our loved ones from much of the evil around us.

The (Most) Recent Loss of the Terrestrial

Since Adam and Eve were cast out of the Garden, this planet has been, generally speaking, in a telestial state. However, from time to time, some groups of people, because of their dedication to living higher laws, have been able to create higher-level societies. As previously mentioned, dramatic examples are seen in the City of Enoch and Melchizedek's Salem, whose inhabitants progressed to near-celestial, Zion societies.

Though certainly not a celestial society, post-World War II, middle-class America of the 50s and 60s managed to provide a largely terrestrial environment, and many of us who grew up during that time inherited a generally terrestrial foundation. We started out in a society that was based in Judeo-Christian beliefs and that promoted terrestrial values of self-control and deferred gratification. People accepted and sought the benefits of hard work, saving money, being faithful in marriage, and so on. Because these beliefs were widely accepted, they were reflected in literature, media, music, day-to-day experience, and almost in the very air we breathed. We did chores before watching TV. Our mothers used lay-away, not credit, to buy things. We watched shows like *Leave it to Beaver*, *Father Knows Best*, *Ozzie and Harriett*, *My Three Sons*, and *The Andy Griffith*

Show.¹⁵ Women were protected, children respected adults, hard work and honesty were valued and expected.

Watching those programs now, it's easy to think those times were naïve and unsophisticated. But perhaps what we call "sophistication" is merely resigned acceptance of increasingly evil practices that have lost the power to shock us. I remember, years ago, using children's literature award lists to find good books for my children to read. But during the early 80s, some of the awards stopped recognizing inspiring stories based on solid values and started honoring children's books dealing with "sophisticated" topics like premarital sex, violence, rebellion, drugs, and drinking. Prime time television started including shows like *The Simpsons, Beavis and Butthead, South Park*, and a host of family sitcoms where the children were smarter than their parents and teachers, so how *could* the kids treat adults with respect? Gone are the days when Andy Griffith's television son, Opie, got into big trouble if he was disrespectful to his teacher, Miss Crump, at school. Now, Andy should just be grateful Opie doesn't drink too much and comes home at night. Yes, the world is more sophisticated.

Alexander Pope described how society's morals decay through repeated exposure, almost without awareness:

> Vice is a monster of so frightful mien
>
> As, to be hated, needs but to be seen;
>
> Yet seen too oft, familiar with her face,

---

15. Younger readers may not be familiar with these television shows unless they watched them on *Nick at Nite*, as my children sometimes did. These shows generally depicted families where parents were good people, not perfect but doing their best to rear children with good values and often showing consistent wisdom and maturity in their behavior and in the examples they set. Children were also not perfect but were typically respectful and responsive to parental teachings and influence.

We first endure, then pity, then embrace.

("Essay on Man," epistle ii, line 217)

So, from the days when parents were scandalized that the new television series *Three's Company* featured a man and two women sharing an apartment as platonic roommates, we have come to a place where parents are grateful when they can limit their kids to watching PG-13 movies, even if they are a lot like the R-rated movies of a few years ago.

We no longer live in a terrestrial society. If we have eyes to see, we recognize the telestial on every side. Children today do not have the advantage of breathing terrestrial air and learning terrestrial principles as the societal default. Still, we don't have to feel vulnerable and helpless. The gospel really does have the answers. This book is intended to help us learn how to understand and apply the gospel in concrete ways to find greater safety, especially in these dangerous times.

CHAPTER TWO

The "Can't Skip" Principle

Building on a Terrestrial Foundation

As we come to better understand how living telestial, terrestrial, and celestial law is a choice we make day by day, we may be eager to focus on living more celestially. However, in order for our progress toward celestial life to be authentic and lasting, it must be built on the foundation of a terrestrial life. With very few exceptions, we progress step by step and cannot "skip" from the telestial to the celestial realm. Consider again Elder Neal A. Maxwell's explanation: "Initially . . . turning [toward God] reflects progress from telestial to terrestrial behavior, and later on to celestial behavior."[1]

FOR OUR PROGRESS TO BE AUTHENTIC AND LASTING, IT MUST BE BUILT ON THE FOUNDATION OF A TERRESTRIAL LIFE.

The "Can't Skip" principle is not a new one. The Lord has always directed his people to first remove themselves from telestial environments and acquire terrestrial control over the natural man before attempting to live more

---

1. Neal A. Maxwell, "Repentance," *Ensign*, Nov 1991, 30.

celestial lives. The Israelites in Old Testament times illustrated this order of progression. After Moses led the children of Israel out of captivity in Egypt, they camped at Mount Sinai while Moses ascended the mountain to be instructed of the Lord. Returning with a celestial order to offer his people, Moses found the majority of the Israelites involved in grossly telestial behaviors, including worshipping a golden calf in depravity and licentiousness. Knowing that a telestial people could not "skip" to living a celestial order, Jehovah took the higher priesthood out of their midst (see D&C 84:25) and added to the basic gospel a more terrestrial, "schoolmaster" law (Galatians 3:24), which contained many performances and ordinances designed to impose a more stringent day-to-day awareness of the need to harness the natural man and stop offending God.

> . . . it was expedient that there should be a law given to the children of Israel, yea, even a very strict law; for they were a stiffnecked people, quick to do iniquity, and slow to remember the Lord their God;
>
> Therefore there was a law given them, yea a law of performances and of ordinances, a law which they were to observe strictly from day to day, to keep them in remembrance of God and their duty towards him (Mosiah 13:29-30).

This law of performances and ordinances was not a punishment, but an invitation for the people to progress and, if they followed the law, acquire mastery over the natural man. Those who ceased their sinful behaviors and began to consistently follow the law became more terrestrial and then, if they chose to become more valiant, could progress toward a higher realm.

Individually, most of us also progress in two stages, moving from the telestial to the terrestrial, and then, if we continue, from the terrestrial to the celestial. Elder Bruce R. McConkie, speaking of how true conversion to the gospel of Jesus Christ comes about, explained that in rare, miraculous cases, conversion is an event. But he went on to explain that for "most people conversion is a process; and it goes step by step, degree by degree, level by level, from a lower state to a higher, from grace to grace, until the time that the individual is wholly turned to the cause of righteousness."[2] Thus we can change from bad to good, and then from good to better.

President Ezra Taft Benson made the same clarifying point, saying:

> The scriptures record remarkable accounts of men whose lives changed dramatically, in an instant, as it were: Alma the Younger, Paul on the road to Damascus, Enos praying far into the night, King Lamoni. . . . Though they are real and powerful, they are the exception more than the rule. For every Paul, for every Enos, and for every King Lamoni, there are hundreds and thousands of people who find the process of repentance much more subtle, much more imperceptible.[3]

Since most of us do not experience those rare, miraculous conversions, we will discuss here the more typical conversion process. Generally speaking, as we are converted, we progress from the natural man state of telestial living to a terrestrial state wherein the natural man is harnessed through self-control and deferred gratification. When we are consistently able to live terrestrially, as honorable men and women, the Spirit can tutor us to a higher state of conversion—and greater valiancy—line

---

2. Bruce R. McConkie, "Be Ye Converted," in *Brigham Young University Speeches of the Year*, (11 February 1968), 12.

3. Ezra Taft Benson, "A Mighty Change of Heart," *Ensign*, Oct 1989, 2, emphasis added.

on line, precept on precept, until we become more like the Savior and are able to live celestial law.

Just as the children of Israel could not successfully skip from a telestial realm to a celestial realm, on a smaller scale and in our own day, we may see the difficulties of trying to skip from the telestial to the celestial in some new converts to the Church. Missionaries tell of "golden" investigators who drink in every lesson with enthusiasm and soon progress to baptism. Sadly, as Christ taught in the parable of the sower (see Matthew 13:18-23), some of these newly baptized members fall away from Church activity rather quickly. Almost certainly, such individuals felt the Spirit and received a witness, but testimonies can quickly fade and new members may fall by the wayside unless their initial excitement is followed by disciplined and consistent compliance with the standards and commandments of the gospel to help them overcome any telestial habits or patterns in their lives. We might call this the *trenchwork of the terrestrial*.

Some new converts stay active as long as certain appetites are satisfied, such as being the focus of missionary attention or warm fellowship from members; or being called to a position they enjoy, feel is important, or where they associate with individuals they like. However, if missionaries are transferred, if supportive fellowship fades, or if new members are called to a position that they feel is less exciting or not as immediately rewarding, they may find it difficult to continue in activity.

Of course, other new members already have or are willing to develop the self-control and discipline of the terrestrial realm. These individuals learn what activity in the Church requires, nod, and say, "Tell me what I'm supposed to do and I'll do it." They don't focus on how they feel about callings or assignments; they have made a commitment, and they can call upon self-control and deferred gratification as necessary to keep that commitment. As with all Church members, standing on a firm terrestrial foundation allows further progress toward the celestial.

The prophets have taught that obedience is the first law of heaven.[4] It's obvious when you think about it. With the Fall, man became carnal, sensual, and devilish (see Mosiah 16:3, 5). To regain the presence of God, we must "yield to the enticings of the Holy Spirit" (Mosiah 3:19), which guides, testifies, and has power to sanctify us, changing us from the carnal, sensual, devilish, natural creature into a more refined, Christlike being. Therefore, in order to progress in any consistent and meaningful way toward celestial life, we must have access to the Holy Ghost. If we are not obedient, we cannot have that access.

> . . . after ye have known and have been taught all these things, if ye should transgress and go contrary to that which has been spoken . . . ye do withdraw yourselves from the Spirit of the Lord, that it may have no place in you to guide you in wisdom's paths that ye may be blessed, prospered, and preserved (Mosiah 2:36, emphasis added).

If we obey, controlling our appetites and subjecting them to the will of the Father, we can exit the telestial realm and have the Spirit in our lives, which then helps us progress toward the celestial realm. If we do not turn from sin to basic—if not yet valiant—obedience, entering a more terrestrial state, the Spirit withdraws from us, and we remain in our fallen state.

Sometimes, without realizing it, we may "skip" the terrestrial by relying on the Spirit to change us before we do the basic, obedient work of correcting our hurtful, telestial behaviors. Tyler came to see me in counseling because he had a problem

---

4. See John A. Widtsoe, *An Understandable Religion*, (Salt Lake City: Deseret Book Co., 1944), 51.

with his temper and it was destroying his marriage.[5] He had grown up in a family that yelled and fought a lot, and he had a hard time accepting his need to change. Rather quickly though, Tyler did come to recognize that his hot temper was seriously damaging his relationship with his wife and kids, and he committed to making a change. However, several months later, Tyler returned to counseling, greatly frustrated. He said that he had been praying continually for mastery over his temper, but the ability to feel different and to curb his anger had not come. He didn't know if he wasn't humble enough or if his faith wasn't strong enough, but he saw that his wife and children were suffering as his temper continued to flare regularly. Although a good and sincere man, Tyler was trying to skip the terrestrial. He was expecting that by showing faith and petitioning the Lord through prayer, his heart would be changed and he would be able to treat his family differently.

I spoke with Tyler about the importance of not skipping over the necessary step of gaining control over his passions even when—*especially when*—things upset him. I suggested that while it is always important to access the blessings of heaven through sincere prayer, God does require of us "all we can do" (2 Nephi 25:23). We discussed concrete ways he could take responsibility for his outbursts, reducing and then eliminating them through the development and strengthening of his self-control and deferred gratification. Tyler was initially quite surprised that exercising his faith and seeking a blessing were not giving him the success he desired. However, he came to understand that he had been skipping an essential terrestrial step. As he addressed himself to gaining self-mastery, he found the success he wanted.

It is not that unusual for people to make the mistake that Tyler did. Quite regularly we hear the idea "If you're not going to do

---

5. All of the names used in personal stories throughout this book have been changed to protect the privacy of the individuals.

the right thing for the right reason, you shouldn't do it at all." Doing the right thing for the right reason *is* the ideal, and the integrated[6]—or wholly blended—life is a requirement for the celestial kingdom. But if we wait to obey until our hearts are purified and our behavior and intent are in complete harmony, we, like Tyler, are trying to skip from disobedience (telestial) to perfect integrity of heart and action (celestial). Except for rare cases of miraculous intervention, as noted above, this doesn't work. What works for most of us is progression from disobedience to basic obedience and then learning to be more valiant and devoted in our obedience, cleansing our hands and then purifying our hearts. For example, it is often said that if we want to gain a testimony of tithing, we should pay our tithing. We are not counseled to withhold tithes and offerings until we feel a burning desire to live off ten percent less for the good of the kingdom. And although it is certainly best to attend church meetings with a worshipful and consecrating attitude, it is never suggested that if we haven't yet wholly attained a communing spirit we may as well stay at home. In both these cases, as well as in other areas of gospel compliance, progressing toward the celestial level of consecration and worshipful communion is not generally accomplished in a single leap, but through a more terrestrial—though not yet wholly valiant—path; a path of tithe-paying even when challenging and of church attendance even when it's tempting to stay home, knowing that the witness, and our more complete conversion and consecration, will come after the trial of our faith (see Ether 12:12).

Children, of course, must follow this same path of progression. Parents, often with the best intentions, mistakenly try to skip the terrestrial stage of helping their children master the natural man and then become frustrated when children don't better

---

6. Often we use the term integrity in reference to honesty, but integrity also means "the quality or state of being complete or undivided: completeness" *Merriam-Webster Online Dictionary*, s.v. "Integrity," http://www.merriam-webster.com/dictionary/integrity (accessed June 7, 2009).

respond to the celestial principles they are being taught. This is such a critical issue in today's world that all of Chapter Seven will be devoted to its discussion.

CHAPTER THREE

Telestial Counterfeits

The Terrestrial Realm's Protection Against Satan's Mimicry of the Celestial

Once we understand the three realms perspective and the importance of the terrestrial, it should be easier to recognize and protect ourselves from the pain and destructiveness of telestial behaviors, situations, and relationships. However, life is not always so straightforward. Satan is a liar. He seeks to deceive. One of his deceptive practices is to imitate what God does—offering telestial choices dressed up to look celestial.

Even in the pre-earth council, when the Father presented His great plan of happiness, Lucifer presented a mimicry, a counterfeit of the plan. Satan presented his plan as if it were basically equivalent—designed to save and exalt us. However, by withdrawing our agency and forcing us to avoid sin, it would actually have made it impossible for us to progress, develop, and *become* like our Father in Heaven, so no one would have been exalted. On this earth, Satan continues to offer counterfeit principles and processes that, in appearance, seem very much like celestial principles and processes, but which, ultimately, violate eternal truths and destroy instead of exalt. Celestial ideas, principles, and practices respect individual agency and seek to lift, bless, and save. The goal of the telestial is to get gain, power, and control through compulsion and coercion. Understanding that the celestial is built on the foundation of the terrestrial helps us distinguish between the ideas, principles, and practices that are truly celestial and those that are telestial counterfeits.

We see telestial imitation of the celestial even in forms of government. For example, we might say that celestial government is theocracy, the rule of God. The Merriam-Webster Dictionary defines theocracy as: "Government of a state by immediate divine guidance or by officials who are regarded as divinely guided."[1] Until the Millennium begins, when Christ reigns personally on the earth, we won't experience theocracy in a purely celestial form. However, the Nephites were governed for a time by a dynasty of prophet-kings—Mosiah I, Benjamin, and Mosiah II—which, according to the above definition, constituted a kind of earthly theocracy. We might conclude that a dictator or an unrighteous monarch would constitute telestial government, given scriptural teachings that "whatsoever thing persuadeth men to do evil, and believe not in Christ . . . is of the devil" (Moroni 7:17) and "how much iniquity doth one wicked king cause to be committed" (Mosiah 29:17). Notice that the *form* of a telestial government is similar to that of the celestial—one man at the top making all the decisions. The *substance*, however, is dramatically different. A dictator uses his power to control others and to achieve personal gain. A prophet-king consecrates his life to serve and bless his people, does not exploit them economically, and never seeks to abrogate their agency.

---

1. *Merriam-Webster Online Dictionary*, s.v. "Theocracy," http://www.merriam-webster.com/dictionary/theocracy (accessed January 26, 2009).

In contrast to the one-man-at-the-top form that seems to characterize both celestial and telestial governments, a safe, good-but-not-perfect, terrestrial government might include democratic or representative systems of government based on the rule of law and conducted by the majority voice of the people.[2] It is interesting to consider, then, that before stepping down as king, Mosiah II instituted a change in the government. He decreed the end of the monarchy and the beginning of a representative form of government that would include the popular election of judges to function as chief governing officers of the nation. This was a change from a more theocratic, celestial system of government—prophet-kings—to a less perfect, more terrestrial system, elected judges. Mosiah explained that such a change would protect the nation from the danger of a telestial government in the person of an unrighteous king. Mosiah explained:

> If it were possible that you could have just men to be your kings . . . then it would be expedient that ye should always have kings to rule over you. . . .
>
> Now I say unto you, that because all men are not just it is not expedient that ye should have a king or kings to rule over you.
>
> For behold, how much iniquity doth one wicked king cause to be committed, yea, and what great destruction!
>
> Yea, remember king Noah. . . .
>
> Therefore, choose you by the voice of this people, judges . . .

---

2. See D&C section 134, which discusses what earthly governments should do and be "for the good and safety of society" (verse 1).

> Now it is not common that the voice of the people desireth anything contrary to that which is right; but it is common for the lesser part of the people to desire that which is not right; therefore this shall ye observe and make it your law—to do your business by the voice of the people.
>
> And if the time comes that the voice of the people doth choose iniquity, then is the time that the judgments of God will come upon you (Mosiah 29:13, 16-18, 25-27).

Since an evil king mimics the same form of government as a righteous king, Mosiah protected his people from a telestial counterfeit of good government by instituting a terrestrial safety net: a government of elected officials—not as good as prophet-kings, but pretty good, and certainly safer than risking the destructive potential of an evil monarchy.

GOOD PEOPLE CAN BE FOOLED BY TELESTIAL COUNTERFEITS.

Good people can be fooled by telestial counterfeits. In the 1940s, some members of the Church became enthusiastic about the rise of communism in the Soviet Union, believing that this was a step toward the establishment of a celestial economic system, the United Order. Church leaders were quick and firm in declaring that communism was a telestial mimicry of God's economic order:

> Communism and all other similar isms bear no relationship whatever to the United Order. They are merely the clumsy counterfeits which Satan always devises of the Gospel plan.[3]

---

3. A message from the First Presidency of The Church of Jesus Christ of Latter-day Saints, delivered in the Assembly Hall on Temple Square, Salt Lake City, Utah, Monday, April 6, 1942, during the closing session of the 112th Annual General Conference of the Church. The message was published in Conference Report, Apr 1942, 88-97, emphasis added.

Telestial mimicry of the celestial is not only found on an institutional level. Such counterfeits can creep undetected into our individual lives and relationships. In individuals, I would suggest that there is not so much a deliberate effort to counterfeit celestial things as there is the confusion that results when an individual feels and demonstrates a connection to elevated spirituality but remains trapped by continued involvement with serious telestial behaviors. Here, too, it is important to remember that we are not generally all telestial or all terrestrial or all celestial as much as we are a combination of behaviors. Nevertheless, *it is essential that we recognize serious inconsistencies that sabotage good intentions.* We are not really progressing toward a celestial realm if we still lie, cheat, steal, or break the laws of chastity. It is only as we eliminate telestial behaviors that we secure a solid terrestrial foundation and can make genuine progress toward the celestial realm.

Let me clarify that *the telestial behaviors, which must be eliminated in order to make solid progress, refer to those particular behaviors stemming from willful rebellion against God's commandments.* I am not suggesting that we must have perfect control of the natural man before we can successfully move forward. For instance, we may struggle with laziness, impatience, overeating, and other such weaknesses during the entire course of our mortal lives. However, if we have the desire to do what's right and make clear efforts to do so, but never completely overcome our faults, this is very different from willful disobedience. Willful disobedience requires a knowledge of the commandment and the conscious choice to rationalize our sin as acceptable. Such disobedience might include the behaviors mentioned above (lying, stealing, breaking the laws of chastity) and other deliberately hurtful and destructive behaviors. When we choose to rebel against God in such willful ways, we cannot have the Spirit with us and therefore cannot yield to its enticings (see Mosiah 3:19), which lead us on the path to a more celestial heart and life.

I remember a girl in high school, let's call her Heather, who seemed so enthusiastic about Church and seminary. Heather immersed herself in the scriptures and loved singing the hymns. She seemed devoted to the gospel. But then Heather would tell me that she regularly fabricated extravagant stories about herself to interest prospective boyfriends. I wondered how someone who seemed so close to the Spirit could still be so quick to lie. Perhaps what I was seeing was the illusion of the celestial by one still choosing to continue in a telestial behavior. That may seem harsh, but consider the scriptural reality that deliberate lying is telestial, not terrestrial, behavior (see D&C 76:103, Proverbs 6:16-17). This is not to say that Heather was totally telestial. She had many good qualities, but she also had a serious telestial problem. Yet, she could still get so enthused about the gospel and seem so spiritually alive that she clearly saw herself as an extremely righteous young woman well on the path to the celestial kingdom.

As we seek to live more celestially, we must honestly acknowledge and eliminate behaviors that trap us in a more telestial realm. Then, our efforts to move forward toward celestial life will not be just an illusion or mimicry but the line upon line, precept upon precept progression that begins with cleaning our hands and ends with purifying our hearts.[4]

There are other circumstances in which we may make, or observe in others, enthusiastic expressions of spiritual commitment without the accompanying consistency of solidly terrestrial obedience. Let's look at what I call "Girls' Camp syndrome." Those familiar with girls' camp have probably noticed that every year there seem to be some girls who attend camp just to give the leaders grief. These girls break rules, they don't show up when they're supposed to, and they bother others. But on the last night of camp, at the "testimony bonfire" they often bear

---

4. See again David A. Bednar, "Clean Hands and a Pure Heart," *Ensign*, Nov 2007, 80-83.

emotional and heart-felt testimonies. Occasionally, however, their own words reveal that they are still struggling with some telestial concerns. They may say things like "I love my mom and dad (celestial effort), even though I don't usually do what they say (telestial problem)." The pattern may continue with, "I love my sister, even though I treat her badly. And I love all of you guys, even though I was a jerk all week."

The expressions seem sincere. And the Spirit can touch anyone who is receptive. This kind of spiritual experience could be the beginning of a new life direction. In that place, in that moment, that young woman may recognize her need for spiritual things and feel a desire to qualify for celestial glory. Nevertheless, such spiritually charged moments can pass quickly. It's not impossible that a young woman can create problems all week at camp, bear a touching testimony, and improve almost overnight, but neither is it all that likely. It is more probable that she will revert to problematic behavior almost immediately.

To effect lasting change, the young woman would need to harness the spiritual energy she felt and turn it toward solid terrestrial efforts at consistent obedience. Her feelings of love for her parents would need to become consistent respect and obedience *even when she feels irritated or impatient with their requirements*. Feelings of love for her sister and others would need to be demonstrated in consistent kindness and consideration *even when she feels frustrated with them*. By doing the right things—even when she doesn't feel like it—terrestrial strengths of self-control and deferred gratification are learned and the young woman can make sustainable progress toward the celestial level she has come to desire.

While it is appropriate and desirable to seek and enjoy deeply spiritual experiences, the "mighty change of heart" (Alma 5:12-14) that accompanies true conversion is not usually accomplished as a result of one such experience. As Elder D. Todd Christofferson explained:

> You may ask, Why doesn't this mighty change happen more quickly with me? You should remember that the remarkable examples of King Benjamin's people, Alma, and some others in scripture are just that—remarkable and not typical.[5] For most of us, the changes are more gradual and occur over time. Being born again, unlike our physical birth, is more a process than an event. And engaging in that process is the central purpose of mortality.[6]

We can and should value, even treasure, the times in our lives when we feel a rich outpouring of the Spirit, but such experiences are not likely to change our lives in a lasting way unless we apply ourselves to securing a terrestrial foundation by overcoming tendencies for telestial rebellion and committing to a practice of consistent obedience even when difficult. Once we are honorable men and women, if we want to more completely fulfill our potential, we can move forward, line upon line, becoming more diligent, devoted, and *valiant* sons and daughters and, ultimately, qualifying for the great gift of eternal life in the celestial kingdom.

Another problem with failing to understand and detect telestial mimicry of the celestial is that we may be easily deceived, confused by, and even vulnerable to the apparent spirituality of an individual who also demonstrates hurtful or dangerous behavior. This can lead to disaster. When choosing friends, roommates, business associates, significant others, and marriage partners (see Chapter Six), it is possible to mistake spiritual expressions or other seemingly positive outward indicators for the consistent presence of the Spirit in the life of a more celestial person. The Lord warned of wolves that would come among

---

5. Here, Elder Christofferson references Ezra Taft Benson's First Presidency Message, *Ensign*, Oct 1989. See Ezra Taft Benson, "A Mighty Change of Heart," *Ensign*, Oct. 1989, 2-5.

6. D. Todd Christofferson, "Born Again," *Ensign*, May 2008, 76-79.

the sheep, telling us to be "wise as serpents" so as not to be deceived or victimized by counterfeits (Matthew 7:15, 10:16). Understanding the need for a first-step, terrestrial foundation to undergird celestial living can help protect us from being deceived. Perhaps even more important, this understanding can protect us from deceiving ourselves into thinking we are on the path to exaltation when, in fact, we are failing to complete basic, foundational requirements.

I worked once with a rather interesting family that was the source of regular confusion and frustration for their bishop. I believe theirs may have been a case of not completely grounding their efforts on a terrestrial foundation. The Trents were a nice family. Brother Trent had a college degree and marketable credentials that could have earned a decent salary with benefits, but he openly stated that working a 9 to 5 job stifled his creativity. Instead, he always had some unusual scheme in the works that he was confident would, in time, yield generous income. In the meantime, he said, "The Lord will provide." The Trents lived in a borrowed home that was in an advanced state of disrepair, and when one of the little boys was seriously injured because of the unsafe housing situation, state child protection services threatened to remove the children. To help make the family dwelling safer, the elders quorum spent a full day fencing off hazards on the property. Brother Trent expressed appreciation in the next fast and testimony meeting, although he had been away from his home on the workday.

Of course, there may have been extenuating circumstances peculiar to the Trents' situation, but let's review some general principles. First, we may have a desire to approach a celestial-like, full reliance on the Lord;[7] but if we reject the limitations of full-time employment, we willfully neglect what might be

---

7. 3 Nephi 13:25, 28 "Take no thought for your life, what ye shall eat, or what ye shall drink; nor yet for your body, what ye shall put on. . . . Consider the lilies of the field how they grow; they toil not, neither do they spin."

considered an appropriate terrestrial step of honorable self-reliance and risk falling into the more telestial sphere of the idler who eats the bread of the laborer, which is condemned by the Lord.[8] Second, we may have a desire to fully magnify our creative gifts in an effort to realize our celestial potential;[9] but if this becomes a reason to avoid less glamorous—but honorable—terrestrial work that provides for our family, we again risk the possibility of the telestial-like failure of meeting responsibilities to provide for our household.[10]

Any of us can make this mistake—thinking in celestial terms, but behaving telestially. For instance, in fulfilling stewardships, we must be mindful of avoiding the telestial counterfeit of unrighteous dominion. Section 121 of the Doctrine and Covenants gives a very strong warning concerning stewardships, beginning with these familiar words, "Behold, there are many called, but few are chosen . . ." (verse 34). A few verses later we read:

> We have learned by sad experience that it is the nature and disposition of almost all men as soon as they get a little authority, as they suppose, they will immediately begin to exercise unrighteous dominion (D&C 121:39).

---

8. D&C 75:29 "Let every man be diligent in all things. And the idler shall not have place in the church, except he repent and mend his ways." Also D&C 42:42 "Thou shalt not be idle; for he that is idle shall not eat the bread nor wear the garments of the laborer."

9. See the parable of the talents, Matthew 25:14-30, especially verses 21 and 23, "Well done, thou good and faithful servant: thou hast been faithful over a few things, I will make thee ruler over many things: enter thou into the joy of thy lord."

10. 1 Timothy 5:8 "But if any provide not for his own, and specially for those of his own house, he hath denied the faith, and is worse than an infidel."

One of the reasons stewardship responsibilities can so quickly lead to unrighteous dominion is that Satan, seeking to deceive, tempts those with authority into counterfeit kinds of leadership—telestial mimicry of celestial principles.

For example, a scout leader may be called who, in his enthusiasm to fulfill his stewardship, *determines* that every young man will get his Eagle Scout award. This may seem a worthy ambition, but—wait—whose plan was it that none should fail? It was Satan's counterfeit plan, rejected in the pre-earth council in heaven. It would have required that our agency be taken away and, as discussed earlier, the removal of our agency would have sabotaged any true spiritual progress or development. Similarly, anytime we, in our stewardships, try to accomplish good by limiting others' choices, even their choice to fail, we are falling for Satan's telestial counterfeit of true leadership—in effect, taking lessons from the loser—and seriously limiting our potential to truly bless or save.

Efforts to *guarantee* Eagle status for every young man may result in what might be termed an "Eagle Mill," with young men receiving rubber-stamped merit badges they didn't really earn, and parents and leaders completing projects or other requirements without much effort—and therefore little or no growth—on the scout's part. I remember attending a Court of Honor for one of our sons. He was awarded several merit badges that night. One badge for motor boating puzzled me. I looked it up in the merit badge manual and asked my son when he would have earned the badge. He replied that there had been a scout activity on the lake and it must have been at that time and place. I read through the specific requirements and asked my son if he had done all those things. He said, "Well, someone did push me behind the wheel for a few moments, but then it was someone else's turn pretty quickly." Our son didn't really learn anything significant or develop any real skill in motor boating, but, nevertheless, he was given the badge as if he had accomplished something fairly meaningful in that area. Now, for a scout to occasionally receive a merit badge on loose terms is not going to do a lot of damage, but neither will it accomplish the fundamental and worthwhile goals of the program. Something is lost. Isolated incidents of this kind are bound to occur in youth programs, at schools, and in our homes, but when they happen regularly, not only does it prevent the development that should have occurred, but it also ends up making awards less meaningful for those who really earn them.

Consider the real-life scouting experiences of two young men, Riley and Jackson. Riley was a sharp young man, a superior student, and a worthy priest. He completed his Eagle Scout requirements, but when his mother spoke to Riley about planning an Eagle Court of Honor, he said he didn't want one. His mother asked why. Riley answered, "I know too many Eagle Scouts I wouldn't trust to the end of the block with one of my sisters. I finished my Eagle because Dad got his and I decided to get mine too, but it doesn't mean what I thought it would."

Jackson's experience was the other side of the coin. Jackson had been a good student and a well-liked and successful young man until he became involved with drugs. Jackson's grades tanked, and he started to get into trouble in school, at home, and eventually with the law. At one point, Jackson was placed on house arrest for physically attacking his father and threatening his mother. His mother recounted all of this to me and explained that Jackson was now beginning some court-ordered anger management classes. Then she concluded, "But the good news is that Jackson is having his Eagle Court of Honor this Sunday."

Do we recognize the major disconnect in all of this? Have we lost the meaning? The Scout Law states: "A scout is trustworthy, loyal, helpful, friendly, courteous, kind, obedient, cheerful, thrifty, brave, clean, and reverent." This is not to say that

Jackson didn't have value and potential, but at that particular point in his life he was none of those things. Does it make sense to give Jackson an award that has no true relevance to the path he is on and the choices he is making? The Lord says very clearly, "I, the Lord, am bound *when ye do what I say*; but when ye do not what I say, *ye have no promise*" (D&C 82:10, emphasis added). The Eagle Scout program is clearly intended to help boys grow into good, honorable men. Of course, we don't expect that even a boy who genuinely earns the Eagle rank will have completely incorporated every one of the scout qualities into his life, but he should be well on his way. If we rubber-stamp the requirements, we may help the boy "achieve" Eagle rank, but he's not really what an Eagle Scout is intended to be. Further, we have sent the destructive message that rewards are available and conferred without appropriate work and effort, which just serves to reduce motivation in what is already being referred to as an "entitled" generation. Ironically, not only do we rob the boy who doesn't really grow and develop as the program intends, but because we award the rank to boys who don't reflect what an Eagle Scout should be, we dilute the meaning and satisfaction the award should have for boys who *do* appropriately complete the program. Significant damage can be done when we fall for Satan's counterfeits.

The dangers warned of in Doctrine and Covenants section 121 are an ever-present trap for the unwary foot: a Primary President who *commits* that each child will complete the Gospel in Action program, a Young Women's president who *vows* that every young woman will finish her Young Womanhood award, or a bishop who *determines* that every young man in his ward will serve a mission. In our church responsibilities, family stewardships, and other areas of our lives, we need to be careful that our efforts to be celestial leaders don't backfire into telestial mimicry. Tragically, in such cases, the well-intentioned leader or parent is completely sincere, but the consequences are different from what was intended.

A repeated theme of this book is that with the change from a terrestrial to a telestial society, the way we used to do things no longer works. The over-lax advancement of scouts is an example of something that we used to "get away with" that in today's more telestial society creates more dramatic problems. Let me be clear. Rubber-stamping requirements or insisting that *everyone* "succeed" in the program was never the Lord's way of fulfilling stewardships. However, in a more terrestrial society, being a little loose on scout requirements, or pushing everyone to complete the program or go on a mission, while still not the Lord's way, did not typically have such dire consequences. Strictly speaking, advancing the underachieving Boy Scout was never a perfect application of principle; neither, however, was it so terribly risky. In more terrestrial times, that scout, while not himself too solidly terrestrial yet, was often surrounded by friends, peers, and a society who were mostly terrestrial and who not only expected him to eventually grow up and straighten out, but supported him in doing so. And because, in more terrestrial times, that underachieving youth was not as likely to be subjected to the aggressive availability of telestial behaviors we are surrounded by in our day, there was a fairly reasonable chance that he could avoid the more seriously destructive behaviors long enough to mature and shape up. Often, that's exactly what happened. Disaster was avoided, terrestrial support was available, and the boy eventually straightened out. But in today's more telestial society, if we advance youth who aren't surrounded by that terrestrial cushion of support and who are subject to the aggressive availability of destructive behaviors, they are much less likely to "automatically" straighten out, and they may become involved in increasingly telestial behaviors. Ironically, if rubber-stamped along the way, such individuals may, nevertheless, carry the "badges" on their life's resume that used to signal meaningful accomplishment and character development.

Celestial desires can also become destructive telestial mimicry in the husband who *is set* upon having a righteous family and is deceived into thinking he *can control or dictate* that outcome. Such a husband needs to remember that "no power or influence can or ought to be maintained by virtue of the priesthood" or, may I suggest, by virtue of any stewardship or even by virtue of having a positive goal. Suppose a young husband and wife are both working before children come. Let's say the husband wants to pay tithing on their earnings, but the wife does not. He is right, of course; both should pay tithing. But if, in a sad fulfillment of section 121, he insists, "As long as I'm head of this family, we *will* pay our tithing," he was right a moment ago, but now he's wrong. A favorite hymn of mine reminds us:

> Know this that every soul is free
>
> To choose his life and what he'll be,
>
> For this eternal truth is given,
>
> That God will force no man to heaven.
>
> He'll call persuade, direct aright,
>
> Bless with wisdom love and light,
>
> In nameless ways be good and kind,
>
> But never force the human mind.[11]

Recognizing how easily the telestial counterfeit can seduce those desiring a celestial experience may help keep us safe from substituting unrighteous dominion for inspired leadership or from thinking the priesthood can be used as a cloak for compulsion or chauvinism. Those seeking to learn celestial leadership must be sure to lead by harnessing their own natural appetites to compel or control others and must learn the more

---

11 "Know This, That Every Soul Is Free," *Hymns*, no. 240.

celestial pattern of stewardship taught in section 121 of the Doctrine and Covenants, which requires persuasion, long-suffering, gentleness, meekness, love unfeigned, kindness and pure knowledge and is sabotaged by any hypocrisy or guile (see verses 41-42).

The ways in which Satan seeks to deceive through counterfeiting celestial principles and practices are unending. But if we understand this pattern of deception we can learn to consider not just the form or appearance of things, but to evaluate the content and substance, as well. We can examine our own behaviors for the consistent obedience necessary to avoid Pharisee-like gospel showmanship, or doing something only for the sake of a righteous (celestial) appearance while continuing to indulge in sinful behaviors (telestial). For instance, a sister who works in the temple and often helps the brides, sadly reported that occasionally a bride comes to the temple with a wedding dress that does not appropriately cover the temple garment. The temple workers, in such cases, offer a cover-up to be worn under the dress. The cover-ups, of course, were not intended for use with immodest dresses, but for use with a short sleeved or open—not low-cut—neckline. The temple worker sister told me that surprisingly often, the girl and her mother will protest that the cover-up garment "ruins the look" of the wedding dress. But is the young bride going to the temple for "the look?" How tragic to think that in the very act of making sacred covenants, the young bride is breaking those covenants—or planning to break them later for pictures and at the reception, since her chosen wedding dress does not allow her to appropriately wear the temple garment. In such cases, the image or idea of marrying in the temple has become a telestial mimicry of joining with God in our marriage covenant. Clearly, the blessings and potential of a temple sealing are significantly limited when not accompanied by obedience.

The more fully we understand the importance of securing a terrestrial foundation, utilizing the "Can't Skip" principle and being on the alert for telestial mimicry of the celestial, the more sure our growth and progress and the safer we can be from serious errors. Further, this understanding can heighten our awareness that we need not only be honorable, but valiant, in order to enter the celestial kingdom, hopefully motivating us to greater diligence and devotion in living the principles of the gospel. Note, too, that membership in the Church of Jesus Christ of Latter-day Saints seems designed to help bring us to a solid terrestrial level, as genuinely faithful involvement requires mastering our appetites, making "bad men good," and then allows those who seek more valiant discipleship to continue toward the celestial level, making "good men better."[12] However, remembering the parable of the five wise and five foolish virgins, we must realize that even full fellowship in the Church cannot purify our hearts—make us celestial—unless we individually yield ourselves "to the enticings of the Holy Spirit" (Mosiah 3:19). Even a temple recommend does not require that our hearts be pure, only that our behavior be sufficiently controlled that we do not overtly offend God or our fellow man. Our temple recommend interviews include questions to help us consider our direction and our desire to focus on the celestial, but generally, if our behavior is in line with basic standards of the Church—tithing, Word of Wisdom, chastity, Church attendance, and so on—our hands are sufficiently clean for us not to offend the Spirit in the temple.

I once heard Truman Madsen tell of renewing his temple recommend. His stake president, a close personal friend, asked Brother Madsen, "Now that you've answered the questions in the book, do you want to answer *my* questions?" Brother Madsen said he was feeling pretty good that day so he agreed to answer his friend's questions. As he recounted the conversation,

---

12. Teachings of Presidents of the Church: Brigham Young (Melchizedek Priesthood and Relief Society course of study, 1997), 21.

Brother Madsen no longer remembered all the questions asked, but they were along the lines of—

> Do you, like the righteous Nephites written of in the eleventh chapter of Helaman, sufficiently understand the true doctrine of the gospel so that you receive "many revelations daily" (see Helaman 11:23)?
>
> Are you living in such a way that at least one of the gifts of the Spirit is operational in your life on a daily basis?
>
> Do you shake at the appearance of sin (see 2 Nephi 4:31)?

Brother Madsen said that he rather quickly decided to stick to the questions in the book.[13] Well, I suspect we all would do better with the questions in the book. From time to time, however, it would be helpful for us all to consider such questions, as well as those suggested by Elder Dallin H. Oaks:

> What is the state of our personal preparation for eternal life? . . . What is the measure of our compliance with covenants, including the sacred promises we made in the waters of baptism, in receiving the holy priesthood, and in the temples of God? Are we promisers who do not fulfill and believers who do not perform?[14]

---

13. From a lecture I heard as a student in an undergraduate philosophy class taught by Brother Madsen. Several years later, in a personal phone call with Brother Madsen, I asked him if he could recall the questions. He said he couldn't exactly, but as I understood the point, I was welcome to make them up.

14. Dallin H. Oaks, "Preparation for the Second Coming," *Ensign*, May 2004, 7–10, emphasis added.

Pondering and then acting on such questions can help us move forward from honorable, terrestrial compliance to valiant, celestial devotion.

CHAPTER FOUR

SAFE DATING AND MARRIAGE CHOICES

USING THE THREE REALM PERSPECTIVE TO SELECT COMPANIONS WISELY

Our Church leaders have repeatedly taught that the most important thing we do in this life is to marry the right person, at the right time, and in the right place.[1] No wonder they say dating is harder in the Church; as the joke goes, where else do people evaluate each other for time and all eternity on the first date? Some may consider it overdone to be thinking in eternal terms while dating, but when so much of our future happiness on earth—as well as our desires for eternal companionship—depends on how good our marriage relationship is, can we be too careful?

We live in an age when about half of first marriages end in divorce—never the goal of those who marry in the temple expecting to be sealed to their spouse for this life and the

---

1. Gordon B. Hinckley, "Life's Obligations," *Ensign*, Feb 1999, 2.

next. Elder Dallin H. Oaks, speaking in general conference to members who have been divorced, said:

> We know that many of you are innocent victims—members whose former spouses persistently betrayed sacred covenants or abandoned or refused to perform marriage responsibilities for an extended period. Members who have experienced such abuse have firsthand knowledge of circumstances worse than divorce.
>
> When a marriage is dead and beyond hope of resuscitation, it is needful to have a means to end it.[2]

Later in the same speech, Elder Oaks wisely pointed out a basic protection from divorce, saying: "The best way to avoid divorce from an unfaithful, abusive, or unsupportive spouse is to avoid marriage to such a person." Of course, people don't deliberately date and marry unfaithful, abusive, or unsupportive partners, but it seems to happen all too often anyway. Happily, the three realms perspective can help identify safer dating and marriage partners.

The decision to marry, of course, should always be one that includes seeking the guidance of the Spirit. Nevertheless, as latter-day revelation has clarified:

> Behold, you have not understood; you have supposed that I would give it unto you, when you took no thought save it was to ask me.
>
> But, behold, I say unto you, that *you must study* it out in your mind; then you must ask me if it be right . . . (D&C 9:7-8, emphasis added).

---

2. Dallin H. Oaks, "Divorce," *Ensign*, May 2007, 70–73.

This chapter suggests and discusses the three realm perspective as a tool in "study[ing] out" potential partners so that we might more appropriately inquire of the Lord.

When society was at a more terrestrial level, more people—as a matter of course—developed self-control and deferred gratification, qualities that made them much less likely to be unfaithful, abusive, or unsupportive. People weren't perfect, of course, but if the major complaints were about partners who watched too much television, women who were bad cooks and housekeepers, and men who were fixated on football or their cars, that was a completely different level of concern from addictions or abuse. In that more terrestrial time, people could "fall in love at first sight," enjoy whirlwind courtships, and make fairly quick decisions about whom to pair up with, and the odds were still not bad that they would end up with a survivable partner who wasn't too tough to live with. But in our time, with so many getting caught up in telestial behaviors and lifestyles even amongst the middle classes and in the Church, the odds are no longer so good. More awareness, discernment, *and more time* are absolutely necessary in making partnership decisions. We must learn to identify telestial behaviors and avoid those who choose them. We also need to distinguish between someone who is making solid, consistent progress toward the celestial realm and someone exhibiting telestial mimicry of the celestial, or what could be termed "the natural man on a good day." Since true celestial qualities can be difficult to measure, a more effective approach to mate selection is to identify people who display consistent terrestrial behavior with the desire to progress to the celestial. Great safety is to be found in dating and marrying terrestrial people.

GREAT SAFETY IS TO BE FOUND IN DATING AND MARRYING TERRESTRIAL PEOPLE.

On many occasions, with single students and clients, I have heard descriptions of the kind of person being sought as a future husband or wife. Descriptions include, "She needs to have a strong testimony," or "He needs to really love the Lord." I appreciate the righteous desires expressed here. Faithful individuals desire faithful partners, someone with whom they can progress to the celestial kingdom, so it may seem logical to focus on celestial characteristics, such as strength of testimony and love of the Lord. However, now that we know about telestial mimicry of the celestial, we must be wary of the *appearance* of the celestial in areas where true content is difficult to measure. For instance, a prospective partner may express fervent testimony and devotion to the gospel and a deep love for the Lord and yet still be largely subject to the appetites of the natural man. I remember a young woman who married a returned missionary at least partly because she was so impressed at how often he attended the temple and how beautifully he bore his testimony. Shortly after their marriage, however, she discovered that he had a vicious mean streak when they disagreed about something and when he was angry he had no limits. He would tell her that she was ugly, stupid, and repulsive to him, but in much nastier language. She had thought his celestial-seeming characteristics made him a good partner, but, in fact, those celestial-seeming characteristics had not been built on a solid terrestrial foundation. He had never harnessed his natural man temper.

Celestial characteristics—love, spirituality, true charity—involve the integration of the heart with the behavior, and are therefore impossible for us to measure. Which of us can accurately measure the deep recesses of the heart? Like the returned missionary above, some individuals seem to display celestial characteristics, but are later found to be very different from what they appeared to be. We have been warned about wolves among the sheep (see Acts 20:29, Matthew 7:15).

It is simply not a realistic expectation to find people in their twenties (or thirties or forties or fifties, for that matter) who have progressed to a consistently celestial level. While there may be many who are moving in that direction, it is not a rapidly accomplished goal. We learn and grow "line upon line and precept upon precept" (Isaiah 28:10-13). In our twenties, many of us are exchanging our childhood testimonies for a personal conversion to the gospel of Jesus Christ. The refining journey to the celestial is still largely ahead of us *and* our prospective spouse. Consider the wisdom of seeking a partner who is solidly terrestrial with the desire to move forward toward celestial living. There is safety in the terrestrial. If we find a partner who consistently lives terrestrial law, we can experience the kind of life where peace, safety, and prosperity are present. Not a bad place for a marriage to begin.

Another advantage of seeking a partner with terrestrial characteristics—consistent behaviors requiring self-control and deferred gratification—is that, unlike celestial characteristics, terrestrial behaviors are mostly measurable and difficult to fake, at least over time. Asking questions like the following can help distinguish a terrestrial partner from a telestial one:

- Does this potential partner pay his bills?

- Is she in significant debt?

- Can he hold down a job?

- Is she often hurtful and offensive?

- Is he in full fellowship with the Church?

- Does she have good credit?

- Is he able to maintain solid relationships and healthy friendships, or does he seem to leave a trail of injury and enmity in his wake?

- Does she control her temper and other appetites?

- Does he honor commitments—attending meetings, fulfilling callings, doing home or visiting teaching?

- Are her decisions based on her own (selfish) desires, or does she consider the wishes and well-being of others?

As you answer these, and other similar questions about a potential spouse, remember that at this stage of life we aren't looking for perfection, but for solid consistency over time. It's true that even these behaviors can be faked, but counterfeits can't "hold their breath" forever. Over time—and it really does help to *take your time*—it becomes fairly evident what kind of mastery an individual has over the natural man.

We are fallible human beings. Just because someone makes mistakes or has weaknesses doesn't mean he or she is telestial. But red flags should go up when a *pattern* of telestial behavior is exhibited. Some individuals seem to go from one crisis to another. They have trouble with their landlord; their bank account is overdrawn; their credit card is "maxed out;" their neighbors are unreasonable; they have fights with roommates and a personality conflict with the boss at work. They may explain such crises in terms of coincidence, unfair treatment, or bad luck—but no one has that much bad luck. It is true that anyone can experience unfortunate or unfair circumstances, but if someone seems constantly "victimized," a closer look often reveals that the individual's choices and behaviors are not consistently in the terrestrial realm. The person is breaking rules, violating basic principles, or offending others, and their choices are generating unpleasant and costly natural consequences.

I once saw a young woman on an emergency basis ("I have to talk to you today!"), which, of course, signaled a crisis. Keri, in her early twenties, was hurt and angry about her parents' disapproval, asking, "How am I supposed to feel any self-esteem?" With a strong sense of ill-usage, Keri told me of a family friend in law enforcement who wanted to prosecute

Keri's ex-boyfriend who had introduced her to illegal drugs. Keri felt responsible for her ex-boyfriend, Mitch, getting in trouble with the law, even though Mitch had returned to drug dealing after serving a prison term for doing so. She had lived with Mitch for a while, but the relationship was tumultuous, so Keri periodically moved out. The last time she moved out and stayed away for a time, Mitch kept all her furniture. Recently, Keri had learned that he had given her a sexually transmitted disease. In spite of all this, Keri was contemplating moving in with Mitch again, rather than staying with a new boyfriend, who was not an ex-felon and who had a stable job. Keri was ready to abandon a relationship with a rather terrestrial new boyfriend to return to Mitch, who was obviously choosing a telestial lifestyle. Incidentally, Keri, still struggling with her own drug addiction and ready to return to her drug-dealing ex, was not a safe choice for her new boyfriend either.

It's important to understand that Keri was a very nice young woman. She was attractive, lively, and fun. She *wanted* to be drug-free and out of debt ("But how am I supposed to pay my bills if I'm in a rehab center?"). Those living at a telestial level are not necessarily unpleasant or "bad" people. Nevertheless, they are allowing appetites and passions to govern their choices and their lives. Sooner or later, the consequences start to pile up for them and for those around them. While not a wholly bad person, Keri was not, at that time, a very safe candidate in terms of potential for marriage or motherhood.

Keri's might seem like an obvious case, but it can be surprising how many red flags people fail to recognize. We might think that individuals living telestially are easy to identify, but that's not necessarily so. Although the telestial life is characterized by unrestrained appetites, remember that appetites and passions are not always evil. Sometimes people feel an appetite for fun, for generosity, for service, or even, occasionally, an appetite for the Spirit and things of righteousness. Because of the telestial pattern of largely unrestrained appetites, when individuals who live by telestial law are in the grip of a positive appetite, they can seem outstanding—in good ways. When such a person is in a fun mood, it can appear that *no one* is more fun. When he feels generous, it seems *no one* is more generous. When he feels the Spirit, it can seem that *no one* is more spiritual. A nursery rhyme that I learned when very young goes like this:

> There was a little girl, who had a little curl
>
> Right in the middle of her forehead.
>
> When she was good, she was very, very good,
>
> But when she was bad, she was horrid.

Those in a telestial realm can be like that. Wonderful when they're good, but scary when they're not. It can be easy to mistake the unrestrained indulgence of good appetites for the celestial, instead of recognizing—again—the natural man on a good day.

Over time—if we know what to look for—we can usually recognize when someone is governed by appetites. This makes it very important not to rush the courtship phase of a relationship. A telestial partner can bring such painful and destructive consequences to a marriage that it is well worth the time it takes to come to know the patterns of behavior of a potential spouse. Sadly, the signs of telestial behavior are often seen during dating and courtship but are not given sufficient weight in the decision to marry. I have heard many people explain that while they saw some disturbing behaviors in their spouse during courtship, they thought those behaviors would disappear or diminish after marriage. But patterns of behavior are exactly that—patterns. The best predictor of future behavior is often past behavior, so an understanding and awareness of the difference between telestial and terrestrial lifestyles can be a tremendous tool in the mate selection process.

Occasionally, a single person may not be currently making the best choices, but has the long-term desire to shape up, become more obedient, and have a solid marriage and family life. This is dangerous territory. Rebecca knew that living the gospel was important, but was compromising her standards to "take it easy" and "have a little fun." She got into the party scene while in college and dated young men who were also choosing that lifestyle. Eventually, she married Mike, a member of the Church though not active. Rebecca and Mike were pretty happy together until Rebecca returned to Church activity and expressed interest in a temple sealing. Mike didn't have that same interest. He was an honest man and a decent husband, but he didn't want to pay tithing or give up social drinking. Rebecca, who felt more and more strongly about going to the temple, particularly when they had children, was heartbroken. She said, "I guess I always thought when we grew up a little, we'd get to the temple."

By dabbling in telestial behaviors, particularly during dating and courtship stages, we are more likely to pair up with someone who is also involved in telestial behaviors. While we may consider such a stage temporary, knowing that eventually we'll get more serious about the gospel, we have no guarantee that the person we marry has the same plan. Since complete family activity in the Church and temple marriage can only be accomplished with two willing partners, once married, we may not have those options if we find ourselves "unequally yoked" (2 Corinthians 6:14).

Of course, as we recognize and seek the great blessing of a terrestrial partner, we must likewise develop in ourselves a consistent pattern of terrestrial living, so we can be safe marriage partners ourselves. And while past behavior is a good predictor of future behavior, we all have the potential to change and improve. A central premise of the plan of salvation is summarized in the second article of faith, which emphasizes that "through the Atonement of Christ, all mankind may be saved by obedience to the laws and ordinances of the gospel." If we recognize that we are involved in telestial patterns of behavior, ruled by the natural man, we can begin to act with more self-control and personal discipline. We can learn to postpone immediate pleasures in favor of more valuable long-term benefits. As we become more grounded in terrestrial patterns, we also become safer potential marriage partners.

Marissa had a difficult early life. Her parents were divorced, and her single mother struggled to support her family. An older brother abused her sexually for many years. As a teenager, Marissa started smoking and drinking, went through a series of bad relationships, was sexually active and often in trouble. She dropped out of high school and left home to live with a drug-dealing boyfriend, so she also became a drug user. But one day, Marissa looked at where she was and wanted something better. She broke up with the drug dealer, found a decent job, got clean and sober, took some adult courses to finish high school, and found satisfaction and peace in her stable life. Then Pete, a returned missionary, met Marissa, and they became friends. Pete asked Marissa for a date, and Marissa laughed, saying, "You have no idea who you're asking out." Pete persisted, and finally Marissa had lunch with him. Their relationship progressed. Marissa had been raised in the Church, although she had never really learned much about the gospel, but now she started attending Church with Pete and really became converted. She stopped smoking and social drinking and completed her repentance process with her bishop. In time, Pete and Marissa married in the temple and, when I met her, they had five children, a good marriage, and were very active in the Church. The Atonement is powerful. Lives can change. Notice, however, that Marissa had a significant track record of terrestrial behavior before Pete

CHANGE, TO BE REAL AND LASTING, MUST BE CONSISTENT OVER TIME.

became involved with her. Change, to be real and lasting, must be consistent over time.

As a potential partner demonstrates a solid terrestrial foundation, we will want to discuss our interest in working toward the celestial realm. If both partners are building on a solid terrestrial foundation and both have a desire to progress, their potential to do so is real. In the Church of Jesus Christ, with our knowledge of the plan of salvation, it makes sense to choose a partner who wants to qualify for the celestial kingdom, consistently demonstrates that desire by making good choices, and lives a solid terrestrial life. If we do the same, the Spirit can help us progress together to the next level.

CHAPTER FIVE

From Victim to Non-Victim

Finding Safety from Victimization in Marriage and Other Relationships

In our increasingly dangerous world, too many relationships involve telestial behaviors that hurt and victimize people. We increasingly hear about bullies on the playground, relational aggression between schoolgirls, unhealthy dating relationships, dishonest business dealings, and abuse in marriage. Because we want to be good people, we are reluctant to think negatively about anyone and we try to be patient and long-suffering with the people who hurt us. This can leave us completely unprotected from people who are choosing telestial behaviors. The three realms perspective helps us know where to apply patience and long-suffering and where we should draw lines in the sand.

Sadly, much of the victimization we hear about takes place in marriage. Too many marriages include telestial behaviors such as adultery, abuse, or addiction. These behaviors always bring pain, violence, and destruction into our lives. Sometimes good people—trying to be patient and forgiving—become perpetual victims of partners involved with telestial problems who never repent or abandon their sins. With a partner who lives at the terrestrial level—a good person, but not perfect—it makes sense to be patient, long-suffering, and forgiving. Those practices help move a terrestrial marriage closer to a celestial level. However, if one partner is living at the telestial level and behaving in seriously hurtful ways, it is wrong for the victimized partner to be long-suffering and forgiving while the unsafe situation continues. Well-intended but misguided efforts to respond in a Christlike or celestial manner to telestial behaviors may become passive acceptance of victimization that doesn't benefit either the victim or the victimizer. The victim remains vulnerable to abuse and, over time, invariably loses respect and love for the victimizer. The victimizer continues unabated on his or her personal road to destruction. A battered wife who repeatedly forgives her husband may be trying to be Christlike but usually ends up stuck in a victim role, while her husband remains stuck in a victimizer role.

The same holds true for any hurtful relationship: a young boy who keeps trying to be nice to the neighborhood bully, a girl who still considers a viciously nasty schoolmate to be her friend, a young woman who continues to go out with a young man who cheats on her, an adult who keeps loaning money to a friend or co-worker who never pays it back, a parent who repeatedly takes in an adult child who steals from the parent to support a drug habit. All these individuals, and anyone else who is chronically taken advantage of or hurt in an ongoing relationship, have accepted a victim role.

TOLERATING TELESTIAL BEHAVIOR IS NOT CHARITY.

There is a terrible irony at play here. Often, the goal of a person with an abusive spouse, friend, co-worker, parent, or neighbor is to act charitably. *But tolerating telestial behavior is not charity.* We typically define charity as "the pure love of Christ" (Moroni 7:47), but we may not fully understand how Christ loves. Christ defined His stewardship in Moses 1:39: "For behold, this is my work and my glory—to bring to pass the immortality and eternal life of man." Christ's resurrection bestows immortality as an unconditional gift. But eternal life is conditional, only available for the obedient and repentant, for "when ye do not what I say, ye have no promise" (D&C 82:10). The Abrahamic Covenant, then, promises salvation for the obedient and also promises that the disobedient will be "reminded" of their covenants.

> For behold, the Lord hath said: I will not succor my people in the day of their transgression; but I will hedge up their ways that they prosper not; and their doings shall be as a stumbling block before them (Mosiah 7:29).

Thus, sometimes charity—the pure love of Christ—is manifested as manna in the wilderness and sometimes as a famine or a plague or a flood. Everything Christ has done, does now, or will do has the purpose of creating the optimal opportunity for us to be saved (see 2 Nephi 26:24). Sometimes that includes letting us hit a brick wall so we change our course from one of self-destruction to one that leads back to Jesus Christ and our Heavenly Father.

It may come as a surprise, then, to consider that someone who patiently tolerates abuse or other telestial behaviors is not *really* acting charitably. Without intention, the long-suffering person is perpetuating the illusion that the behavior of the erring friend, associate, or partner is "good enough" to maintain a relationship. If the victim is also agreeing to keep telestial behaviors hidden from family, friends, officials, or Church leaders, he or she is supporting the lie that the victimizer is acceptable to the community and worthy of membership in the kingdom of God.

What about our obligation to forgive the sinner? Should we not forgive "seventy times seven?" (Matthew 18:22). Forgiveness should be our ultimate goal, but there is a difference between forgiveness and remaining vulnerable to abuse. President David E. Sorensen, of the Presidency of the Seventy, spoke plainly about that difference:

> I would like to make it clear that forgiveness of sins should not be confused with tolerating evil. In fact, in the Joseph Smith Translation, the Lord said, "Judge righteous judgment" (JST, Matthew 7:1). The Savior asks us to forsake and combat evil in all its forms, and although we must forgive a neighbor who injures us, we should still work constructively to prevent that injury from being repeated. A woman who is abused should not seek revenge, but neither should she feel that she cannot take steps to prevent further abuse. A businessperson treated unfairly in a transaction should not hate the person who was dishonest but could take appropriate steps to remedy the wrong. *Forgiveness does not require us to accept or tolerate evil.* It does not require us to ignore the wrong that we see in the world around us or in our own lives. But as we fight against sin, we must not allow hatred or anger to control our thoughts or actions.[1]

Trying to move directly from suffering abuse (which traps us in a telestial realm) to forgiveness (a celestial ideal) violates the "Can't Skip" principle. First, the relationship must move into a safe, terrestrial realm. Safety begins with a clear communication that the victim is not willing to continue being subjected to telestial behaviors. Thinking rationally and pragmatically (good terrestrial skills), the injured party needs to establish a

---

1. David E. Sorensen, "Forgiveness Will Change Bitterness to Love," *Ensign,* May 2003, 10, emphasis added.

terrestrial boundary in the relationship (e.g. the friendship or business association will end, or an abused wife refuses to stay in the home if the abuse continues). The offender can then either repent and improve (often the choice of rational individuals) or escalate, trying to coerce the other back into a victim role. One way or another, the relationship has a clear prognosis—either it will improve or it won't, in which case it may have to end.

Sally's husband sometimes locked her and their children out of the house when he got upset. Joe wasn't a terrible man—he was a committed member of the Church, he fulfilled responsible callings, he loved his wife and children and provided well for them. But while Joe's behavior was milder than some more blatantly destructive marriage problems, he was nevertheless doing a telestial thing when he lost his temper and locked the doors against his family. Sally had tried to be patient and long-suffering, which she thought was the Christlike response, but this destructive pattern was destroying her personal dignity and her love for her husband. It was also, not incidentally, terrible modeling for the children. She felt herself becoming bitter.

I explained the three realms perspective to Sally and suggested she draw a terrestrial boundary with her husband. Sally agreed to always wear clothes with pockets. In the pockets, every morning, she put her driver's license; cash, credit card, or checkbook; and keys. With the keys, Sally could have unlocked the door, but we didn't want to risk getting into a tug-of-war over the doorknob, so, instead, Sally packed the trunk of her car with a change of clothes and supplies for herself and her children, and then told her husband that *she* would no longer accept behavior they *both* knew was unacceptable to God. If he locked the door on her again, Sally said, she would take the kids and go somewhere they would be safe and not feel like beggars at their own door—perhaps the library, a park, a movie, or a restaurant. When she felt ready, she would call him to see if he was ready to get some help with his problem. Joe never locked the door on Sally again, and he came into counseling. The relationship moved into a safer place, and Sally's love for her husband was rescued from almost certain destruction.

Holly told me she wished she had learned earlier the importance of not tolerating sin. Holly's husband, Bill, had become emotionally involved with a woman he met at the gym. Holly admitted she and Bill had grown apart; he was very involved in his career, and she was busy with children and community activities. Bill justified his relationship by saying it was just a friendship. As long as he wasn't sleeping with the woman, he said, Holly shouldn't complain, even though Bill regularly met the other woman for lunch or a movie and was essentially dating her. Yes, things would have been worse had the relationship progressed to physical adultery, but Bill was having an emotional affair and violating his marriage covenants.

For three years, Holly prayed for patience and forgiveness, while she disintegrated emotionally. She almost ceased to function, pulling out of all her involvements in Church, in the community, and even in her family, leaving too much responsibility for household and younger siblings to the older children. Holly knew things were bad, but felt she was doing "the right thing." One day, in desperation, she prayed, "How long do I have to live like this?" The answer came quietly, but clearly: "You don't have to live like this, and you shouldn't." Holly was stunned. She had thought that she was doing the best thing for her husband and family. She finally realized tolerating Bill's sin was not best for any of them: Bill, the kids, or herself. She was surprised, but empowered. Holly went to her husband and said, "If you see that woman again, our marriage will end, not because I want it to, but because you will have chosen to end it." He responded with the equivalent of, "Well, in that case, I won't see her again." He didn't, and Bill and Holly started working to heal their relationship.

For years, Holly and her children paid a terrible price for the telestial choice her husband was making. Bill, himself, paid a terrible price as he pursued a path of spiritual self-destruction. Patience with the telestial behavior allowed the destruction to continue. Think how all involved might have been protected if a terrestrial boundary line had been drawn sooner—right away, in fact. Bill would not have traveled so far on a path taking him away from God, nor would he have had as much to repent of. Holly would have been spared tremendous pain, misery, and loss. The children would not have been without a functioning mother and would have more quickly regained a father who could act as the leader and example he should be.

> GOD HAS ALMOST INFINITE PATIENCE WITH OUR TERRESTRIAL IMPERFECTIONS BUT A ZERO TOLERANCE POLICY CONCERNING SIN.

Some may still feel that it is wrong not to continue in patience with a telestially erring friend or family member, but God has said, "I the Lord cannot look upon sin with the least degree of allowance" (D&C 1:31). God has almost infinite patience with our terrestrial imperfections but a zero tolerance policy concerning sin. This is not the rejection of a harsh deity, but the proof of love so profound it gives sin no quarter—because sin destroys His children. If we are to become "even as He is" (3 Nephi 27:27), then we, too, must be intolerant of sin. To be patient with someone's telestial behavior is not charity; it is victimhood.[2]

In our age of extended adolescence, we see many parents struggling to find the right balance between charity and victimhood with adult-aged children. Marie's son, Tate, was twenty-eight years old. Tate usually lived with his widowed mom, although from time to time, he moved in with friends. Tate worked occasionally, but his use of cocaine kept costing him jobs. When he ran out of other resources, he came home

---

2. Additionally, by continuing to tolerate abusive or destructive behavior, we may end up in the position of *enabling* the behavior.

to his mother's place. Marie periodically helped Tate with bills or emergency "loans" that were never repaid. After some recuperation time, he moved out again, usually stealing money or taking valuable objects with him. Marie was hurt and angry every time, but the next time Tate came around, she didn't have the heart to turn him away. Marie's other children were getting more and more angry at Tate's behavior, and they were upset at Marie for letting herself be so exploited. They saw their mother's stress skyrocketing, her health deteriorating, and her financial situation becoming jeopardized. Marie loved her children, but her relationships with all of them were tense and strained. She was angry at Tate's taking advantage of her. She was also hurt and frustrated with the criticism and pressure she was getting from Tate's siblings.

It wasn't easy, but Marie finally changed things. She realized she was subsidizing Tate's self-destruction. He was caught in telestial behaviors and, by protecting him from the harsh consequences of his choices, Marie was not only trying to delay the inevitable, but she was also letting herself get chewed up and spit out by Tate's choices. She told Tate she loved him but she would no longer give him money or allow him to live in her home. Her door was open to him only under the condition that he entered a rehabilitation program and followed through with it. As with many parents in similar circumstances, she had to deal with her fears that Tate might destroy himself more quickly without her intervention. But Marie finally realized she couldn't forever prevent that outcome if Tate didn't decide to turn his life around. She saw that by giving Tate a soft place to land, she was making it easier for her son to avoid acknowledging the mess he was making of his life. Marie also had to stretch her faith and remember that God loved Tate even more than she did and would be mindful of him.

Drawing a terrestrial line may prompt the victimizer to repent, rather than continuing to self-destruct. But whether or not

From Victim to Non-Victim

the victimizer repents, drawing a terrestrial line turns victims into agents, and *it is essential that victims become agents.* It was never part of God's plan for us to passively accept a victim role. Living as victims destroys our sense of self, our motivation, our health, every part of our well-being, and it sets a terrible example for those around us. There is also the possibility that we may reach our limit and decide, "I've taken it long enough; now I'm dishing it out," at which point we end up becoming another telestial victimizer. There is no positive outcome to tolerating ongoing victimization.

Sometimes a victimized spouse, trying to escape the misery of tolerating sin or abuse, also turns to inappropriate behavior. Ellen was impossibly controlling and demanding, constantly demeaning her husband, Matt, and their children. Matt tried to live with this situation patiently, but eventually his love for his wife died, and he become involved in another relationship with a woman at work. This further complicated an already toxic family situation. When Ellen discovered Matt's affair, she could easily ignore her own contributions to the failure of their marriage and, instead, rise up in supposed righteous indignation to condemn Matt. Of course, Matt's behavior was horribly wrong and nothing justifies sin, but in the furor over *his* mistakes, it was all too easy for Ellen's contributing sins to be ignored and unaddressed. The children couldn't even begin to find their way through the resulting maze of confusion and make sense of what had happened to their family. It would have been so much better for everyone had Matt drawn a terrestrial line and addressed Ellen's abusive behavior before his love for her was destroyed.

About 20 years ago, I saw a greeting card I liked so much I decided to buy several but never sent one of them. I'm sure they are safely in a storage box somewhere, and if I ever come across them again, I'm going to frame one. On the front it read: "A wise man once said, 'If you look through the rain long enough, you'll see the rainbow.'" Inside: "And an even wiser man said, 'If you're getting wet, get the hell out of the rain.'" While healthy, capable, and righteous people are sometimes victimized by the evil actions of others, adults cannot be consistently victimized over time without a measure of their own assent. We have access to too many resources to remain in a victim role without a measure of passive acceptance of the victimization. We were not sent to this earth to become or to remain victims. We are meant to become agents, not acting inappropriately toward others (as victimizers) nor being acted upon inappropriately (as victims).

I remember teaching this principle to our son, Adam, when he was about ten years old. We had moved into a neighborhood where there weren't that many boys, but conveniently, Jared, exactly Adam's age, lived just a few houses away. Jared attended a private school, but, every day after school, the two boys played together. A few months into this comfortable routine, Adam came home from school on a Friday afternoon, changed his clothes, and went out to play with Jared. But Jared had brought a couple of school friends home with him for the weekend, and the three boys rudely rejected Adam's efforts to join in with them. Adam came home feeling stunned and betrayed. We made a point to stay busy as a family that weekend, but when Monday came, after school, Jared knocked on the door and asked Adam to come out and play as if nothing had happened. Adam excused himself and came to ask me what to do. We reviewed the obvious alternatives: go ahead and stay friends with Jared or never play with him again. The first left Adam vulnerable to being hurt again; the second would create an obvious feud in the neighborhood, never a good situation. I proposed a third alternative: continue to play with Jared when convenient *but don't trust him*. This would protect Adam from future hurt, while allowing the relationship to continue as long as it was convenient to both boys. Adam would be safe from being victimized and would avoid victimizing back. I remember that Adam asked, "Shouldn't I forgive Jared? And what if he changes? Shouldn't I trust him again?" I explained that when he was safe from being hurt—and in this case, to be safe Adam just needed to lower his expectations of loyalty and watch his back—it would be pretty easy to forgive. Further, if Jared became a more loyal friend, time would tell and Adam could easily adjust his expectations and invest more in the friendship again.

Adam caught the vision of how to stay safe while still maintaining a friendly relationship with Jared. The boys continued to play together pretty regularly but Adam didn't hesitate to politely and quickly excuse himself if he felt like doing something else, or if, for whatever reason, Jared's attitude or behavior became unpleasant. Adam also cultivated other friendships with boys who were more consistently loyal. Jared, himself, actually seemed to improve, and he was never again so directly hurtful. It was a convenient association and kept peace in the neighborhood without leaving Adam vulnerable to continuing victimization.

When the early Saints were suffering severe persecution, the Lord revealed a powerful non-victim principle in section 98 of the Doctrine and Covenants.

> Now, I speak unto you concerning your families—if men will smite you, or your families, once, and ye bear it patiently and revile not against them, neither seek revenge, ye shall be rewarded;
>
> But if ye bear it not patiently, it shall be accounted unto you as being meted out as a just measure unto you.
>
> And again, if your enemy shall smite you the second time, and you revile not against your

enemy, and bear it patiently, your reward shall be an hundredfold.

And again, if he shall smite you the third time, and ye bear it patiently, your reward shall be doubled unto you four-fold;

And these three testimonies shall stand against your enemy if he repent not, and shall not be blotted out.

And now, verily I say unto you, if that enemy shall escape my vengeance, that he be not brought into judgment before me, then ye shall see to it that ye warn him in my name, that he come no more upon you, neither upon your family, even your children's children unto the third and fourth generation.

And then, if he shall come upon you or your children, or your children's children unto the third and fourth generation, I have delivered thine enemy into thine hands;

And then if thou wilt spare him, thou shalt be rewarded for thy righteousness; and also thy children and thy children's children unto the third and fourth generation.

Nevertheless, thine enemy is in thine hands; and if thou rewardest him according to his works thou art justified; if he has sought thy life, and thy life is endangered by him, thine enemy is in thine hands and thou art justified.

Behold, this is the law I gave unto my servant Nephi, and thy fathers, Joseph, and Jacob, and Isaac, and Abraham, and all mine ancient prophets and apostles (D&C 98:23-32).

God tells Joseph that when hurt, we should bear it patiently. If someone hurts us and we immediately hurt back, God sees us as equally offensive and doesn't want us to bother Him about it. I used this verse of scripture when my children tried excusing aggressive behavior by saying, "She started it!" I told them this scripture makes it clear that if we strike back when struck by another, both of us are pretty telestial, and God isn't too interested in who actually struck first. There's not enough difference between us to matter. We should never go from victim to victimizer, though we can, and should, take measures to stop getting hurt.

The Lord told Joseph that a second and even a third offense could also be borne patiently, and the Lord would bless us for our patience. But after a third offense, the Lord uses strong, directive language, saying, "*See to it* that ye warn him in my name, that he come no more upon you, neither upon your family" (emphasis added). In other words, the Lord is telling us not to stay victims forever. When the Lord says "I have delivered thine enemy into thine hands . . . and if thou rewardest him according to his works thou art justified," we need to place this direction in the context of all gospel truth. Of course, God does not authorize or condone a free-for-all, vigilantism, or vengeance. Those things are never acceptable to God. However, neither is the continual victimization of His people acceptable to God. He wants a kingdom of agents, not victims. He wants us to study, learn, identify available resources, and stop being victims. We can't change other people, but, remember, chronic victimization is a terrible dance that requires two, a victimizer *and* a victim. If the victim uses appropriate resources to get safe, it's like learning a new dance step, and the victimizer is going to have to find a new place to put his feet.

A serious caution must be given here. Drawing terrestrial boundary lines usually generates one of two responses from the offender. One is that the offender backs down and makes efforts to improve in order to save the relationship. This is the outcome we hope for. It's possible, however, that someone too deeply involved in a telestial life may intensify or escalate hurtful behaviors in an effort to force the other person back into a victim role. *If violent response is a possibility, do not encourage anyone to confront a victimizer without backup.* In other words, don't send a wife on her own to confront a husband who beats her up, and don't send your child unsupported to stand up to the playground bully. An abused wife must be accompanied by a male family member, a priesthood leader, or someone who can guarantee her safety, if necessary. A child must be backed up by parents, older siblings, or school officials. Take similar precautions in any situation where there is a chance of a violent response. Make a plan that provides for everyone's protection.

The Marriage Covenant

Another sad irony is one I have heard expressed dozens of times by suffering spouses who have thought it best to tolerate telestial behaviors. They say something like, "We were sealed in the temple, so I feel I need to do whatever is necessary to make it work." It is true that we should not take temple sealings lightly. On the other hand, we need to remember that temple sealings invite, but do not guarantee, eternal marriage.

Celestial marriage is available only to those sealed for time and all eternity in the temples of the Most High. Through this sacred ordinance, husband and wife covenant to enter into the patriarchal order, to become one with each other and God. But a temple sealing alone does not guarantee a celestial or eternal marriage. Temple covenants, like all other covenants, are conditional. Only husbands and wives who keep the covenants of marriage by growing together into a celestial relationship will have their marriage covenant sealed by the Holy Spirit of Promise, binding their covenant on earth and in heaven (see

D&C 132:7). Occasionally, a person sealed in the temple, but unhappy in the marriage, expresses concern about being bound to their partner forever despite the painful condition of the relationship. That won't happen. Marriage sealings are an invitation and an opportunity, not a prison sentence. And keeping the covenant includes liking each other. If we don't *want* to be with our partner forever, we won't be.

Even if we *do* want to be with our partner forever but the relationship is plagued with telestial patterns on the part of one or both spouses, we are not in the running for an eternal marriage, whether or not we have been sealed in the temple. So to tolerate destructive behaviors—sin—in an attempt to preserve a temple sealing is not only painful but meaningless as well. If we are being victimized by telestial behaviors, the best thing we can do to fight for our eternal marriage is to draw a terrestrial line in the sand and find out, once and for all, if the marriage can improve enough to someday become eligible for the sealing promises of eternity.

Choosing Safety

This chapter is directed, of course, to those victimized in any relationship. Let me clarify that while there is much that can and should be done by anyone being victimized, this is not to say that the victim is responsible for being victimized. *It is never correct to blame the victim.* It is the victimizer who is responsible for his or her behavior and who will be accountable for sins that are not fully repented of. When confronted with a terrestrial boundary, some victimizers express surprise that their behavior was so offensive or intolerable, but there is little, if any, legitimate excuse for an adult, or even a child in most cases, to claim ignorance about the destructive force of hurtful behaviors in a relationship. As members of the Church, we constantly hear lessons, talks, and conference addresses about how we should treat each other. Even outside the Church, it is no mystery that each person is entitled to respect and decency. Claiming ignorance of the proper treatment of human beings is an inadequate defense. Nevertheless, consider this: if a man is mugged in the street, it is not his fault. It's the mugger's fault, and the mugger will be accountable. But if the man gets mugged every day, he's walking down the wrong streets. Or maybe he's hanging twenty-dollar bills out of his pockets. There is something he can and should do about either or both of those things.

Adults who are victimized in an unrighteous relationship have a responsibility to find safety by developing and maintaining a terrestrial boundary. Adults should teach and support children in creating safety in their relationships, as well. Maintaining terrestrial boundaries in our relationships may end up blessing the victimizer, too, since healthy boundaries may "wake up" the victimizer to his need to repent and improve. Either way, the victim who stops accepting victimization and becomes an agent becomes healthier and happier, models appropriate life choices to others, and becomes more like the Savior.

CHAPTER SIX

MOVING TOWARD CELESTIAL MARRIAGE

In the previous chapter, we used the three realms perspective to understand the need to end victimization and maintain safe relationships. Several marriage examples were used, as marriage is one of life's primary relationships and, sadly, telestial marriage situations are plentiful. But, having discussed the dangers and challenges of telestial marriage and the importance of securing safer, more terrestrial marriage relationships, it only seems right to go a bit further and discuss the potential that exists for building a celestial marriage.[1] Whether currently married or single, it is useful to know what the goal is.

All too many people suffer the misery and desperation of telestial marriage, while remaining hidden behind the carefully maintained picture of a happy, successful relationship. Some

---

1. Please remember that telestial, terrestrial, and celestial designations are not intended to imply hard and fast categorization but rather to indicate patterns of behavior and/or interaction that seem consistent with telestial, terrestrial, or celestial outcomes. As used in this book, these terms are intended to help us better evaluate our own behaviors and life situations and to find ways to improve them. They are not intended to make final judgments of others or ourselves.

fortunate couples enjoy a strong, happy, terrestrial marriage—not by chance, but because they live good terrestrial lives. Husband and wife get along, treat each other well, enjoy being together, are faithful and loyal to one another, and both know and feel they are loved. Then there are some marriages, even on this planet, that grow beyond good, solid terrestrial success toward unified, celestial partnership. These celestial marriages are those ultimately sealed by the Holy Spirit of Promise and will continue forever in fulfillment, completion, and joy (see D&C 132:19).

Leo Tolstoy began his book, *Anna Karenina,* by observing: "Happy families are all alike; every unhappy family is unhappy in its own way." Similarly, we can say that *telestial* marriages include any number of tragic conditions. A telestial marriage could be characterized by authoritarian, oppressive, dictatorial unrighteous dominion on the part of either husband or wife. Telestial marriage includes marriages where one or both partners is involved with destructive behaviors, such as physical, emotional, or sexual abuse; addiction; explosive, demeaning anger; infidelity; or pornography. Telestial marriage could also include marriages where one or both partners are unwilling to participate in the relationship. It might be a husband who, though able, refuses to work to support his wife and children (see 1 Timothy 5:8). It might be a wife who, though able, decides she will no longer fulfill her normal responsibilities toward her husband and children. It might be a marriage where one partner demands intimacy, without regard for the health of the relationship and with no consideration for the spouse's feelings. Or it might be just the opposite, where one partner withdraws completely from marital intimacy, again without regard for the feelings of the spouse. There can be no comprehensive list of the ways a marriage might be telestial, but such a marriage is characterized by at least one partner's selfish focus on his or her own appetites and desires, to the exclusion of concern for the spouse.

Terrestrial marriage is more consistent in content and characteristics. This kind of marriage might be described as an equal, democratic partnership where negotiation, compromise, and taking turns create a peaceful, workable co-existence. In terrestrial marriage, both partners feel safe and respected. Each partner consistently controls appetites and desires, taking into consideration the comfort and wishes of the spouse. Both partners contribute consistently to the marriage and family, fulfilling their share of family work dependably and recognizing the contribution of their spouse. Both partners are loyal and faithful to spouse and family. They don't routinely behave in deliberately or carelessly hurtful ways. When, in the course of normal, human imperfection, they do hurt their spouse, they apologize quickly and sincerely and make honest and successful efforts not to repeat hurtful behavior. They show genuine affection to each other and share a healthy intimate life that considers each partner's needs and desires and is based in love, not lust. Terrestrial marriage is not free from stresses and disagreements, but terrestrial troubles arise from normal human imperfections and are not destructive or demeaning. A spouse who watches too many sports programs on television, who is chronically late, who doesn't clean up often enough, or perhaps is too finicky about cleaning, can be hard to live with, but patience, kindness, and long-suffering are the response that ultimately works best for everyone involved. (Note: Although not obviously destructive, almost any imperfect behavior, if carried to the extreme, can become destructive and telestial.) The partners in terrestrial marriage observe appropriate boundaries when angry, never crossing the line into name-calling or foul, profane, or abusive language. And physical or emotional violence, threats, or intimidation are never present. The terrestrial couple has developed a workable system of communicating about problems and disagreements. They are able to consistently reach negotiated compromises that keep both partners feeling engaged, listened to, respected, and cared for. One party doesn't do all the compromising or sacrificing; both sacrifice appropriately to safeguard the relationship.

A celestial marriage does not replace terrestrial marriage, but rather it builds on the health and satisfying foundation of the terrestrial. *The Family: A Proclamation to the World* affirms, "Fathers and mothers are obligated to help one another as equal partners." The *celestial* form of marriage—a patriarchal order—is built upon the principles of equal partnership, which include divinely appointed roles for husband and wife.

A man is to provide for, preside over, and protect his family, while a woman has primary responsibility for nurturing the children and being a *help meet* to her husband.[2] This divinely established division of labor between husbands and wives designates basic areas of stewardship for each partner. Part of Adam's stewardship was to till the earth and work in the fields, and "Eve also, his wife, did labor with him" (Moses 1:1). Undoubtedly, while Eve cared for and taught her children, Adam was often there with her, doing the same (see Moses 5:10-12). Thus, despite the difference in primary stewardships, each shared in the other's stewardship and actively helped the other fulfill the measure of his or her creation.

In marriage, too, the telestial mimics the celestial and, no doubt from the beginning, some husbands have attempted to use the priesthood and patriarchal authority as a cloak for chauvinism, leaving the Church vulnerable to criticism concerning the treatment of women. But true implementation of the patriarchal order never dominates or subjugates women; it's exactly the opposite—a relationship in which a humble, loving, worthy, priesthood-holding husband accepts the admonition to act the part of a savior for his wife and family, sacrificing whatever

---

2. "The Family: A Proclamation to the World," *Ensign,* Nov 1995, 102. See also Howard W. Hunter, "Being a Righteous Husband and Father," *Ensign,* Nov 1994, 49.

is necessary to secure temporal and eternal well-being and happiness for his stewardship (see D&C 121:34-45, Ephesians 5:22-33). Again, section 121 of the Doctrine and Covenants makes it clear that coercion or compulsion is *never* a part of divinely sanctioned patriarchal or priesthood authority. When a wife disagrees with her husband, *even if he is right and she is wrong*, a righteous patriarch employs the qualities discussed in an earlier chapter—"persuasion, long-suffering, gentleness, meekness, and love unfeigned"—as his response. If he tries to control, dictate, force, or manipulate, his authority is revoked (see D&C 121:37).

Just as men can inappropriately seek to maintain power or influence in a marriage, women, too, may exert power or influence inappropriately. A woman who demands that her husband pay tithing, or call family prayer, or direct family scripture reading, is also out of line with the order that God has established. To emphasize again, "no power or authority can or ought to be maintained" by virtue of any stewardship, or even by virtue of having a correct or positive goal (see D&C 121:41). It is true that husbands and fathers have a stewardship that includes leading and directing family prayer, scriptures, family home evening, Church attendance, and so forth. However, a man's failure to fulfill this stewardship does not authorize his wife—or anyone else—to turn the gospel into a club and beat him up with it.

Leading righteously is a challenging task, but brings blessings to all involved and strengthens, rather than weakens, relationships. One young husband gave an impressive example of righteous patriarchy when his wife, a few weeks after giving birth to their first child, announced that she was going back to work. The husband was surprised and disappointed, as he had understood that his wife planned to be a full-time mother, and he wanted that for his children. He had a good job and could provide comfortably for the family with his income. The wife said she had considered staying home, but she liked her job too much to quit, so she planned to continue her career and had found daycare for the baby. The husband didn't want his child in daycare but never fought or argued or tried to "pull rank" and insist that his wife stay home. He did, occasionally, talk to his wife about his desires for their family, but the tone of those discussions was positive and sharing, not contentious, and he didn't let those expressions become harangues. While he did sometimes reference the counsel of the prophets, he didn't use the gospel as a weapon against his wife. Perhaps most impressive, although his disappointment was significant, he didn't let this situation compromise the love he felt for his wife or allow it to damage their relationship. This continued for a few years until the birth of a second child. The wife then told her husband she had decided to stay at home full-time with the children. Gently, over time, she had been persuaded of the importance of being at home.

The true patriarch does not compel, force, or insist. He leads, teaches, and persuades. His goal is to help bring to pass the eternal life of all within his stewardship. Thus, while the superficial structure of a patriarchal marriage may be similar in appearance to a marriage with an unrighteously domineering husband, the two differ tremendously in content. One hurts, controls, and destroys; the other blesses, serves, and saves.

In his epistle to the Ephesians, Paul encourages wives to submit themselves to their husbands, *as the husband submits himself to the Lord* (see Ephesians 5:22). If a husband fails to follow the will of God, amen to the authority of that man (see D&C 121:37). This is not to say that a wife should require her husband to be perfect or that she has the right to endlessly challenge her husband's direction. If he has established a pattern of righteousness, she should counsel with him in righteousness and support his position as family leader. Nevertheless, if it becomes clear that a husband is living or seeking to lead in unrighteousness, a wife has the responsibility, based on her stewardship over herself and her children, to choose a safer course. The story is told of a woman who approached President Brigham Young on the streets of Salt Lake City. With indignation, the woman said, "President Young, my husband told me to go to hell!" Brigham simply responded, "Sister, don't go!" God does not require, or more accurately, God does not *desire* that a woman follow her husband in unrighteousness. However, with the normal differences of opinions and disagreements that come up in any marriage between two good but imperfect partners, a wife's response should also follow the pattern established in D&C section 121 of persuasion, long-suffering, gentleness, meekness, and the other qualities taught there, the development of which improves us and makes us more like Jesus Christ.

Paul reminds husbands of the magnitude of their responsibility toward their wives: "Love your wives, even as Christ also loved the Church, and gave himself for it" (Ephesians 5:25). The stewardship of a patriarch, like all other stewardships, is to bless and save. A husband who understands this celestial pattern for marriage does not try to lead his family *in his own way* but takes responsibility to learn through study, righteous living, and revelation how to lead his family *in the Lord's way*. Note that in verse 39 of D&C section 121, the Lord, speaking of priesthood holders, says, "As soon as they get a little authority, *as they suppose* . . ." (emphasis added). The Lord seems to be making the important point in those three words, "as they suppose," that it is not *their* authority, it is *His* authority. When God gives men authority to act in His name, they should understand the authority is not theirs, it is His, and whatever calling or position they hold is not license to do things their own way but a responsibility to find out how to do things His way. If these basic stewardship principles are understood by both husband and wife, there is no need for the anxiety and aversion some women feel towards the patriarchal order of marriage.

When a marriage is firmly established on a terrestrial foundation, the husband and wife can be taught by the Spirit, line upon line, precept upon precept, how to progress to a patriarchal order. Remember that the celestial order of any institution is only available when founded upon the terrestrial base. In marriage, that means equal partnership. Submitting to a husband who values his wife as an equal partner is not a matter of subjugation, then, but acceptance of God's organization for the family. For a husband to love as Christ loves the Church means that he is willing to do anything to promote—not compel—the salvation of his wife and children. This will involve not only developing the characteristics of Christ (persuasion, long-suffering, kindness, gentleness, etc.), but will also involve learning to receive revelation for the family. The husband's responsibility and opportunity in the patriarchal order is to become like Moses to the children of Israel, the vehicle by which light, truth, and blessings come to his stewardship. The righteous patriarch becomes a conduit between heaven and earth. And through that conduit flows power to lift, bless, serve, and save all within his stewardship.

Though many women have felt concern over the idea of submitting to a husband, how difficult is it to submit to the leadership of a man who devotes his life to becoming a blessing to his wife and children? A true patriarch will never oppress or demand or coerce. He would throw himself off a cliff before hurting, or allowing anything else to hurt, those within his stewardship. In like manner, the wife who seeks to correctly live the patriarchal order will support her husband as a help meet in all things. The terrestrial "safety net" of equal partnership can give us the security to progress to a more celestial realm.

I remember hearing from one woman about an event in her marriage, which helped her understand the great blessings that the patriarchal order of marriage—celestial marriage—can bring to a wife. Lisa spoke of a very demanding time of her life when most of her children were still at home. She had recently been inspired to go back to school for a graduate degree. Her husband, Cal, was very supportive of her schooling and had taken on more cooking, cleaning, shopping, helping with the kids, and other activities to allow her more time to study. At the time, Lisa also taught early morning seminary and an adult religion class for the stake. Then, another stake president asked if she would teach a class for his stake, too. Lisa was inclined to say yes, but she wanted to consider carefully whether she would be "run[ing] faster than [she had] strength" (Mosiah 4:27). She knew taking on another class might not just tax her energy and time but might also exact an inappropriate level of sacrifice from her husband and children. Lisa believed in putting family first and did not want to pursue other interests at her family's expense. She discussed the situation with Cal, who appreciated her caution, but also understood the contribution she felt she could make in teaching. Lisa told Cal, "I have prayed about this decision, and I'm unclear on what Heavenly Father wants me to do. I feel like I could teach the class, but I'm not sure if that's just my own desire or the will of the Lord. Would you go to the Lord for me and get the revelation I need?"

Consider how deep a trust a wife has in a husband when she genuinely puts her life in his hands and asks him to find out which direction she should go. She has to know he will not use such an opportunity to impose his own will or preference. She has to know her husband is a man of sufficient worthiness that he can draw upon the heavens for revelation and receive and recognize it when it comes.

Cal went to the Lord to find an answer for his wife. He fasted and prayed for her, and then, when reading scriptures, he came upon a verse and knew he had found the answer. The scripture read: "And all this for the benefit of the church of the living God, that every man may improve upon his talent, that every man may gain other talents, yea, even an hundred fold, to be cast into the Lord's storehouse, to become the common property of the whole church" (D&C 82:18). Cal told Lisa that he felt the Lord wanted her to "cast [her talents] into the Lord's storehouse" and teach the second stake adult religion class. Both Cal and Lisa were surprised. Both had thought it might be more logical and prudent for Lisa to avoid adding to her schedule, but both felt the confirmation that Cal had received the right answer.

The story doesn't end there, however. Here's the *really* patriarchal part. Cal asked Lisa, "What do you need me to take off your list, so you will be able to fulfill this new assignment?" Added to what he had already taken on to help Lisa through graduate school, Cal started taking care of the laundry and doing even more cleaning and other jobs Lisa had handled. With deep emotion, Lisa concluded, "If you think I loved and trusted Cal before, how much more do you think I love and trust him now?"

In the patriarchal order, a man is invited to be the conduit between his family and the powers of heaven, a vehicle for counsel, guidance, direction, comfort, and miracles. Of course, wives and children can and should receive revelation for themselves, but in the same way that each Church member is blessed by following the living prophet, wives and children can be blessed by having inspired leadership at the head of the home.

Inspired leadership never includes compulsion or coercion, especially in this most important stewardship of a marriage relationship. Again turning to the direction given in section 121 verse 41, it is only *by persuasion* that we should try to resolve disagreements, excluding those which involve telestial, destructive behaviors (see Chapter Five for a discussion of appropriate responses to telestial behaviors in marriage).

Persuasion seems a lost art in our world. Too often, people skip right over persuasion and try to manipulate, leverage, bribe, or threaten. Persuasion implies conversion to a new way of thinking. When we try to persuade, we are acknowledging each individual's right to act in harmony with his own beliefs, but we are asking him to examine his beliefs and consider exchanging them for another perspective, opinion, or belief. Why is persuasion so uncommon? Perhaps because it requires the development of so many other characteristics. It seems to me that the other characteristics necessary for persuasion are in the list that follows "persuasion" in verse 41: long-suffering, gentleness, meekness, love unfeigned, kindness, pure knowledge, no hypocrisy, no guile. Let's look at each one.

Long-suffering—This is unlikely to be anyone's favorite quality. It sounds difficult and demanding and requires *so much* patience. But to persuade, we need to willingly allow the time necessary for the individual to thoughtfully consider exchanging his or her current beliefs for a new way of believing. Persuasion is not a quick process. Further, when pushed or pressured, people are more likely to dig in their heels and cling stubbornly to their current opinion.

Gentleness—This is an essential component of persuasion. When people are aggressively confronted, they feel attacked and criticized, and, again, the tendency is to hold tightly to their opinion.

Meekness—This is another component of persuasion; I once heard it defined as appropriately harnessed power. There is power in truth or in a correct idea, but that power should be moderated and restrained, not aggressively unleashed, to allow for the process of conversion to a new idea.

Love unfeigned—Genuine love and concern for the individual are essential. We have often heard that "no one cares how much you know until they know how much you care." Perhaps trite, but certainly true. The one trying to persuade must honestly care about how the new principle or understanding will bless the other person's life, not just about being right.

KINDNESS—This is a necessary part of every successful interpersonal human interaction.

PURE KNOWLEDGE—This is important because we need to be sure that the idea we are promoting is correct.

WITHOUT HYPOCRISY—Any attempt to persuade another out of hypocrisy can never bring lasting change or conversion and merely illustrates that the point on which we hope to persuade is not compelling enough for us to apply it in our own lives.

WITHOUT GUILE—having guile means we have an agenda of our own and that the well-being of the other person is not our real concern.

Bryan and Wendy, married only a couple of months, came to see me. It was a second marriage for both of them, and they were already talking about divorce. Wendy had a two-year-old daughter from her first marriage, and the child had become accustomed to sleeping with her mother. Bryan understandably wanted Wendy to put the little girl in her own room at night; Wendy resisted doing so. Bryan argued almost constantly with Wendy about the situation, bombarding her with books, magazine articles, and the opinions of family, friends, and neighbors, all saying Bryan was right—the little girl should sleep on her own. Wendy wouldn't even talk about it any more.

In my office, Bryan explained all the reasons he was right and then said, "Besides, I'm the patriarch in our home, and she should follow what I say." I pointed out that priesthood authority was never license to compel, but should only be used with persuasion. Bryan quickly challenged, "How do you know I'm not using persuasion?" I pointed to Wendy and asked, "Does that look like the face of a woman who is being persuaded?" Wendy was looking at Bryan with a steely glint in her eyes, a jaw like granite, and clenched teeth. Bryan did a quick double-take and admitted that maybe he wasn't being all that persuasive.

If Bryan had referred to our checklist of qualities involved in persuasion, he would have known that whatever he was doing, it really wasn't much like persuasion at all. He wanted immediate results, so long-suffering was definitely not in his plan. He was not gentle nor meek nor kind. Granted, he had done his homework and was right that everyone, not least of all the little girl, would be better off with the child in her own room. However, he certainly had his own agenda in all of this, and it was fairly obvious that his main focus was his comfort and satisfaction, more than the happiness or comfort of his wife and daughter.

Bryan might have asked, "What if I do all the things I'm supposed to do, in all the right ways, and the other person still isn't persuaded?" The answer is that if we work to acquire all the qualities and traits listed in section 121 verse 41, we get to become more like the Savior, Jesus Christ, because those are His qualities and traits. Then, even if the other person is not persuaded, we come closer to fulfilling the measure of our creation. Not a bad consolation prize. Let's not, however, ignore the reality that when we honestly seek to persuade someone, not for our benefit but for theirs, and we use correct means, the truth will resonate in the honest heart and many, if not most, will eventually be persuaded. Everyone involved can be blessed in the process.

Frankly, I can't count the times I have explained the need for and the process of persuasion. Bryan and Wendy are certainly not the only couple I have worked with who needed to turn away from conflict and contention and develop and apply the qualities of persuasion. In fact, all who seek celestial life need to learn and internalize these qualities. Some individuals respond well, working hard to overcome the tendency to insist or compel and humbly focusing on their part in improving the way they handle disagreements, rather than stubbornly waiting until their partner "gets it right." Others remain stuck in their pattern of contention and unrighteous dominion. Unfortunately, Bryan was one of those. He seemed to feel it was more important to prove he was right than to rescue the marriage, which died a swift death.

To make a very brief point of an idea worthy of much greater consideration, let me suggest that *putting God first in the marriage* is what so often makes the critical difference between couples that progress toward celestial marriage and couples that don't. The Proclamation on the Family declares that "marriage between a man and woman is ordained of God,"[3] and when a man and woman are sealed in the temple, they covenant with God to create a marriage that can become celestial. President Joseph Fielding Smith taught:

> Those covenants are made in the presence of God and angels at the altar in the temple of the Lord. How, then, can a man and a woman with the love of God in their hearts ever turn away from the solemn covenants that they make that they will be true and faithful all the days of their lives in mortality and that their faithfulness will continue after death? That is the covenant that they make.[4]

Let's face it, there are times when we may not want to change to please our spouse but, if we truly put God first, we are willing to change to please Him. Christ warned: "What therefore God hath joined together, let not man put asunder" (Matthew 19:6). If we truly believe that our marriage covenant includes

---

3. "The Family: A Proclamation to the World," *Ensign*, Nov 1995, 102.

4. Joseph Fielding Smith, "The Eternity of Temple Marriage," Conference Report, April 1961, 48.

God, we must not let our own natural man, in the form of pride and stubbornness, tear that marriage apart. Focusing on what God thinks of our behavior as husbands or wives helps us get past those stumbling blocks to get on with the business of repentance, improvement, and growth.

Returning to the topic of persuasion, I learned something valuable from one of my sons. I was recounting to Graydon a conversation I had with his father, Chris, that left me astonished. I am one of those people who have pretty strong opinions about almost everything (this will not come as a surprise to anyone who knows me, or probably to anyone who is reading this book). I said something to Chris about his changing my mind, and he expressed surprise, saying, "I don't think I've ever changed your mind about anything." I was amazed. My husband has helped change my opinions about some vital issues, beginning before we were married.

Chris and I dated before his mission. Once he asked about my plans after high school. I said I planned to get a Ph.D. and teach at the university level, like my mother and father. Without disapproval or challenge, Chris asked if I planned to have children. I said, "Yes, maybe three or four." (We have eight children, so I obviously had no clue as to what my future life would be.) Chris, again without censure, asked who would take care of them while I pursued my career. As foolish as this sounds, it was the first time I paused to consider that French grandmothers, like the one who lived with us as my sisters and I grew up, do not come standard issue.

Chris didn't belabor the point, but it started me thinking. I considered my future plans and more intently listened to the messages at general conference. The Equal Rights Amendment was a hotly debated issue at that time, and the prophet counseled members of the Church to oppose its passage because of the cost to families. Many speeches were given on women's divine roles. My entire life's direction changed as I *was persuaded* that if I married and could have children, I would be a full-time mother, which I was for almost 20 years. Even had I not married Chris, I would have been eternally grateful to him for having begun that process of persuasion and conversion to a different way of thinking.

Over the years, my husband has gently and kindly and, no doubt, with much long-suffering, introduced me to new ways of thinking about other important principles. As I explained this to Graydon, I again expressed my astonishment that his dad didn't realize this. Graydon's comment was, "Well, that's probably because when people are persuaded in the right way, the new direction of thought can seem like their own idea," which is what true persuasion is all about, when you think about it. Graydon continued, "And the honest and humble *persuader* isn't keeping score or taking credit, so he doesn't always notice." Out of the mouths of . . . well, insightful teenagers. I think that's exactly what was going on. We can all see the added advantage to a relationship when we drop the score-keeping statements such as, "I told you so," or "I'm the one who told you that," or "You have to admit I was right."

My husband has said for some time that section 121 of the Doctrine and Covenants is perhaps the greatest scriptural treatise on relationships. Before leaving this discussion on moving toward more celestial relationships, we need to also consider verses 43 and 44, with their oft-quoted direction:

> Reproving betimes with sharpness, when moved upon by the Holy Ghost, and then showing forth afterwards an increase of love toward him whom thou hast reproved, lest he esteem thee to be his enemy;
>
> That he may know that thy faithfulness is stronger than the cords of death.

"Betimes" means as close to the time of the offense as possible. Without publicly embarrassing anyone, we should give needed correction as soon as is appropriately feasible. "With sharpness" has sometimes been thought to excuse harshness or aggressive reproof, but "sharpness" refers to the need for clarity, or pinpoint sharpness, when giving correction. It's not very helpful to tell someone, "You're a jerk." That leaves the offense unspecified and only does damage. Sharpness is more along the lines of, "I felt hurt and unimportant when you forgot to pick me up after work."

The most important direction concerning reproof is in the phrase "when moved upon by the Holy Ghost." Think about that for a moment. When was the last time we waited to tell someone off? We can be so quick to volunteer, and although we haven't begun to give the time, space, or stillness that would allow us to feel the whisperings of the Spirit, we convince ourselves that we are righteously indignant as we express anger.

But that's not how the Spirit works. If the Holy Ghost is going to "move upon" us to reprove someone, it will follow established celestial patterns. First, it would involve a stewardship situation, as the Holy Ghost would not inspire us to reprove someone over whom we have no stewardship. Second, the *purpose* of the reproof would be to bless the life of the other person, giving him an opportunity to make needed correction in his behavior, so he can continue along the path to eternal life. The Holy Ghost would *not* inspire us to reprove someone so we can vent our frustration and angry feelings.

Perhaps one sign that we are truly being inspired by the Holy Ghost to reprove someone would be that we are reluctant to do so. If we're eager to reprove, we're probably doing it wrong. If we follow inspired instruction to have a stewardship interview with someone who needs correction, the conversation is motivated by our desire to help that person understand that his behavior is unacceptable to God, not just hurtful to us.

When we genuinely feel the Spirit and desire to help someone progress, it is natural to show "forth afterwards an increase of love toward him whom thou hast reproved" because the entire communication is made out of love and concern.

Expressing love as part of a loving communication has meaning and authenticity, as opposed to dutifully tacked on expressions of love that follow expressions of anger. I remember as a young parent always telling my children I loved them after administering my best efforts at parental justice. Years later, my children said it always puzzled them to be told they were loved immediately after being chastised or punished. Ending with an expression of love doesn't mitigate the impact of anger. If we wish to follow the Savior's pattern of correction, the interaction doesn't just end with love, it begins with love.

Genuinely cultivating the qualities of persuasion—Christlike qualities—and seeking the guidance of the Spirit in our relationships requires a lifetime of determined and committed effort. It is not the path of least resistance, but it is the path that leads toward a more celestial life. Sadly, we may not see—or be aware of—very many examples of couples moving toward more celestial marriage. It doesn't exactly take a keen observer to recognize that marriage is currently under attack. Even marriages that begin as terrestrial partnerships can weaken, ending in divorce or unhappiness. Marriage is challenging and, in my opinion, constitutes part of the Refiner's fire. But if we can remove telestial elements and secure terrestrial elements, our marriages can be safe, happy, and satisfying. If we learn and act on the principles of the patriarchal order, our relationships can progress toward the ideal of celestial marriage, be sealed by the Holy Spirit of Promise, and qualify for the promised joy of eternity with a partner we love and trust. Telestial marriage destroys. Terrestrial marriage is quite satisfying and can bring enjoyment and contentment. Celestial marriage, through a long process of changing, growing, and refining, yields not only the kind of relationship we would look forward to continuing forever, but fulfills the very promise and potential of mortality, helping us become more like the Savior, Jesus Christ.

CHAPTER SEVEN

Better Parenting

A Three Realms Parenting Application—
Help for You and Your Children

This is not a book on rearing children, and the ideas discussed here do not constitute a complete approach to parenting. The three realms perspective, however, can help us understand why parenting seems to be especially challenging in our day. It can also give us reinforcement and confidence in addressing that new level of challenge.

Parenting has always been a tough job, but parenting in a telestial world is harder than parenting in a terrestrial world. We have discussed how, in recent history, our society has turned toward increased wickedness. President Boyd K. Packer, in February of 2004, said:

> Satan uses every intrigue to disrupt the family. . . . Profanity, vulgarity, blasphemy, and pornography are broadcast into the homes and minds of the innocent. Unspeakable wickedness, perversion, and abuse—not even exempting little children—once

> hidden in dark places, now seeks protection from courts and judges.[1]
>
> These are days of great spiritual danger for our youth.[2]

As prophesied, wickedness will increase up until the Second Coming of Jesus Christ.[3] So the world in which our parents reared children was, by definition, not as telestial as today's world, and the world in which our children will rear our grandchildren will be more telestial still.

This has huge implications for parents. Let's start with a simple example. Over the last couple of decades, I have heard more and more parents express frustration that their children treat them with disrespect. "I would never have spoken to my parents the way my children speak to me," they complain. Some frustrated parents have gone to their own parents and asked what *they* did to command basic respect. These grandparents consider for a moment and then usually respond, "We don't know." Of course, this just increases the frustration. The fact is, when the grandparents—or perhaps great-grandparents—were parenting, the world was more terrestrial. Disrespect from a child to an adult was not much modeled or tolerated. Children generally showed respect to adults; that was the world we lived in. Naturally, there were some kids who showed disrespect, but when that happened, you could literally hear the gasps.

---

1. Boyd K. Packer, "On the Shoulders of Giants," (J. Reuben Clark Law Society devotional address, Brigham Young University, Provo, UT, February 28, 2004).

2. Boyd K. Packer, "The One Pure Defense," (address to CES religious educators, Salt Lake Tabernacle, Salt Lake City, UT, Febraury 6, 2004).

3. "There has never been such a dire day as this. Iniquity abounds; all the perversions and evils of Sodom have their devotees. And the revealed word assures us that conditions will get worse, not better, until the coming of the Son of Man." (Bruce R. McConkie, "'Who Hath Believed Our Report?'," *Ensign,* Nov 1981, 46.) See also 2 Timothy 3:1.

The shock and disapproval of practically everybody acted as a powerful incentive to improve behavior. Not so today. As the values in society have changed and terrestrial patterns of belief and behavior are replaced by telestial beliefs and behaviors, "normal" is now very different. As mentioned earlier, even mild family fare on television regularly portrays parents and adults as rather stupid. Frequently, it's the kids who come to the rescue, so the shows seem to justify all jokes at the parents' expense. A laugh track lets us know how acceptable, and even clever, it is to lace every conversation with zingers and put-downs. And it won't stop here. Tomorrow's children will face the next level of deteriorating respect and decency.

Parents in a telestial world have to parent more pro-actively than parents in a terrestrial world. In decades past, parents may not have needed to think very much about teaching their children to respect adults; society did much of that for them. But society won't teach today's children to be respectful; their parents will need to do it. Society won't teach today's children the difference between true, modest beauty as defined by God and trendy, immodest, but increasingly popular behavior and attire; their parents will need to do it. Society won't teach our young men to respect and protect women; their parents will need to do it. Society won't teach today's children the importance of sexual abstinence before marriage and complete fidelity in marriage; their parents will need to do it. And this will be the case with more and more of the standards and behaviors that we may have taken for granted when we grew up. They can't be taken for granted now.

Today's and tomorrow's parents need to be more educated and skilled at parenting. Repeating the parenting practices of even excellent parents will often be inadequate. The world is deteriorating too fast and too dramatically.

Looking back on my own youth—quite a while ago now—it seems that amongst my Church member peers, there were some who stayed worthy and married in the temple almost by accident. Don was a high school friend who was pretty casual about following the rules. All of his friends were members of the Church and consistently observed the standards, but Don occasionally drank coffee and beer and decided not to serve a mission. Eventually, however, Don married a nice girl in the temple and sort of "grew up" as a member, serving as a seminary teacher and then as a bishop. I don't mean to undervalue the temple marriage of any worthy individual, but my point is that a few decades ago, some young people sort of drifted along with a crowd of good kids and ended up in a good place, without having to make very significant sacrifices or intentional efforts. Today, I don't know that it's likely that many of our youth will end up worthily married in the temple unless they are determined, focused, and willing to sacrifice to achieve that goal. There are so many aggressively available opportunities for our youth to indulge in drinking, drugs, immodesty, pornography, premarital sexual activity, and so on that it seems fair to say they have to be more *intentional* about staying worthy. They have to be increasingly different from their peers. And each succeeding generation up until the coming of the Lord will have to be "a [more] peculiar people" (1 Peter 2:9) than the one before.

To help our children successfully negotiate safe passage through our increasingly dangerous world, parents need to teach celestial law and principles, but enforce terrestrial law and principles. Church members understandably want their children to someday become celestial, but while we can and should teach children celestial ideals, we must realize we cannot *make* our children celestial. Celestial life is a state of being, an integration of purified hearts and righteous behaviors. Parents, no matter how strong their desire and how diligent their efforts, can't change the hearts of their children. Only the Lord can give them "a new heart . . . and a new spirit" (Ezekiel 36:26).

When society was more terrestrial, parents could, with perhaps less effort, help children learn to live a terrestrial standard. Then, having been taught celestial ideals and having learned terrestrial behavior, the children were ready to move forward if they chose to, with ready access to the Spirit, so they could build on a solid foundation and work effectively toward "a new heart . . . and a new spirit." In a more telestial society, parents can still teach celestial ideals, but if they don't make deliberate and intentional efforts to teach and enforce a terrestrial standard, children may instead learn the telestial behaviors they are constantly exposed to just by living in our increasingly telestial society. I have heard many good parents lament that their children are rude, disrespectful, spoiled, lazy, disobedient, and quick to fight with siblings. If we expect such children to accept and live a celestial standard while displaying telestial behaviors, we are essentially asking our kids to skip from the telestial to the celestial, and we know that doesn't usually work well. And if the children aren't consistently terrestrial, their telestial behaviors will offend the Spirit and leave them without the necessary guidance and sanctifying power needed to progress toward the celestial. Today's parents are more often successful when they create a structure that makes it worthwhile for the child to develop terrestrial patterns of self-control and deferred gratification.

ONE ETERNAL NEED THAT MAY ESCAPE THE NOTICE OF PARENTS IS THE NEED FOR CHILDREN TO LEARN TO MASTER THEIR APPETITES AND HARNESS THEIR NATURAL MAN TO CORRECT PRINCIPLES.

Every child is born into this world as the quintessential natural man. Each child is innocent, but as his spirit is cloaked in a tabernacle of flesh; the flesh makes him a creature of desires, appetites, and passions. When he is tired, he cries; when he is hungry, he cries; when he is cold or bored or uncomfortable, he cries. Of course, we meet the needs of infants and children, but one eternal need that may escape the notice of parents is the need for children to learn to master their appetites and harness their natural man to correct principles.

A friend once told me of a sacrament meeting in which her family sat behind a young family with several children, the oldest of whom was probably ten years old. After the opening prayer, the mother began unpacking a large bag and distributing the contents to the children, including goldfish crackers, apple slices, gummi bears, small sandwiches, and fruit juice boxes. The picnic continued throughout the meeting with just a small pause for the sacrament. One wonders why we expect children who can't get through a 70 minute meeting without food to control their hormones when they hit puberty.

Some parents talk about their children's difficult and unpleasant behavior—their yielding to the desires and passions of the natural man—as if the behavior will automatically improve as the children grow older. How often do we hear parents dismiss tantrums as "the terrible twos?" Yes, developmental stages exist and can bring specific challenges, but in a telestial world, there is no guarantee that improvement—self-control and deferred gratification—will come with age. We have only to look around us to see that more and more children go from the terrible twos to the terrible threes, fours, and fives. Many eventually grow into adolescence and adulthood without ever having learned to consistently master their desires and appetites.

It is parents who can most effectively teach self-control and deferred gratification, the laws of the terrestrial, to their children. This chapter will review only a few ideas on effective parenting practice. These are not new techniques nor should they be seen as a complete treatment of the subject. There are, however, excellent resources available to help parents become more skilled at rearing their children. Considering the time and money we often spend on pre-school programs, gymnastics, soccer, little league sports, art and music classes, etc., to enhance the lives of our children, it only makes sense to also invest in books or classes to learn how to more effectively parent. For now, though, let's consider a few ideas to help us as parents.

Focus on Concrete, Terrestrial Behaviors

A number of good parents get caught in the trap of trying to skip their children from the telestial to the celestial realm. Teresa, the mother of six school-age children, told me that she was constantly frustrated by how much her children fought and argued with each other. She and her husband made serious efforts to teach the children to get along better but with no noticeable improvement. Teresa was so troubled about the contention that she could no longer bring herself to sing "Love at Home," in Church meetings. The words of the hymn made her feel so guilty she would leave the room, rather than hear it sung.

I asked what Teresa had done with her children to try to improve things. Besides constant reminders, she and her husband had planned several family home evening lessons and activities focused on learning to love each other as family members. She told me of successful lessons in which everyone felt a really special spirit of love, but five minutes after the closing prayer the children were fighting over refreshments. She was completely at a loss as to what more she could do to lessen the contention in their home.

The three realms perspective confirms what Teresa already knew and worried about—contention is a telestial behavior. Love amongst siblings is a celestial principle and definitely should be taught in our families. However, we cannot change the hearts of our children and make them love each other. And when children are at a fairly telestial level of fighting and quarreling with each other, to try to get them to love each other violates the "Can't Skip" principle. Teresa and her husband needed to continue to teach the celestial ideal of family love but also focus on the terrestrial safety net behavior of not fighting with each other.

Let's say our two children, Johnny and Susie, are fighting—again. It doesn't work to say, "Johnny and Susie, you shouldn't be angry with each other. You need to love each other, and I'm going to wait right here until you do." Hearts don't change on demand, and they can't leap from telestial fighting to celestial loving. But we *could* say, "Johnny and Susie, I know you're really upset with each other (and frankly, I'm not too crazy about either of you myself, right now), but *you can't hit; you can't break each others' things, you can't call each other those names."* In this way we focus on harnessing the natural man (terrestrial) as opposed to trying to change their hearts (celestial). The children may still be upset with each other, but if they are not allowed to give free rein to angry feelings, they can move from telestial behavior to terrestrial behavior.

If we utilize a system of natural and logical consequences, we make it worth our children's while for them to control themselves. Note the difference between *controlling* our children's behavior and making it *worth their while* for them to *control their own* behavior. We want our children to develop within themselves the self-control and deferred gratification that harnesses the natural man in each of us and allows the Spirit into our lives. Helping, even requiring, our children to build a terrestrial foundation sets the stage for good things to happen. For instance, if we appropriately motivate our children to treat each other with respect and we prevent them from hurting one another, their hearts can change and love can grow. Family life, with its intense opportunities to share and build memories, usually yields loving, enduring attachments as long as family members are respected and safe.

While rearing my own children, I remember fielding complaints one child would bring to me about another child. I did my best to appropriately address misbehavior with the erring child, but before dealing with a guilty sibling, I sometimes took a moment to explain to the first child that I could impose consequences and correct behavior, but I couldn't *change hearts*. (If I could have changed their hearts, I would have done so long ago.) But although I couldn't change the way my children *felt* about things, that didn't stop me from addressing my children's behavior on two levels: first, setting up a structure that required self-control and deferred gratification (securing the terrestrial); and second, teaching them the gospel principles behind the standards of behavior that we required (inviting them to become converted to celestial ideals). The former I could regulate, the latter I could only teach and offer. But when parents consistently require terrestrial behavior from their children, the Spirit can be consistently present in the home, making it possible and more likely that children will be converted to celestial ideals.

A second common mistake made by parents in this area of skipping from telestial to the celestial levels with their children involves a misapplication of a well-known statement by Joseph Smith. When asked how he governed the people of Nauvoo, the Prophet answered, "I teach them correct principles and they govern themselves."[4] Quite often, I hear of parents using this statement as their entire parenting approach. Yes, the Prophet's statement applies to parenting, in terms of the ultimate reality that children reach a point at which, for better or worse, they govern themselves. And certainly, parents should teach correct principles. However, I would suggest that this principle has greater application to terrestrial adults than to the parenting of young children.

Consider, first of all, the differences between the Nauvoo citizenry and the children who come into our homes as infants. Most, if not all, of the Nauvoo citizens were, at least, terrestrial. These people had, for the most part, harnessed the natural man. Their presence in Nauvoo meant they had already paid a heavy

---

4. Quoted by John Taylor, in *Millennial Star*, Nov 15, 1851, p. 339.

price for membership in the Church, enduring hardship and persecution and then reclaiming a mosquito-infested swamp to build the greatest city of its time in that part of the country. Nauvoo did not even have a jail—there wasn't the need—further demonstrating that the inhabitants were not much afflicted with telestial behaviors. When our children come to us, they are innocent, but just beginning their struggle with man's dual-nature. They are *spirits* of great worth and divine potential cloaked in *flesh*, which from the Fall of Adam has become carnal, sensual, and devilish (see Alma 42:10, Moses 5:13, Moses 6:49). Their appetites exert a powerful influence. It doesn't make sense, then, to instruct small children on the danger of playing with knives or fire and then leave the choice up to them. We don't teach a young child about the value of education and then allow him to choose whether or not to go to school. And hopefully, we don't explain to our children that smoking, drinking, and drugs can have seriously harmful outcomes but tell them "Whatever you decide is all right with me."

Analisa told me that her six-year-old daughter, Brittany, threw tantrums all the time and Analisa couldn't get her to stop. I asked for a recent example. Analisa said Brittany would often insist on having cookies just before dinner, even though Analisa would tell her dinner was almost ready and Brittany should wait till after. Analisa said she tried to teach Brittany about good nutrition and explained why it is better not to spoil one's appetite with sweets, etc., but Brittany would throw fits, screaming and yelling at her mother. This had happened again just the day before. I asked how Analisa responded. She gave Brittany a cookie. But the cookie was broken, so Brittany threw it across the kitchen and yelled that she wanted one that wasn't broken. I asked what Analisa did then. She gave Brittany an unbroken cookie. Analisa would tell Brittany her behavior was inappropriate and unpleasant, but Brittany's appetites were obviously running the show.

Enforcing Terrestrial Behavior—Costs and Payoffs

We must not only teach correct principles, we must create and enforce a structure that includes rewards and penalties that make it worthwhile to comply with gospel and family standards. The structure that generally works best is based on costs and payoffs.[5]

When all is said and done, human behavior is motivated by costs and payoffs.[6] We do what we feel rewarded for doing, and we stop doing things that cost us too much. Since children are completely dependent, especially to begin with, parents can appropriately manipulate the costs and payoffs for certain behaviors. This can begin early in the child's life and motivate the child to learn to control his or her appetites.

When we were expecting our first child, my husband and I heard many parents complain that they spent a lot of sacrament meetings in the foyer of the chapel with noisy children. We noticed, however, that children often spent "foyer time" playing on the furniture, walking in and out of the doors, or generally running and tumbling around. It occurred to us that any child would rather run around the foyer than sit quietly on a bench in the chapel. Kids probably figure out pretty quickly

---

5. This is a brief review of a basic behavior-modification approach found in many, many parenting books and seminars.

6. That may seem harsh, but consider that to a great extent, each of us individually defines what we consider a cost and what we consider a payoff. Some, even as adults, are motivated by food, money, laziness, popularity, or other worldly treasures. But others choose to be motivated by the desire to be acceptable to God and to qualify for the great gift of eternal life. The Lord addressed different motivators when He taught "Lay not up for yourselves treasures upon earth, where moth and rust doth corrupt, and where thieves break through and steal: But lay up for yourselves treasures in heaven, where neither moth nor rust doth corrupt, and where thieves do not break through nor steal: For where your treasure is, there will your heart be also" (Matthew 6:19-21).

that if they make enough noise in the chapel, they get to go to the foyer and have a good time. Their parents may not be too happy with them, but overall, the payoff exceeds the cost. We decided that when we had to take a child out of the chapel, we would go to an empty room—or if a room wasn't available, to the back seat of our car (the front seat is too much fun)—and hold him firmly in our lap, until he was ready to go back in the chapel. The choice was simple: did the child want to sit in a boring place, no stories, no songs, no toys, not allowed to move around and play, or would the child rather return to the chapel and play with his quiet book and do other chapel-appropriate activities? It worked. It was worth their while for our kids to control themselves and stay in the chapel.

Individual adaptation is absolutely necessary. Not all children define costs and payoffs in the same way. Human beings differ tremendously, but we're all pretty much the same in one way— no one keeps putting his hand on an electrified fence. So, as parents, we need to make misbehavior feel a little bit like putting your hand on an electrified fence. An immediate caution: if you find yourself too enthusiastic about creating "electrified fences" for your children, *slow down* and *pull back*. Effective parenting *never* includes harsh, mean, punishing responses.

On the other hand, if you are trying to increase the costs and decrease the payoffs of an undesirable behavior in your child and the behavior persists, recognize that the payoffs are still too high and the costs are still too low. One mother told me that her four-year-old son kept playing too roughly with his baby brother. "Every time he hurts his brother, I put him in his room," the mother said. I asked if that was working. "Not really," she said, "he still plays much too roughly." It seems the payoffs were still exceeding the costs. This is one reason I have sometimes questioned the effectiveness of "time out" as a consequence. Many children don't mind enough when sent to their rooms. And why should they mind? Some rooms are equipped with iPods, televisions, DVD players, computers, video games, and cell phones. Even without the latest electronic entertainment, some children are content enough to be in their rooms just reading or resting. If time out—or any other imposed consequence—isn't working, change the consequence. Remember, when payoffs exceed costs, behavior continues; when costs exceed payoffs, behavior stops.

Mary told me that her teenage son was out of control and she felt helpless to do anything about it. I asked a few questions. Whose car does he drive? Who pays for the insurance? The gas? Does he have a cell phone? Who pays for it? Does he have access to a computer? Whose computer is it? Who pays for the Internet? Our society has cultivated such entitlement for our children that parents sometimes buy into the idea that their kids deserve access to a number of parent-provided luxuries with no strings attached. Parents may need to consider that removing or limiting some of those privileges is a logical consequence that may shift the balance of costs and payoffs for children.

It is important for parents to recognize that when they impose a cost on their children, the parents too will pay a price. If the price is too high for the parent to follow through with the consequence, that consequence should not be threatened or imposed. Years ago, I taught early morning seminary. The week after report cards came out there were always some students whose parents took away their car keys because their grades were too low. I asked how long the student would be unable to drive, and the answer was often, "Oh, it's supposed to be for the whole term, but after getting up at 5:30 a.m. to drive me to early morning seminary for a few days, they always give me back the keys." Better to choose a different consequence.

When possible, consequences should be logically connected to the issue being addressed. This can help reinforce the principle being taught. For instance, siblings who aren't getting along well can be required to treat each other respectfully and kindly or forfeit opportunities to play with friends and neighbors.

It's easy to be respectful and kind with friends, but family relationships are more important. If a child takes two hours to settle down and go to sleep at night, the bedtime ritual can begin two hours earlier so the child sees that it's important to get to sleep by a decent hour. If siblings fight over the television or computer or games, access to those things can be denied until the children are willing to take turns and respectfully negotiate their differences. Decent grades can be a requirement for driving a car, as there is a clear connection between the self-control and deferred gratification required for good grades and the qualities that make a safe driver (a connection known by insurance companies and reflected in reduced, good-student rates). But parents would have to follow through and drive the child to early-morning seminary or anywhere else he needs to be until grades improved.

We benefit our children not at all by allowing them to continue with telestial behaviors, subject to their appetites and desires. We don't let infants and toddlers govern themselves. We don't let school-age children govern themselves. Even adolescents should not be left to grow up without parental involvement and supervision, perhaps receiving suggestions but facing no consequences for their choices. *It is as children begin to display the consistent terrestrial ability to self-regulate that we gradually allow them to start governing themselves.*

When parents use a let-them-govern-themselves approach before children have learned to control their appetites, the upshot of that parenting style is permissiveness. Many caring parents fall into this category, teaching their children celestial and terrestrial principles, but without a structure to motivate and teach self-mastery. In such circumstances, children are likely to exploit the permissive parenting and let the natural man rule. Parents may then wait hopefully, painfully, and usually in vain for a magic moment of maturation, at which time rebellious children will finally embrace the correct principles they've been taught. That moment may never come. Elder Neal A. Maxwell made this sobering statement:

> I have no hesitancy, brothers and sisters, in stating that unless checked, permissiveness, by the end of its journey, will cause humanity to stare in mute disbelief at its awful consequences.[7]

As a family counselor, I am already seeing the fulfillment of this prophetic warning. As neighbors and citizens, you are seeing it, too.

Our Children's Agency

Occasionally, I speak with good parents who teach their children the gospel but sometimes feel unsure about how much they can demand of their children. The parents don't want to be overly controlling or dictatorial, and they worry about "taking away my child's agency." These parents are confusing freedom with agency.[8] Freedom can certainly be limited or taken away by others, appropriately or inappropriately. Even God sometimes takes freedoms away. One vivid example was when He stopped Pharoah's chariots with a pillar of fire to allow the children of Israel to cross through the Red Sea on dry ground, He was limiting the freedom of the Egyptians, but not their agency (see Exodus 14:24-29). Indeed, God will not take away the very gift He gave us, the gift He would not allow Satan to take from us. Agency is the power given to man by God to allow us "to choose liberty and eternal life, through the great Mediator of all men, or to choose captivity and death, according to the captivity and power of the devil" (2 Nephi 2:27). The truth is that *no one can take agency from another*, because it happens in the heart. Even in a prison cell or a concentration camp,

---

7. Neal A. Maxwell, "Becometh As a Child," *Ensign*, May 1996, 68.

8. See Appendix B for further discussion of this idea.

each individual can choose eternal life or spiritual captivity and death by choosing God or rebelling against Him.

As parents, we have a stewardship over our children that includes—regularly, at first, and then less often as they mature—limiting their freedom to engage in telestial behaviors that are destructive of themselves or others. Such limitations of freedom do not, and never will, constitute the taking away of children's agency. Parents can feel confident in setting limits for their children, using their understanding of what constitutes telestial behaviors to draw a clear line in areas that offend God or hurt others.

Protecting Children from Telestial Parenting

Another three realms application to parenting concerns the well-accepted idea that parents should present a united front in parenting their children. Yes, there are good reasons for a united parental front. Children can benefit from having parents show their agreement in the standards and expectations of family life, in measures of discipline, and in other decisions that affect family functioning and practice. It is also important to avoid the danger of triangulation, where children may attempt to circumvent or undermine parental authority by using a "divide and conquer" approach that pits the parents against one another. *However, if one parent is behaving telestially, the terrestrial parent should not support the more telestial partner in parenting practice for the sake of presenting a united front.*

Consider a sad, but not unfamiliar problem of a family with an abusive parent. Let's say the father of a family, Bill, has a terrible, uncontrolled temper that sometimes explodes against the children so that he is too physically rough with them and speaks to them in vile, demeaning language. Ann, the mother, hates to see the children subjected to Bill's temper, but doesn't want to undermine Bill's parental authority and believes she needs to support Bill's role as patriarch. Further, she is sure that if she interferes with Bill's parenting he will openly accuse her of not supporting him and be furious.

Ann needs to consider a different perspective. First, Bill is not behaving like a patriarch. Section 121 makes it clear that when priesthood positions are abused to compel or injure others, "amen to the authority of that man" (verse 37). Second, she should *not* support Bill in telestial parenting. Bill's abuse of the children is not going to lead to positive outcomes but will only generate the pain, violence, and destruction that telestial behavior always brings. Third, Ann admits that she is concerned, even afraid, of Bill's temper. So consider how terrified *the children* must be of their father's temper. Ann needs to intervene between Bill and the kids as needed, even if that means drawing Bill's fire. If Ann thinks the situation could become dangerous, she needs to seek out and employ appropriate backup resources to support her in protecting the children. Fourth, if the more terrestrial parent won't advocate for and protect the children, who will? Children have such limited access to supportive resources. *But parents are supposed to protect children.* Of course, *both* parents should protect children, but if instead one of the parents is actually hurtful to the children, the children need more than ever the protection of the other parent.

I have spoken to many adult children of abusive parents. The injury can be deep and long-lasting, but with the application of true principles and the Atonement of Jesus Christ, healing is always available. In the process of working through such injuries, however, it sometimes surprises the adult child to realize that not only do they have to process the anger they feel toward the abusive parent, they also have to process the anger they feel toward the non-abusive parent. Sometimes those feelings of anger and betrayal almost seem deeper. They ask, "Why didn't that parent protect me?"

If we have a partner who is solidly terrestrial (or better) and we sometimes have differences of style or opinion in parental matters, we should exercise caution, discuss differences away from the children as much as possible, and work unitedly in our parental efforts. But if our partner is indulging in telestial behaviors, we need *not* to back them up in parenting situations where our children are being hurt. *We must protect our children.*

What God Requires of Parents

All this is not to say that parenting is the only factor in determining how children behave. Boyd K. Packer has said,

> The measure of our success as parents . . . will not rest solely on how our children turn out. That judgment would be just only if we could raise our families in a perfectly moral environment, and that now is not possible. . . . It is not uncommon for responsible parents to lose one of their children, for a time, to influences over which they have no control. They agonize over rebellious sons or daughters. They are puzzled over why they are so helpless when they have tried so hard to do what they should. It is my conviction that those wicked influences one day will be overruled.[9]

Good parents throughout the history of the world have done their best to rear children in the gospel in spite of telestial elements all around them. Many of these good parents have felt the heartache of seeing their children turn away from those gospel teachings. These parents sometimes feel great guilt for what they see as their failure as stewards over the precious children of our Heavenly Father. Over the years, my husband,

---

9. Boyd K. Packer, "Our Moral Environment," *Ensign*, May 1992, 68.

who is also a marriage and family counselor, has reassured parents that the Lord does not measure us as parents based on what our children do, He measures us as parents based on what *we* do *with what we know.*

While parents are not accountable before God for the choices their children make, there is evidence in the scriptures that God does hold parents accountable if some lines are not drawn in the parents' tolerance or subsidy of their children's telestial behaviors. For instance, in King Benjamin's address to his people, he told parents:

> And ye will not suffer your children that they go hungry, or naked; neither will ye suffer that they transgress the laws of God, and fight and quarrel one with another, and serve the devil, who is the master of sin, or who is the devil spirit which hath been spoken of by our fathers, he being an enemy to all righteousness (Mosiah 4:14).

This was a scripture I used when stopping fights or arguments between my children. I would point out that if I allowed them to continue, *I* would have to answer to God. ("And if you think I'm going to let you jeopardize my standing with God, you're crazy.")

Certainly, as noted, children have agency and will make choices for which *they* are responsible, not their parents. However, King Benjamin taught that parents must not "suffer" their children to "transgress the laws of God." In the Old Testament, we read of two fathers whose children were unrighteous, Eli and Samuel. God held Eli responsible for "suffering" his sons' behavior, not the case with Samuel. The Bible Dictionary says that Eli was: "High priest and judge, a descendant of Aaron . . . The blot on his character was his toleration of the wickedness of his own sons."[10] The scriptural record tells us that his sons were "sons of Belial" (1 Samuel 2:12), defined in the Bible Dictionary as "worthless" or "wicked."[11] A few verses later, we read that Eli heard of his sons' evil doings, "how they lay with the women that assembled at the door of the tabernacle of the congregation" (v. 22). Eli confronted his sons, telling them off, but "they hearkened not unto the voice of their father" (v. 25). Samuel, given to the Lord by his mother at a young age and placed in the charge of Eli at the tabernacle, "became the great prophet and judge of Israel . . . and is a signal example of faith, patience, integrity, and self-sacrifice through a long and trying career."[12] The record says, "When Samuel was old . . . he made his sons judges over Israel . . . [but] . . . his sons walked not in his ways, but turned aside after lucre, and took bribes, and perverted judgment" (1 Samuel 8:2-3). Samuel is not rebuked by the Lord as far as we know. Eli, however, is condemned because he "honour[ed his] sons above [the Lord]" (1 Samuel 2:29). The Lord continues, "His sons made themselves vile, and he restrained them not" (1 Samuel 3:13). Both Eli's sons were slain in battle on the same day, and Eli, distraught at hearing the news of his sons' death and that the ark of the covenant they bore had been captured by the enemy, fell, broke his neck, and died (see verse 18), exactly as the Lord had foretold.

While the Old Testament record may be a bit sketchy, it's clear that God held Eli responsible for the telestial behaviors of his adult sons but He did not hold Samuel similarly culpable. We know that God is "no respecter of persons" (Acts 10:34; D&C 1:35, 38:16), so it was not a matter of His liking Samuel

---

10. Bible Dictionary, *Holy Bible,* King James Version, The Church of Jesus Christ of Latter-day Saints, s.v. "Eli."

11. Bible Dictionary, *Holy Bible,* King James Version, The Church of Jesus Christ of Latter-day Saints, s.v. "Belial."

12. Bible Dictionary, *Holy Bible,* King James Version, The Church of Jesus Christ of Latter-day Saints, s.v. "Samuel."

better than Eli or applying a double standard. It may be that the difference lay in the fact that Eli's sons were officiating in priesthood responsibilities over which Eli had direct stewardship and yet Eli did not release them from those priesthood callings even when he heard of their telestial offenses toward God.

I remember hearing of Pete—almost eighteen years of age—whose younger brother, Josh, was turning sixteen and was scheduled to be ordained to the office of priest in the Aaronic priesthood. Josh's entire family knew that he was seriously involved in illegal drug use, but nothing was said to the bishop and clearance for the ordination was given. When Josh was presented to the ward for a sustaining vote, Pete did not sustain his brother. When those opposed were given an opportunity to so indicate, he raised his hand. Pete's actions were based in two strong emotions: a profound respect and reverence for God and His priesthood and a deep enough love for his brother that Pete did not want to participate in Josh making a mockery of sacred things. The story of Eli prompts us to consider that in such a case God may expect parents to speak to the bishop about behaviors that render a child unworthy for participation in sacred ordinances or responsibilities.

A mother of another teenage boy once came to speak with me about her son's deep involvement in pornography and masturbation. She said the bishop did not know about her son's problem, so the son continued to officiate at the sacrament table and still went to the temple to do baptisms. The mother had mixed feelings about speaking to the bishop. She knew her son had a problem with worthiness but hated the thought that he might be embarrassed or that he might not be able to enter the temple. Is it possible that God might consider the mother's silence to be honoring a son above the Lord? It may be that God would expect a parent to stand at the temple gate, if necessary, to prevent a child from mocking sacred things while simultaneously protecting the child from personal damnation for participating unworthily in the ordinances of salvation (see 3 Nephi 18:29).

While God does not hold parents responsible for their children's exercise of agency, God apparently expects parents not to tolerate or subsidize their children's sins, particularly in areas that involve making a mockery of sacred things or violating the trust of priesthood authority.

Finally, remember that parents should *teach* celestial law and *require* terrestrial behavior. We can't change the hearts of our children, but if we invest in developing the knowledge and skills of effective parenting, particularly in our children's early years, we can modify their behavior so they are much less likely to be offensive to God or their fellows. In doing so, we give them a better life now and make it possible for the Spirit to work on their hearts, preparing them for a better eternity.

PARENTS SHOULD TEACH CELESTIAL LAW AND REQUIRE TERRESTRIAL BEHAVIOR.

I remember hearing the story of a woman who, with several young children, got on a city bus. The bus driver looked at all the kids and asked, "Lady, are those all your kids or are you taking the neighborhood out for a picnic?" The woman responded, "They're all mine, and it's no picnic." Granted, parenting has never been a picnic, but as the world becomes more telestial, parents must recognize that *increasing* awareness, study, skills, and energy are all necessary to do an effective job of parenting. Terrestrial times have ended, and parents now have the additional challenge of dealing with the deterioration of societal values and the aggressive evils so readily available to our children. Nevertheless, if we come to understand these basic principles and learn to apply them in our parenting stewardships, we can still get the job done in a manner acceptable to our Heavenly Father.

CHAPTER EIGHT

Worst Things First

Not All Problems are Equal—Prioritizing Our Approach to Problem-Solving

Not all sins are equal in offense toward God. While all sin separates us from God and true followers of Christ seek to eliminate all sin from their lives, the Lord communicates that there are differences of degree amongst certain offenses. When the Lord refers to adultery as "the sin next to murder" (Alma 39:5),[1] this communicates that murder is a particularly heinous offense (not difficult to understand) and that adultery is very nearly as destructive and offensive. This, and other serious sins, are designated by the Lord as so grievous that they prevent us from worthily partaking of the sacrament, entering the temple, or serving a mission. While all commandments are important and all sin is serious, some sins are clearly *more* serious than others.

---

1. See also "The Law of Chastity," in *Gospel Principle* (Salt Lake City: Intellectual Reserve, Inc., 1997), chapter 39.

The three realms perspective establishes a hierarchy—a ranking—of concern when we are trying to decide which problems, behaviors, and issues to address first to make effective progress in improving our lives. Because telestial behaviors bring pain, violence, and destruction, they are the most crucial to address and correct. This includes adultery, stealing, lying, or dishonesty of any kind. It also includes addictions such as pornography, substance abuse, gambling, violence, intense expressions of anger, and so on, as well as any abusive behavior. This is not a complete list, of course, as telestial behaviors include all actions and attitudes that constitute *willful rebellion* against God and His commandments—behaviors that damage and eventually destroy individuals and relationships.

Terrestrial problems are not nearly as destructive, although they can certainly be irritating to live with. Some terrestrial problems might include procrastination, being messy, watching too much television, being a workaholic, being lazy, being too finicky, being unorganized, being a fanatic sports fan, etc. These behaviors may be bothersome to live with and certainly are behaviors that could and should be improved, but they are not as overtly and directly destructive as telestial behaviors. Remember that if a terrestrial problem is taken to the extreme, it can start to cross over into the realm of destructive (telestial) behaviors. But even at that level, there is a significant difference between, for instance, someone who is obsessed with sports to the point that it is painful to live with and someone who is physically abusive, or between someone who never cleans up after him or herself and someone who is having an extramarital affair.

All Problems Are Not Created Equal

In marriage counseling, I've sometimes seen partners with telestial problems try to convince their spouse that his or her terrestrial problems were just as big a factor in the marriage as the telestial problems. For instance, I remember a husband who sometimes used illegal drugs. During periods of drug use, he became abusive to his wife. In one counseling session, the husband asked when he would be able to list *his* complaints about his wife's shortcomings. I invited him to go ahead. He said she began every year by making a goal to exercise regularly and drop a few pounds, but then she would slack off in a few months. His second complaint was that his wife wasn't consistent about regulating the children's household chores and responsibilities. She didn't always check their work, so occasionally the next child assigned to the task would complain that the job hadn't been properly completed the last time. I asked if there were any other complaints. He said not really, but he considered it a critical concern that "my wife sets a bad example to the kids of not completing goals and doesn't teach them to be 'finishers' on their jobs." He worried that the children would grow up to be irresponsible and unsuccessful—this, in spite of the fact that his eldest daughter had been accepted to a prestigious university because of high achievement.

After he finished discussing his wife's shortcomings, I asked him to consider that on the one hand (I held out my left hand, palm up) his wife didn't continue her exercise goals for very long and didn't always check up on the children's chore completion, and on the other hand (I held out my right hand, palm up) he used illegal drugs, on occasion became physically and emotionally abusive, and was unworthy of a temple recommend. I looked from one hand to the other for a moment and then let my right hand drop as the "scales" tipped heavily on the side of the destructive telestial behaviors. I asked if he sincerely considered her failings to be equivalent to his. He seemed startled, but admitted they were not.

In working with many clients over the years, I have become aware of this pattern of exaggerating terrestrial problems and minimizing telestial problems. The Savior referred to this pattern, condemning those "which strain at a gnat, and swallow a camel" (Matthew 23:24). *Minimization*—not acknowledging the severity of one's own destructive behavior—is swallowing the camel. *Blaming and criticism*—magnifying lesser imperfections in the spouse—is straining at the gnat. It is not uncommon that the more terrestrial spouse, who is genuinely trying to be a good person and a good partner, takes in all that blame and criticism and starts to feel seriously browbeaten. Further, the terrestrial partner, trying to be fair and teachable, is more likely to look inward and self-scrutinize. So the terrestrial partner, ironically, may begin to seriously question his or her own value and worth.

Consider the following situations:

- A husband, addicted to pornography, blames his wife for not being more physically affectionate.

- A wife who is verbally abusive and emasculates her husband, even in front of their children, complains that her husband plays too much golf and doesn't give enough service.

- A husband who has had an affair tells his wife he can't trust her because she "betrayed" him to their bishop.

Sadly, there are many such situations. Moral relativism, a predominant social philosophy in our society for some time now, requires that we withhold judgment. Political correctness seems to reject anything other than equal sharing of responsibility and doesn't want to assign blame or shame to anyone. We have no-fault insurance, no-fault divorce, and now no-fault marriage and relationship evaluation. While blaming others isn't useful, to have come to the point where sinners need not take responsibility for sin is ridiculous. God has made it clear that He "cannot look upon sin with the least degree of allowance" (Alma 45:16), yet we sometimes are so concerned about anyone feeling bad that we hesitate to label any behavior as sin. And in our information age there are plenty of euphemisms available. We can substitute words like problem, issue, weakness, disorder, disability, or genetic tendency. Of course there are people with genuine challenges or weaknesses that should be taken into consideration, but we can go too far, as in the case of a man whose wife had always been physically and emotionally abusive. I asked why he was still married to her. The man replied, "Well, I saw the results of a personality test my wife once took. The test showed that she was narcissistic,[2] so I feel I need to make allowances for her behavior." I tried to explain to him that in spite of the fact that narcissism is listed as a disorder in the *Diagnostic and Statistical Manual*,[3] in many respects, narcissism is more a *sin* than a *disorder*.

WE NEED TO ACKNOWLEDGE THAT SOME SINS ARE INDEED WORSE THAN OTHERS, AND SHOULD BE ADDRESSED WITH MORE WEIGHT AND URGENCY.

With society's tendency to avoid anything that sounds like stern judgment, we too can easily fall into the trap of "calling good evil and evil good" (Isaiah 5:20), or in a more subtle distortion, calling evil "not-so-bad" or "not any worse than your (terrestrial) problems." But if we are going to successfully problem-solve in our own lives and in our relationships, we need to acknowledge that sin exists and some sins are indeed worse than others and should be addressed with more weight and urgency.

Rachel came to see me after separating from her husband, Trent. She had been married to Trent for about seven years and throughout that time had tried to be patient with a number of extremely hurtful behaviors, including verbal and physical abuse, pornography, and demands for brutal and demeaning

---

2. "Narcissism: extreme selfishness, with a grandiose view of one's own talents and craving for admiration." *The Oxford Pocket Dictionary of Current English*, s.v. "Narcissism," http://www.encyclopedia.com/doc/1O999-narcissism.html (accessed May 29, 2009).

3. The DSM is a publication of the American Psychiatric Association and specifies diagnostic criteria for mental disorders.

sex. In addition, Trent was frequently out of work and made minimal effort to stay employed, so Rachel worked full-time and largely supported them. Trent spent hours playing violent video games that were extremely disturbing to his wife. Rachel had repeatedly tried to get Trent to agree to marriage counseling, but he refused. When Rachel finally moved out, Trent seemed shocked and became extremely conciliatory, saying he had no idea she was so unhappy and she should come back so they could try again. Trent found dozens of conference talks and *Ensign* articles about the importance of preserving marriage and keeping temple covenants—yes, they had been sealed in the temple—and told Rachel she was out of line for abandoning their marriage. Trent's family became involved in his efforts to save his marriage. His aunt wrote the following to Rachel:

> Please don't just run away from the problems. You are both equally responsible for the trouble in your marriage. It's true that Trent has problems with addictions, anger, selfishness, etc. but you have low self-esteem and never stand up for yourself.

No doubt, Trent's aunt had good intentions and hoped to help. However, look at the comparison being made between Rachel's "low self-esteem" and inability to stand up for herself and Trent's "addictions, anger, selfishness, etc." Remember that the "etc." included physical and sexual abuse and a pornography addiction. The aunt's conclusion that Trent and Rachel were "both equally responsible for the trouble in [their] marriage," is a monumental error. Trent's problems were telestial and destroyed the relationship. Rachel's problems were terrestrial issues that she was, incidentally, more than willing to address.

Trent also wrote to Rachel:

> I admit I haven't always treated you right, but I do love you. I knew there were times I was frightening you, but I didn't realize you lived in constant fear. I

> don't think you know how much I care about you. I truly believe that our problems all boil down to a lack of communication!

Trent's and Rachel's problems did *not* boil down to a lack of communication. Trent was utilizing the common response of many offenders in minimizing his telestial behaviors. Rather convenient to characterize physical and sexual abuse, pornography addiction, not working to support his family, and other problems, as "a lack of communication."

In another letter, Trent wrote:

> You have more serious issues than you are addressing. I think your shyness and lack of confidence are more significant than you are admitting. I hope you're being honest with yourself.

Like his aunt, Trent was maximizing the severity of Rachel's problems and, in combination with minimizing his own telestial issues, it allowed him to shift focus from his own guilt and responsibility to Rachel's less-than-perfect (aren't we all?) life.

Rachel was confused by these messages. She had an innate feeling that something was wrong with the logic somewhere, but she didn't know how to respond to these challenges. Because Rachel had a solid testimony and a desire to do the right things—as demonstrated by consistent, concrete, and productive efforts—she was quick to look to herself. She wanted to be accountable and to make sure she wasn't being too hard on Trent. As so many spouses do in these situations, Rachel constantly asked herself if she was being too demanding or unrealistic in her expectations. She worried that the Christlike response was to patiently endure Trent's abusive behavior, although she felt she had come to a breaking point where she could no longer endure. She worried that this was a failure or weakness in herself. But, as Rachel came to understand the basic distinctions between the telestial and terrestrial realms, her confusion dissipated and she was eventually able to respond to her husband with the following:

> Trent, I want you to know that I don't agree with what your aunt said about my being equally responsible for our problems. I am responsible for my own behavior, but I am not equally responsible for what has happened in our marriage. I didn't ask to be treated with disrespect or to be your personal servant and maid. I didn't ask to be emotionally, verbally, physically, and sexually abused. I didn't bring those behaviors into our marriage, you did. You can't ignore your covenants for five years and then make me the bad guy when I walk out. It's not your place to decide, "My wife, who has been keeping her covenants for five years, is obligated to stay with me and work it out."

Some spouses, when confronted with a similar clarification, finally acknowledge and take responsibility for their telestial behaviors and begin the process of addressing and overcoming them. Others don't ever seem to get it. Even when directly confronted with the severity of their behavior, they quickly resume the but-you-have-problems-too or the we-are-equally-responsible stance. Because we don't fix things we don't believe are broken, a spouse who brings telestial behaviors to the marriage but who won't acknowledge that his or her behavior is "broken," is not going to fix it.

A side note: when choosing a marriage counselor, it's important to find a clinician who is not reluctant to assign priority to the presenting problems of each spouse and focus first on eliminating destructive, telestial behaviors. One woman told me of going to a therapist for help in dealing with her husband's sixth extramarital affair. The therapist told her that maybe if she didn't nag her husband and tried being more affectionate and loving, her husband would stop seeking out other women. The woman left the therapy session feeling doubly brutalized.

It is not only in relationship problems that we need to be aware of the order of operations. In our personal efforts to progress, we may also find ourselves caught in the trap of incorrect focus or emphasis. Katrina had a serious problem with cutting herself in response to her loneliness and the stresses of her life. She had made progress, but Sundays continued to be difficult days for her. She lived alone, so after Church Katrina found herself back in her apartment alone and usually ended up cutting. While we worked on improving her emotional stability and coping skills, I also wanted Katrina to consider changing her Sunday schedule immediately, to break the pattern of self-destructive behavior on that day. I suggested she get out of her apartment and be with other people for most of the day. She had no family in the area and didn't feel comfortable calling on neighbors or ward members, so I suggested that, while not normal Sabbath behavior, she could go to a mall and walk around or even go to a movie or a concert. Katrina was horrified at the suggestion. "I can't do those things on Sunday!" she protested. I asked her, "Which do you think God would prefer, that you go to a movie on Sunday or that you stay home and cut yourself?" The goal was to get to a point where she could be safe on Sundays and observe the Sabbath correctly, but she needed to fix the more destructive problem first.

Couples may make this mistake together. Years ago, I met with a husband and wife who had been married for about ten years and who had four children. They were ready to file for divorce, but their bishop had made them promise to meet with a counselor a few times before doing so. Not exactly a promising beginning. Nevertheless, I asked them what, if anything, might save their marriage. They both agreed that their problem was communication. After our initial meeting, I met with each spouse individually and then we had another session all together. I began by telling them that their problem was not communication. They were surprised and rather indignant. "Yes, it is!" they protested. "No, it's really not," I maintained. "Well, what is it, then?" they challenged." My answer: "You're mean to each other." I continued, "You're actually communicating quite effectively, but the substance of your communication is pretty nasty, and it's destroying your marriage."

This couple had confused telestial and terrestrial offenses in their self-assessment. Both had minimized the telestial behavior of mean, hurtful interaction and had framed it as a terrestrial problem of poor communication. They—under the direction of their bishop, at least—wanted to improve their communication skills, rather than acknowledging and addressing the mean-spirited words and behaviors that characterized their relationship. To give them great credit, both husband and wife began to take responsibility for their hurtful behaviors and, together, they saved their marriage and family.

Parents sometimes send confusing messages to children about which behaviors are most destructive. For instance, if parents come home to find that the kids played ball in the living room and broke a lamp, the parents would do well to consider their response and the message it will send to their children. Yes, it's irritating and needlessly expensive to repair that error, but how grave an offense is it in the grand scheme of things? Will horseplay, resulting in some broken furniture, prevent that child from getting to the kingdom of God? Not unless it's deliberately and maliciously done, which is not generally the case.

If parents become enraged at broken furniture, children, trying to avoid their parents' anger, may end up lying about their actions. Now lying *is* a behavior that prevents us from getting to the kingdom. So, as parents, it is important to respond to misbehaviors at levels consistent with the significance of the offense. This doesn't mean a child should not be corrected for horseplay, and depending on circumstances, perhaps levied a consequence to help restore what was broken. But parents should clarify that while the child's behavior ignored rules and showed a careless lack of responsibility and poor judgment, lying would have taken the problem to a deeper, telestial level, offending God.

Failure to clarify different degrees of offense can lead to critical misunderstandings. More than one birth parent social worker has reported puzzling interviews with young, unwed, LDS girls who are pregnant. The worker may be speaking with a fourteen or fifteen-year-old girl, and in the course of the interview the worker asks, "So, is the father of the child a boy you've been dating?" The young girl looks shocked and offended, responding, "I wouldn't date! I'm not sixteen!" Apparently, we have failed to communicate important information to this young woman concerning the relative significance of two gospel standards. While it is recommended that young people delay dating until age sixteen, and blessings and protections are available to those who follow that counsel, if young adults ignore this guideline, they may still take the sacrament and enter the temple. On the other hand, premarital sexual activity involves the sin "next to murder" (Alma 39:5). There is no question but that sexual immorality is a telestial behavior and a severe offense to God. We do not condemn or shun individuals who commit this sin or any other, but those who are involved in serious sins are not worthy to enter the temple and may jeopardize their status as members of the Church—a far more serious situation than that of a more terrestrial offense, like dating before age sixteen. Even armed with correct information, children may still make bad choices (adults do it all the time). With the framework of the three realms perspective, however, they can understand better which sins are most serious and, hopefully, put their greatest efforts toward avoiding telestial behaviors.

When we recognize different levels of offense, we can address personal and relationship issues in a more effective manner, focusing first on the most destructive behaviors. Three other positive outcomes also result. First, we legitimize, empower, support, and bring hope to those victimized by telestial behavior. Second, the telestial offender has a better opportunity to arrive at true contrition and genuine repentance. Third, understanding the difference between terrestrial and telestial offenses allows for a more realistic expectation of when healing and forgiveness can occur.

Let's look at each of these more closely. First, by understanding telestial versus terrestrial offenses the terrestrial victim can sift through the confusion so often generated by the telestial offender. The offended can be more confident about holding the line on telestial behaviors, without feeling guilty or worrying about not being sufficiently Christlike.

Second, the offender has a better opportunity to arrive at true contrition, a state of "sincere remorse for wrongdoing; repentance."[4] Confronted with his minimizing of his sins and his maximizing of others' problems or imperfections, the offender can choose to acknowledge the gravity of his sins and repent in figurative "sackcloth and ashes" (Matthew 11:21, Mosiah 11:25). This scriptural phrase refers to the practice of wearing a simple garment made of coarse fabric and sitting among the ashes or rubbing ashes on one's head and skin as a sign of deep grief, mourning, and sorrow. In our day, this term is not to be taken literally, of course, but signifies that remorse, sorrow, and repentance for hurting someone should be demonstrated by noticeable actions, and groveling should probably be involved. If someone is really sorry for causing another person pain, the injured party should be able to recognize that sorrow in the actions of the offender, not just take the offender's word for it.

When my kids were little and one of them had hurt a sibling, I, like many parents, insisted the offending child apologize to the one hurt. Sometimes the first apology wasn't very convincing,

---

4. *The American Heritage® Dictionary of the English Language*, 4th ed., s.v. "Contrition," http://dictionary.reference.com/browse/contrition (accessed June 7, 2008).

coming out with a snide tone and sarcastic expression. That wasn't good enough. I would say, "No one here is convinced you're sorry. Why don't you try again?" The offending child wasn't off the hook until a convincing apology was made.

Some offenders want the offended to forgive even when no convincing apology has been offered. Joy told me her husband, Dustin, had never apologized for having a chat room affair that became very sexualized. Dustin was seeing a counselor who told Joy that Dustin had a "shame response" from emotional injuries in his youth that were hard for him to deal with, so Joy shouldn't press for an apology because it could induce shame in Dustin.

Well, we *should* feel ashamed when we sin. And that shame should be accompanied by our best efforts to "make it up" to anyone we have offended. Instead, when a person seriously injures someone else, we often see a "no-fault" response that comes across as, "Well, too bad this happened (but it's not really my fault). Let's just repair our own cars and drive on." That just doesn't heal broken hearts. Repentance should include *many* convincing apologies, humility, and sincere, extra, and prolonged service to the person offended. Such a response—if genuinely offered—soothes and heals those who were wounded. And the truly repentant person, who wants to help heal those he has injured, needs to not tire of those efforts too quickly.

Tom had become involved with another woman and was trying to repent and make things right with his wife, Kara, who had already forgiven him of more than one extramarital involvement over the 20 years of their marriage. Tom seemed to be genuine in his efforts to show remorse and serve his wife, but he did complain to me privately that sometimes things would seem to be going "so well," and then something would remind Kara of those injuries. She would tell Tom what she was thinking and how hurtful the memory was. He would usually respond with something like, "Well, don't think about that any more," or

"Try to forget those things." Tom thought Kara needed to try harder to move on and worried that she would never be able to put the past behind them. I suggested he take a different tack. When something reminded Kara of the deep hurts she had suffered at her husband's hands, I suggested Tom create out of those moments an opportunity to apologize again and to reaffirm the promises he had made. He could say something like, "I am so sorry for ever hurting you, and I am finally aware of how destructive my sins have been to our marriage, but I hope you'll keep giving me the chance to prove I'll never hurt you like that again."

Finally, understanding the severity of the damage done by telestial offenses allows for a more realistic timetable for healing and forgiveness. Often the offender is in too big a hurry to be forgiven. This is another kind of minimization. Telestial behavior is horribly destructive, and even after the behavior stops, healing and forgiveness will take time. Kent told me that his wife, Laura, had had an affair. She was secretly involved for quite a while, but finally confessed to her husband and then began her repentance process with their bishop. Almost immediately, Laura expected Kent to forgive her. When he said he didn't feel forgiveness at that point and wasn't sure when he would, Laura told him that if their marriage ended, it would be Kent's fault for not forgiving. That's not true. Adultery would be the primary cause of destruction in that marriage. Let's not so easily dismiss the sin next to murder. Further, consider how offensive and inappropriate it is to frame this situation as Kent's fault. That turns the knife in the wound.

Whether or not Laura repents, Kent needs to come to a point where he forgives. (Whether or not the marriage continues is a different issue involving many variables, including the sincerity of repentance.) God does expect us to "forgive all men" (D&C 64:10), although there is no specific time requirement in which forgiveness must be completed. We should never deliberately withhold forgiveness, *but in order for forgiveness to be healthy and genuine, it must come after we are safe again.* Forgiving before we are safe—like the battered wife who forgives but then is battered again—is not really forgiveness, it's accepting a victim role. Elder Richard G. Scott noted that forgiveness does not need to be rushed, saying:

> While an important part of healing, if the thought of forgiveness causes you yet more pain, set that step aside until you have more experience with the Savior's healing power in your own life.[5]

Both offender and offended are benefited if there is a realistic understanding that healing and forgiveness may take some time and are made more difficult if pressure is applied to rush the process.

Relationship problems are painful and challenging enough without complicating things by straining at gnats and swallowing camels. Understanding and applying the three realms perspective can help us clear up confusion, avoid victimization, and put first things first.

---

5. Richard G. Scott, "To Heal the Shattering Consequences of Abuse," *Ensign*, May 2008, 40-43, (emphasis added).

CHAPTER NINE

How to Be Anxiously Engaged Without Being Anxious

A Three Realms Perspective on Dealing with Stress

The primary message of this book concerns using the three realm perspective to help us find safety in a dangerous world. A secondary message reminds us that it is possible to become too comfortable at a terrestrial level when we should be rousing ourselves to greater valiancy. This chapter, however, uses the three realm perspective in a different way: to help us evaluate and manage life's stresses. There will be some overlap with ideas discussed in previous chapters, but since stress is an ongoing concern for so many of us, I think it worthwhile to consider it on its own. God knew how stressful life would become for his children living on the earth today and, of course, He has provided the information we need to deal with it successfully.

Even stress can be usefully categorized as telestial, terrestrial, and celestial. Some might think that all stress should be considered telestial, because it is pretty unpleasant, but in fact, some stress is terrestrial and, perhaps surprisingly, even celestial stress exists. As members of the Church, we sometimes have a particular vulnerability to terrestrial stress, but each level of stress may touch our lives and to find real solutions, we must understand each level and know how to address each kind of stress correctly.

Telestial Stress—The Soap Opera Syndrome

I like to call telestial stress the "soap opera syndrome," named for an experience I had many years ago. My husband, Chris, and I had moved across the country just in time for him to start a master's degree in the Social Work program at the University of Oklahoma. I already had two preschoolers, I was nine months pregnant, I was severely anemic, and the baby was overdue. After our new daughter was born, three weeks late, I would sit on the couch for hours, exhausted, just holding her. I started watching TV, but after a while, I got tired of the game shows and found the only other option (we only had five or so channels in those days)—a soap opera. I watched, then watched again . . . for about four or five months. I hoped the kids weren't paying any attention, but one day my four-year-old said, "Mom, why is that man yelling at that lady?" Now, I believe children's questions deserve answers, but I wondered how to respond without going into the sordid details of the last three weeks' episodes leading to this fight. I thought for a moment and said, "Okay Adam, this is the answer: these people are making really bad choices; they're breaking all kinds of Heavenly Father's commandments—and it makes them miserable." Adam looked up at me, and, with that child's instinct for the jugular, he asked, "Then why are we watching it?" Ouch! I turned off the TV and have never watched another soap opera since. Years later, this event came to my mind as I considered how to define telestial stress. Telestial stress is the misery that results when we live in ways that are contrary to the commandments of God.

We know that the outcomes of indulging the appetites and passions of the natural man are pain, violence, and destruction. The scriptures warn of "sowing the wind and reaping the whirlwind" (Hosea 8:7, Mosiah 7:30). There are, of course, innocent victims who suffer because of the telestial choices of others, but for the most part, if we avoid sin our lives are more peaceful and safe. The commandments are not arbitrary hoops God asks us to jump through in order to win a prize. They are advance information about which behaviors bring happiness and which bring sorrow. As Alma so succinctly summarized, "Wickedness never was happiness" (Alma 41:10) and, in fact, a great deal of stress in life comes as a result of sin. Thus, active, obedient membership in the Church, particularly at the level of temple worthiness, generally frees us from the majority of telestial stress.

Too often, individuals may have the mistaken idea that agency is free—meaning they can do whatever they want *and get away with it*. This is one of Satan's great lies. As President Boyd K. Packer has emphasized, agency is not free.[1] Agency has consequences. Moral agency allows us to choose good or evil, and in making that choice, we also choose the good or evil outcomes. In other words, agency means we can go to hell if we really insist. Some try to argue their right to break commandments by protesting, "I have free agency!" but more accurately, they could say, "I can destroy myself if I choose, and God won't stop me because He allows me that choice."

Some are confused about the connection between sin and misery because the consequences of sin are often deferred. In

---

1. See Boyd K. Packer, "Our Moral Environment," *Ensign,* May 1992, 66.

this life, people even sometimes get away with murder. However, if we expect actions to always bring immediate consequences we misunderstand the plan. Consider what would happen if every time we did something good, an immediate reward appeared—maybe a hundred dollar bill in our pocket—and if every time we did something wrong a lightning bolt zapped us just enough to hurt us badly. No one would sin—or at least not much—but all it would prove is that we can keep our hands off an electrified fence. Receiving immediate rewards or punishments would not give us a way to develop and demonstrate virtue or help us become more Christlike. It would be a kind of "cattle prod salvation." The reality is that we become more like God as we make correct choices *without* an immediate reward, and sometimes even with a significant cost attached. Christ taught, "For if ye love them which love you, what reward have ye? Do not even the publicans the same?" (Matthew 5:46). It is when we love those who don't love us back that we come closer to developing Christlike love. Likewise, it is as we keep commandments without a hope of immediate reward, and even if we're getting kicked in the teeth for doing the right thing, that we truly become more like Jesus Christ.

> WE BECOME MORE LIKE GOD AS WE MAKE CORRECT CHOICES WITHOUT AN IMMEDIATE REWARD, AND SOMETIMES EVEN WITH A SIGNIFICANT COST ATTACHED.

Alma taught that a "space," or a period of time, is needed between action and consequence, sin and punishment, or virtue and reward to allow for the exercise of agency and to give meaning and purpose to the plan (see Alma 12:12). It is easier to understand the times when life seems unfair if we understand these two truths: first, immediate consequences for our choices would sabotage the exercise of agency; and second, the Day of Judgment—accountability for us all—will eventually come.

Although complete accountability for our choices may not come until the final judgment, some consequences do come in this life. Several years ago, a rather gruesome cover story in *Time* magazine called "7 Deadly Days"[2] reported how many people had been killed in this country in one week (there were 464). Pictures of the victims were included, with names, ages, and brief synopses of how they each died. After reading through the article, I was surprised to find myself feeling strangely comforted. I realized that in the majority of cases, the murder victims were living telestial lifestyles—and my family does not live like that. Many victims were involved in the commission of a crime; many involved alcohol or drugs; and some were involved in domestic violence or bizarre love triangles, which exploded in violence. These were ugly situations, the kind we are protected from if we obey basic commandments, largely freeing us of telestial stress. The article reported some innocent victims—one man, for example, was killed in the violence of a video store robbery—but they were clearly the exception. Yes, the telestial realm can invade terrestrial or celestial lives, but overall, when we do not sin, we are much safer from telestial stress. The solution to telestial stress is simply to repent and obey.[3]

Terrestrial Stress—The Martha Syndrome

Terrestrial stress could be called the "Martha syndrome" in honor of the good woman, sister to Mary and Lazarus, who is depicted in a painting hanging in many Relief Society rooms all over the world. The painting shows Martha and her sister, Mary, with Christ as they fed him in their home one evening. The story is told in the last four verses of Luke chapter 10. We read that Martha complained to the Savior because Mary wasn't helping in the kitchen. The Savior responded with

---

2. Ed Magnuson, "7 Deadly Days," *Time*, July 17, 1989.

3. If we are subject to telestial stress because of the actions of people close to us, the solution may be in developing healthier boundaries, or in extreme cases, may require ending the relationship. See Chapter Five—From Victim to Non-Victim.

words we have often heard, "Mary has chosen the better part, and it shall not be taken from her" (Luke 10:42). Just before those words, however, are other important words that I believe define terrestrial stress: "Martha, Martha: thou art careful and troubled over many things" (Luke 10:41).

Martha was "careful and troubled"—stressed—over terrestrial things; at that moment, it was cleaning up after a meal. Like Martha, we can become troubled over many things that fall into a terrestrial category. These are not evil things; in some ways, evil could be identified and eliminated more easily. With terrestrial stress, the things that burden us are good or necessary, but nevertheless *of the world*. In order to free ourselves from terrestrial stress, we must reduce and simplify some of the good, but temporal, things in our lives.

Women, in particular, seem to have problems with the Martha syndrome. We have much "care and trouble" over cooking, cleaning, laundry, bills to pay, holidays to prepare for, decorating, and gardens. Mothers worry about children's homework, the science fair, soccer practice, music lessons, cub scouts, PTA, and keeping all the baby books and scrapbooks up-to-date. There are birthday parties to plan, worthwhile community involvements, vacations, and food storage to be obtained and rotated—and, oh yes, we should be cooking with locally-grown, organic produce. We may feel guilty if we aren't actively supporting the political candidate of our choice. We may worry that our homes aren't more like the temple, or at least more like the "after" pictures in home decorating magazines. We try to provide our children with any number of good experiences and struggle to find time to exercise. The list could quite literally consume many pages. Every time we look at a magazine cover in the grocery store, browse the television channels, or notice what our neighbors are doing, we find more to add to the list.

In the 1980s, Margaret B. Black and Midge W. Nielsen wrote a piece called "Patti Perfect." It started like this:

> Patti gets up very early and says her personal prayers. She zips her slim, vigorous body into her warm-up suit and tiptoes outside to run her usual five miles (on Saturday she does ten). Returning home all aglow, she showers and dresses for the day in a tailored skirt and freshly starched and ironed blouse. She settles down for a quite meditation and scripture reading, before preparing the family breakfast. The morning's menu calls for whole wheat pancakes, homemade syrup, freshly squeezed orange juice, and powdered milk (the whole family loves it).
>
> With classical music wafting through the air, Patti awakens her husband and ten children. She spends a quiet moment with each and helps them plan a happy day. The children quickly dress in clothes that were laid out the night before. They cheerfully make their beds, clean their rooms, and do the individual chores assigned to them on the Family Work Wheel Chart. They assemble for breakfast the minute mother calls.[4]

Patti combines all our best intentions and unrealistic ideals into a perfect day. Every baby book is up to date, she makes whole wheat bread, fellowships the non-member neighbor, does her visiting teaching, writes genealogical inquiries, sends letters to the ward missionaries, volunteers at the local elementary school as a clinical psychologist, has perfect children, a perfect husband, a perfect life.

---

4. Margaret R. Black and Midge W. Nielson, "Patti Perfect," *Exponent* 10, no. 2 (1984).

During my years as a full-time mother, my husband and I would occasionally hear the "Patti Perfect" story read or referred to. At one point, my husband turned to me and said, "You know, Lili, I don't think you get it."

"Of course I get it," I protested.

He insisted, "No, I don't think you get it."

I finally asked, "Okay, what am I not getting?"

He answered, "You think you can *be* Patti Perfect."

I blinked. He was right. I did think if I tried *just a little harder*, I could accomplish all those wonderful things in my own family and home. And after all, my terrestrial stress included some very satisfying things: learning to make and stitch pieced quilts, getting really good at pie crusts and rolls, making homemade Christmas gifts, having a vegetable garden, canning produce, doing my own preschool for my children, even themed Halloween costumes (one year my kids were the signers of the Declaration of Independence and their wives; we have pictures; I can prove this), and much more that helped me learn and develop valuable skills.

I am not suggesting we should altogether eliminate these good terrestrial activities. Terrestrial stress can be so challenging precisely *because* it does not come from sins to be eliminated. The Savior was not telling Martha she should never cook or clean the kitchen again. He was warning her that she could get caught in the terrestrial realm, focusing on good things of the world to the exclusion of more important things, or as Elder Paul H. Dunn put it, "getting caught up in the thick of thin things."[5]

---

5. Paul H. Dunn, "'Because I Have a Father'," *Ensign*, May 1979, 7.

Today, women are bombarded with images of Patti Perfect's many younger sisters. We see so many good, terrestrial ways to spend our time and money, whether single, married, or mothers. We go to the gym, further our education, develop careers, drive children everywhere, recycle, scrapbook, Facebook, Twitter, blog, and run the blood drive. If we don't make the tough choices about what we realistically can and cannot do, we can easily get trapped in terrestrial stress.

Men get trapped in terrestrial stress, too. Employment is a necessary, even divinely ordained (see Moses 5:1),[6] temporal concern; but if allowed, it can draw too much of a man's focus, time, and energy, and a man may find himself "run[ing] faster than [he has] strength" (Mosiah 4:27). Along with employment, there are plenty of other temporal concerns that compete for attention: house maintenance and repair, gardening, landscaping and yard work, keeping the cars running, coaching kids' teams, and whatever other responsibilities husbands and fathers assume. And these are just the productive ways we can spend our time! With movies, television, video games, the Internet, sports, hobbies, online social networking, and many, many other things that fill our time and take our money, we add to our terrestrial stress. To eliminate it, we may need to make very difficult decisions, reducing the number of things we allow to take priority and learning to streamline and simplify the necessary tasks of life.

A caution here: sometimes we are fooled into thinking that more money can eliminate terrestrial stress. While money can allow access to some helpful services and conveniences and while insufficient financial resources can add to our stress, experience repeatedly demonstrates that money does not solve the problem of crowding our lives with too many good, but temporal, concerns. In fact, too often, the more money people

---

6. See also "The Family: A Proclamation to the World," *Ensign,* Nov 1995, 102.

have, the more they seem to need, so money does little to reduce stress in any significant sense.

WHILE IT MAY SEEM OBVIOUS THAT OUR SECULAR LIFE ACTIVITIES SHOULD BE MODERATED AND SIMPLIFIED, WE SHOULD BE AWARE THAT EVEN CHURCH SERVICE CAN GET OUT OF BALANCE.

Another potential trap is thinking that things will be better as soon as a certain event has passed or project is complete. "When the holidays are over," "After football season is done," "When we move into a bigger house," and similar expectations anticipate that life will get less hectic just around the next corner. It's true that the passing of major events or the completion of a large project can bring some relief, but generally speaking, we find that new or returning activities and demands take up the slack so quickly we don't really get much lasting relief. While it may seem obvious that our secular life activities should be moderated and simplified, we should be aware that even Church service can get out of balance.

Elder M. Russell Ballard, in October conference of 2006 spoke plainly:

> Occasionally we find some who become so energetic in their Church service that their lives become unbalanced. They start believing that the programs they administer are more important than the people they serve. They complicate their service with needless frills and embellishments that occupy too much time, cost too much money, and sap too much energy. They refuse to delegate or to allow others to grow in their respective responsibilities.[7]

Certainly, dedicated Church service is one of the great blessings and responsibilities of membership in the kingdom of God.

---

7. M. Russell Ballard, "O Be Wise," *Ensign*, Nov 2006, 17-20.

Accepting and serving willingly in our Church callings is part of an obedient life and is part of God's plan for us to lift others as we ourselves are lifted. But sometimes, learning *not* to run faster than we have strength while still serving God with all our heart, might, mind, and strength (see D&C 4:2) is a challenge. As we seek to serve "in [His] own way" (D&C 104:16) we should listen carefully and respond to the warning voice of our latter-day prophets who are increasingly telling us to simplify our lives, including the way we perform Church callings. As we then try to serve in a dedicated, consecrated, acceptable manner, following the counsel of prophets and apostles, we can be freed from the stress that could otherwise accompany the best intentions to serve diligently. Elder Ballard again warned:

> As a result of their focusing too much time and energy on their Church service, eternal family relationships can deteriorate. Employment performance can suffer. This is not healthy, spiritually or otherwise. While there may be times when our Church callings require more intense effort and unusual focus, we need to strive to keep things in proper balance. We should never allow our service to replace the attention needed by other important priorities in our lives. Remember King Benjamin's counsel: "And see that all these things are done in wisdom and order; for it is not requisite that a man should run faster than he has strength" (Mosiah 4:27).[8]

My husband and I were exposed to the wise example of a member of our stake presidency in Oklahoma when my husband was in graduate school. This good brother told us that he had realized he was allowing too much of his family time to be taken by members of his stake wanting to talk to him about their problems. He wanted to help, but he had a wife

---

8. Ballard, "O Be Wise," 2006.

and eight children who were not getting a balanced part of his time and attention. He counseled with his wife, and together they made a schedule of when he could meet with stake members. Many of those hours were during the day because he had some flexibility in his work schedule. People would call to schedule an appointment and he'd say, "I can visit with you at this time on Thursday." Sometimes people would instead ask to see him during evening hours. This brother would ask, "What do you do when you've got a toothache?" They answered that they took time off work to see a dentist. His reply: "When it hurts as much as a toothache, give me a call." Previously, he had been too "careful and troubled" about everybody else's scheduling convenience, slipping into the Martha syndrome of trying to be all things, to all people, all the time. However, when we listen to and follow the counsel of our leaders, we too can bring greater wisdom and order to our lives, families, and stewardships by making sure our priorities are appropriate.

The Church has made at least two significant program changes to encourage members to simplify—and in some ways, we have circumvented both. One change was the consolidated schedule, designed to provide more family time during the week and on Sunday. As Elder Boyd K. Packer explained:

> There will be . . . fewer activities, fewer programs. That will leave a vacuum. Nothing likes a vacuum. We must resist, absolutely resist, the temptation to program that vacuum. That space belongs to families. When we cut down on Sundays to the block plan that consolidated our meetings and left some time open, you know what happened. Now brethren, it is their time. Let them use it as they feel to do—for better or for worse. . . . If we do, then

that vacuum will be filled with prayer and work and study . . . with faith and reverence.[9]

In spite of such warnings, sometimes more programs *were* added—more meetings, more interviews, or more activities—undoing the good that could have been done by the consolidated schedule. Eight years later, President Packer tried to communicate this message again:

> We must be careful lest programs and activities of the Church become too heavy for some families to carry. The principles of the gospel, where understood and applied, strengthen and protect both individuals and families. Devotion to the family and devotion to the Church are not different and separate things. . . . I do not want anyone to use what I say to excuse them in turning down an inspired call from the Lord. I do want to encourage leaders to carefully consider the home lest they issue calls or schedule activities which place an unnecessary burden on parents and families. . . . Every time you schedule a youngster, you schedule a family—particularly the mother.[10]

Church leaders have tried to remind us and encourage us to follow this direction. In February of 1999, a letter from the First Presidency was read in sacrament meetings expressing concern for the youth of the Church. It included this plea:

> However worthy and appropriate other demands or activities may be, they must not be permitted

---

9. Boyd K. Packer, "Let Them Govern Themselves," (address presented at the Regional Representative Seminar, March 20, 1990).

10. Boyd K. Packer, "Parents in Zion," *Ensign,* Nov 1998, 22.

> to displace the divinely-appointed duties that only parents and families can adequately perform.
>
> We urge bishops and other Church officers to do all they can to assist parents in seeing that they have time and help, where needed, as they nurture their families and bring them up in the way of the Lord. Wherever possible, Sunday meetings, other than those under the three-hour schedule and perhaps council meetings on early Sunday mornings or firesides later in the evening, should be avoided so that parents may be with their children. As we strengthen families, we will strengthen the entire Church.[11]

While some leaders responded, it seems that to others any and all meetings *can* be seen as essential. Prophetic warnings have continued.

> Church leaders should be aware that Church meetings and activities can become too complex and burdensome if a ward or a stake tries to have the membership do everything that is good and possible in our numerous Church programs. Priorities are needed there also. . . . Stake presidencies and bishoprics need to exercise their authority to weed out the excessive and ineffective busyness that is sometimes required of the members of their stakes or wards. Church programs should focus on what is best (most effective) in achieving their assigned purposes without unduly infringing on the time families need for their "divinely appointed duties."[12]

---

11. First Presidency Letter, Feb, 11, 1999, "Strengthening Families," http://www.lds.org/pa/display/0,17884,5154-1,00.html.

12. Dallin H. Oaks, "Good, Better, Best," *Ensign,* Nov 2007, 104-8.

At a worldwide leadership training broadcast, Elder Dallin H. Oaks emphasized this idea again:

> Let me speak to bishops and stake presidents, who preside over ward councils and stake councils. Let's have parental time on agendas as we make up schedules, not just fitting every conceivable meeting and activity into the Church calendar without regard to what that does to families.[13]

The Church is trying to give us back our time—for prayer, meditation, and family life. But even if programs and meetings are streamlined, we can sabotage that blessing by amplifying our perception of what our callings require, increasing the terrestrial, unnecessary, non-redeeming stress in our lives.

A second change that the Church instituted, in part to help us simplify, was the revision of the budget program. President Thomas S. Monson clearly explained that the change in the budget allowance program was intended "to reduce financial burdens on members" and that "priesthood leaders should reduce and simplify activities," which should require "little or no cost, build testimonies, and provide meaningful service to others."14 The idea was that with limited budgets we would have to simplify the programs, alleviating some of the stresses that come from financial and time obligations. If we, however, with the best intentions, circumvent budget allowances—asking members to bring supplies, furnish refreshments, or contribute money in order to continue hosting activities that are more elaborate than would otherwise be covered by the budget—we still end up trapped in terrestrial busy-ness, despite the Church's best efforts to help us "reduce and simplify." It is all too easy to forget that the budget allowance was not intended to save the

---

13. Dallin H. Oaks, (address, worldwide leadership training satellite broadcast, February 2008).

14. Thomas S. Monson, "The Lord's Way," *Ensign,* May 1990, 92.

Church money through increasing contributions or donations from members, but—again—to "reduce financial burdens on members" and that "priesthood leaders should reduce and simplify activities."

Excessive terrestrial emphasis on embellishing activities and assignments has caused some members to experience burnout in Church service (perhaps not surprising when we consider what can sometimes happen with programs like Girls' Camp). How tragic that some may blame the programs of the Lord's Church instead of recognizing that the problem is our failure to obey. The Lord warns, "I command, and men obey not; I revoke and they receive not the blessing. Then [after disobeying] they say in their hearts: This is not the work of the Lord, for his promises are not fulfilled" (D&C 58:32-33). If we complicate our lives with terrestrial stress, if we fail to follow repeated admonitions to simplify, it's not appropriate to blame our callings, the Church, or the Lord when we feel overwhelmed and overburdened. The Lord gives us guidelines to bless us and our families. If we ignore those guidelines, He won't demand or compel our compliance, but the blessings are lost.

In the next chapter, we will discuss that the terrestrial realm is a good realm, filled with good, honorable men and women who do good things, but who ultimately are not fully acceptable for the Lord's kingdom. It is not enough to do good things in *our way*, we must be willing to do things *in the Lord's way*, as revealed by his prophets.

It is rare to attend a women's meeting without a tablecloth and a centerpiece, and sometimes a magnet, laminated bookmark, or some other gift for everyone to take home. Of course, there is nothing wrong with doing nice things, but we must be careful not to *over*do them to satisfy our own expectations and desires, rather than seeking to understand how the Lord would have us complete our assignments. It is sometimes too easy to get caught worrying about how well we *appear* to be fulfilling our stewardships, rather than remembering that all stewardships are about helping to bring souls to Christ.

I have spoken at many stake women's conferences where sisters find me during the luncheon and tell me they wished they had been able to attend my presentation, but, because they were on the food committee, they had been busy putting the garnish on the dessert. The picture of Mary and Martha has been on Relief Society walls for so many years, reminding us where the Lord would have us place our priorities, and yet sometimes we may still miss the message. Even worse, some get caught thinking that each event has to be better, more elaborate than last year; so we try to do more and be more, jumping higher and running faster, in spite of inspired counsel to the contrary. From Elder Oaks:

> The instruction to magnify our callings is not a command to embellish and complicate them. To innovate does not necessarily mean to expand; very often it means to simplify.[15]

And from President Dieter F. Uchtdorf:

> It is possible to take even good things to excess. . . . Even some programs of the Church can become a distraction if we take them to extremes and allow them to dominate our time and our attention at the expense of things that matter most. We need balance in life.[16]

Of course, sometimes we do see delightful simplicity. At one stake auxiliary training meeting, the brethren were in charge of refreshments. After the closing prayer, all were invited into the cultural hall where two men were setting up a table. There

---

15. Dallin H. Oaks, "Good, Better, Best," *Ensign,* Nov 2007, 104-8.

16. Dieter F. Uchtdorf, "We Are Doing a Great Work and Cannot Come Down," *Ensign,* May 2009, 59–62.

was no tablecloth, no decorations, no theme. In the kitchen, another brother took some brown cardboard boxes out of the freezer. A couple of guys brought those to the table, ripped them open, and invited us to help ourselves to ice cream sandwiches. One fellow brought in a large garbage can, set it next to the table and said, "You can put your trash in here," and a very thoughtful brother got some coarse, brown paper towels from the restroom, set them on the table and said, "Here—if you need a napkin." It was not elegant, but it was quick, simple, there was a treat for those who wanted one, and no one missed any part of the spiritually instructive and uplifting program because they had been "busy putting the garnish on the dessert."

Again, none of this is to say that we can never appropriately plan and carry out special events, including tablecloths and decorations, but only that we need to be cautious to not focus so much on the extras that we inadvertently demand of ourselves, our families, and perhaps others more time, effort, or expense than is consistent with "wisdom and order."

There are other ways that we can miss opportunities to reduce and simplify in our service, denying ourselves, and others, the blessings that could be ours. At the age of twenty-two I was called to be Primary president. Our new presidency began to meet regularly, and after a few weeks my husband asked how our meetings were going. I said, "Great! These are wonderful women."

He asked, "How long are your meetings?"

I said, "Oh, two and a half or three hours sometimes. There's so much to do as we get organized."

"Whoa!" was his response.

So I said, "Okay, teach me."

My husband quoted Elder J. Golden Kimball, that insightful and colorful man, who once said "It has to be a damn good meeting to be better than no meeting at all."[17] Then my husband went on to teach me some important, simplifying skills, including how to make an effective agenda and distribute the agenda a couple of days early so each person could be ready to report on assignments. My husband counseled, "Whatever you do, have your opening prayer on time and your closing prayer sixty minutes later. If you can't do it in sixty minutes, it most likely doesn't need to be done that week." He was right. I became a more effective leader and reduced the burden on those sisters and their families. I felt their gratitude, and I was grateful too. Our meetings had taken up too much of everyone's time.

When we fail to simplify our callings, we may end up imposing unnecessary, terrestrial burdens of stress on others. A counselor in a Young Women's presidency told me of a time when they planned special refreshments for New Beginnings. Eight women came to the president's house and spent about eight hours making patchwork sugar cookies from cookie dough, dyed in the value colors. Beautiful icing bows at each junction put the finishing touches on these little artistic marvels that now looked like patchwork quilts. Admittedly, those cookies were a work of art, but it's doubtful the girls ate those cookies much more slowly than they would have eaten an Oreo. Might not those sixty-four man-hours have been put to more effective use? Elder Jeffrey R. Holland reminded us:

> Elder Scott said sometimes to magnify your calling is to do less, not more. You've brought more focus to it, you've exercised better judgment. You've increased the quality, but the sheer mass may be smaller, not greater. That's an equally liberating thought, I think—not to shirk, not to be a slacker,

---

17. Claude Richards, J. Golden Kimball: The Story of a Unique Personality, (Salt Lake City: Bookcraft, 1966).

but to really, seriously look at the big picture, including the big picture of the family, and maybe sometimes do less.[18]

One barrier to simplifying is tradition. We tend to repeat elaborate activities because "that is the way it has always been done." General Relief Society president Julie Beck, in the worldwide leadership training meeting, warned:

> A good reason to have a ward activity or a stake activity is because we need it and it will strengthen our families and individuals. A bad reason to have an activity is because it's a tradition or there's a certain holiday we have to celebrate. When we talk about gospel patterns, we know the needs. Let's plan the activities around those needs, and if something was a wonderful activity last year, it doesn't mean we need to build it into a tradition.[19]

Occasionally, we may be tempted to justify ignoring the counsel to simplify by thinking of some of the good outcomes of previous, elaborate programs—a less active youth who felt the Spirit, a shy sister who bore her testimony, or a less active brother who started coming to Church. But a positive outcome in such cases is not likely to be *because* we are ignoring guidelines, but *in spite* of it. God has always made lemonade out of lemons. God will bless any who are ready to feel the Spirit, but just think what an outpouring of the Spirit could happen if we would increase our obedience and simplify as our leaders have pled with us to do. We must always remember: "To obey is better than sacrifice, and to hearken, than the fat of rams" (1 Samuel 15:22)

---

18. Jeffrey R. Holland, (address, worldwide leadership training satellite broadcast, February 2008).

19. Julie Beck, (address, worldwide leadership training satellite broadcast, February 2008).

Another barrier to simplifying is our tendency to "[look] beyond the mark," as Jacob warned (Jacob 4:14). Sometimes we reverse the "ends" and the "means," and the program itself becomes the goal, rather than a means by which individuals can be brought to Christ. A Relief Society president once called me in some distress. Her stake Relief Society leaders had heard that sisters serving in the Primary and Young Women's organizations felt the loss of attending Relief Society, so to address this loss, the stake Relief Society presidency decided to have a lesson taught on fast Sunday evenings for all sisters who could not attend their ward Relief Society meetings on Sundays. They tried to keep it simple by rotating the assignment to teach amongst ward Relief Society teachers, who could repeat a lesson they had already given. The first month, three sisters in the stake attended. The second month, one sister attended. The third month, two sisters came. It was a nice idea, but, as much as some sisters in the stake may have expressed sadness that they couldn't attend Sunday Relief Society meetings, it obviously wasn't worth it to those sisters to leave their families on a Sunday evening to have a Relief Society lesson. It would have been logical to cancel the program at that point, but instead, the stake Relief Society presidency sent a message to ward Relief Society presidencies telling them they needed to attend the fast Sunday evening meetings in order to "support the program." The Relief Society president that called me in distress had a young family that already made significant sacrifices for her to fulfill her calling. Sunday evenings were precious family time.

General Relief Society president Julie Beck has said:

> When a ward council meets together or a presidency meets together, oftentimes they discuss, "How can we get people to support us in our organization?" or "We had a lot of people there; we had a lot of support." And that's really backward. When a ward council meets or a presidency meets, if they would begin by saying, "How can we support the family?"

> Then what we do is an outgrowth of things that will support the family and not the other way around; I think we could all turn that lens backward.[20]

If we lose sight of the purpose of programs, which are intended to strengthen families and bring people to Christ, we may end up sacrificing individuals and families to support programs. Thus, the tail wags the dog, and terrestrial stress increases.

Elder Boyd K. Packer said on one occasion that the Brethren sometimes feel they are losing their ability to correct the course of the Church.[21] This should be a sobering, even a frightening, thought. Our prophets receive revelation and teach us the will of the Lord and then, so often with good intentions, we may completely disregard their prophetic pronouncements. Again, as the Lord has warned: "I command, and men obey not. I revoke and they receive not the blessing" (D&C 58:32). If we insist on complicating our lives with terrestrial stress against the counsel of God and His earthly stewards, we deny ourselves the blessings He would give us.

There are so many good things in the world that we can enjoy and in which we can participate. And much good is brought to pass from being "anxiously engaged in a good cause" (D&C 58:27). As many have pointed out, however, the scripture does not tell us to be anxiously engaged in *all* good causes. We must choose, in wisdom, our level of involvement in good things, lest we succumb to terrestrial stress.

---

20. Julie Beck, (address, worldwide leadership training satellite broadcast, February 2008).

21. Boyd K. Packer, "Let Them Govern Themselves," (address, presented at the Regional Representative Seminar, March 20, 1990).

Celestial Stress—The Wilderness Syndrome

Although celestial stress may seem a contradiction in terms, full participation in the plan of happiness requires what could be described as a stressful "wilderness experience." In the scriptures we read about many individuals and groups that were called into the wilderness before being led to the promised land: Moses and the Israelites, Lehi and his family, the Jaredites, even our latter-day pioneers.

Similarly, God calls each of us to enter a *spiritual wilderness* to prepare for the kingdom: "Come out from among them and be ye separate" (2 Corinthians 6:17), "Go ye out from . . . Babylon" (D&C 133:14), "Friendship of the world is enmity with God" (James 4:4). We need to spiritually leave the world and shed our worldly baggage in order to be prepared to receive experience His Spirit and His kingdom and His promised land forever. Shedding worldly baggage is stressful, and this preparatory, refining stress awaits us in the spiritual wilderness.

The wilderness experience of celestial stress helps us become more celestial people and can include many different refining experiences and trials, some of which we will discuss in Chapter Eleven. One source of celestial stress that we will discuss in this chapter is taking upon oneself the standard of Christ.

Second Nephi chapter 4 from verse 17 through the end of the chapter, has been referred to as the *Psalm of Nephi*. It begins with these beautiful, but painful, words:

> O wretched man that I am! Yea, my heart sorroweth because of my flesh; my soul grieveth because of mine iniquities.
>
> I am encompassed about because of the temptations and the sins which do so easily beset me.

And when I desire to rejoice, my heart groaneth
because of my sins (2 Nephi 4:17-19).

These words may, at first, sound like the pain of a sinful man, but Nephi wasn't sinful, particularly at this point in his life. What failing, then, is he so concerned about? Nephi names the problem he is wrestling with in verse 27:

Why should I yield to sin because of my flesh? Yea, why should I give way to my temptation that the evil one have place in my heart to destroy my peace and afflict my soul? [And here it is—Nephi's problem:] Why am I angry because of mine enemy? (2 Nephi 4:27, emphasis added).

Who were Nephi's enemies? Laman and Lemuel, his brothers. Nephi was probably angry with them because they kept trying to kill him. Many of us, judging by even good terrestrial standards, would say Nephi's distress was an overreaction. He was not a sinful man. Compared to the world, Nephi was a front-runner. Nephi, however, was not measuring his behavior by the standards of the world; his standard was Christ. Nephi saw where he was lacking in his efforts to become like the Savior, and this gave him stress, *celestial stress*, because he wanted to close the gap. To truly acquire Christ's image in our countenance (see Alma 5:14), to be like him when he appears (see Moroni 7:48), requires a monumental commitment and enduring effort—*all* that we can do, in addition to the grace of Christ (see 2 Nephi 25:23). This effort may sometimes cause our souls to groan with the realization of our weaknesses. Nevertheless, this is the business of life, the purpose of the great plan of happiness, to invite us into the spiritual wilderness to experience spiritual growing pains on our path to perfection.

A question that characterizes this effort to become Christlike is, "What lack I yet?" (Matthew 19:20). To become like the Savior, we have to hitch our wagon to a celestial star and stop worrying about the measurements of the world. We have to leave all worldly baggage along the way; we must be prepared to lay it all on the altar, determinedly breaking the chains that bind us to Babylon.

Other ways we experience celestial stress may include suffering failure of our dreams and personal ambition; being subjected to criticism or rejection—perhaps even by friends and family—for our efforts to serve God before all others (see Matthew 10:34-37); struggling through the anguished loss of a loved one or the pain of a failed marriage; accepting the loneliness of a life without marriage; submitting to a crippling disability, accident, or disease, as well as to "all things the Lord seeth fit to inflict upon [us]" (Mosiah 3:19). Of course, such difficult experiences can happen to any individual, whether he is living at a telestial or terrestrial level, or trying to lift himself to a more celestial life. What makes these difficult experiences celestial stress rather than merely painful and destructive is: first, that we are not living in such a way that they are merely a consequence of our own telestial choices, but rather, we are trying to live in a way that is acceptable to God; and second, our response to the trials is a yielding to the refining process rather than an angry and rebellious spirit. In our yielding, we allow the Spirit to work with us and in us to cleanse, refine, and purify not only our actions, but also our thoughts and motives. In this process, we allow the Lord to "consecrate [our] afflictions for [our] gain" (2 Nephi 2:2).

None of this is easily accomplished. It's a process that includes broken hearts and contrite spirits, discussed in the next chapter, which considers the related issue of how we progress through the realms. Also discussed in Chapter Eleven is the solution to celestial stress: enduring to the end. Each person who determines to come unto Christ must willingly submit to refining celestial stress. It is an individual journey. No one can push or pull us along this path. We must choose it.

THE CHOICE IS OURS

We do not have to be subject to every kind of stress. We choose the kind of stress we allow in our lives. Some choose to waste their lives with telestial stress. The world constantly invites us to "eat, drink, and be merry" (2 Nephi 28:7). There are wasted lives all around, the lives of those who flout the commandments of God, even with impunity. Eventually, they will reap the whirlwind (Hosea 8:7), for the ultimate outcome of telestial stress is destruction, tragedy, waste.

Though not as outwardly devastating, the trap of terrestrial stress ensnares many good people. Such people may accomplish significant temporal good, but ultimately, they get lost in the "thick of thin things." The problem for these "honorable men of the earth" (D&C 76:75) is that although they may be largely free of telestial stress and obedient to basic commandments, they are so busy with terrestrial concerns that they do not ever move into the spiritual wilderness and get about the *true business of life*. It's tragic that by concentrating so much on performing *good works*, we may prevent ourselves from ever beginning the *essential saving works*. We can get caught up in the urgent at the expense of the vital. Many temporal tasks have deadlines attached: "If I do not put gas in the car, I'll be in trouble;" "If I do not pay this bill on time, I'll be in trouble;" "If I do not get the Christmas shopping done, I'll be in trouble." Too often these urgent tasks get in the way of the vital ones, which generally have no clear deadlines attached. If we don't study the scriptures today, the house won't fall down. If we don't have a bonding family time this week, we'll get by. If we don't have meaningful prayer and learn to receive revelation—well, maybe we can work that in next week. We get caught, again, putting things that matter most at the mercy of things that ultimately matter much less.

Some individuals who are trapped in terrestrial stress eventually burn out and then throw the baby out with the bath water, eliminating not only terrestrial stress but perhaps the marriage, the family, or the Church as well; mistakenly blaming those institutions for "requiring" too much of them.

Our third, and only worthwhile choice, is celestial stress. If we repent of our sins and lead obedient lives, then learn to appropriately balance terrestrial concerns, we can choose the celestial stress of a spiritual wilderness. Following the admonitions of the prophets, we simplify and leave the world—worldliness—behind, still in the world, but no longer of it (see John 17:11-19). We come to know the Savior, for He has promised, "I will also be your light in the wilderness; and . . . inasmuch as ye shall keep my commandments ye shall be led towards the promised land; and ye shall know that it is by me that ye are led" (1 Nephi 17:13). This is a path of individual tutelage; only the Savior can teach us how to become like Him. He can whisper through His Spirit those precious communications concerning what we personally must do. It is too noisy in the rest of the world. Indeed, if we are caught up in the terrestrial, we won't hear that voice.

Isaiah, seeing our day and time, asks this very relevant question:

> Wherefore do ye spend money for that which is not bread? and your labor for that which satisfieth not? hearken diligently unto me, and eat ye that which is good, and let your soul delight itself in fatness.
>
> Ho, every one that thirsteth, come ye to the waters, and he that hath no money; come ye, buy and eat; yea, come, buy wine and milk without money and without price (Isaiah 55:2, 1).

Choosing telestial or terrestrial stress is like spending money and labor on things that can never satisfy us. The gospel of Jesus Christ, a gift without price and yet priceless, does have the answers to our stressful lives. Our best choice, the only choice that allows us full participation in the purpose of the plan, is to follow the prophet and get ourselves into that celestial spiritual wilderness, where the real work of life can begin. There we can fulfill the measure of our creation—ultimately, completely—and become *men and women of Christ*, a force for good, for building the kingdom. Whether or not we are here upon the earth when Christ comes again, we are influencing the generations that will be here to receive Him. We must teach and exemplify the principles of the gospel that will likewise apply to their busy and stressful lives. In doing so, we will come to know the Savior; He will be our light and lead us to our promised land.

CHAPTER TEN

A Stepping Stone, Not a Stopping Place

The Terrestrial Realm as a Bridge to the Celestial Life

The greater part of this book has been focused on *finding safety from the telestial elements that surround us.* However, the doctrine of three levels of glory—three realms of law, light, and life—offers us a second powerful message and tool that is also vital to our successful completion of God's plan for our happiness. *Understanding the terrestrial realm gives us power to realistically examine ourselves and to guard against becoming complacent with our good, terrestrial lives, thereby sabotaging our hopes for a greater, celestial glory.* This chapter discusses the second idea.

Because all truth is intricately and beautifully interwoven, the better we understand the terrestrial realm, the better we can understand both the telestial and the celestial realms. Understanding the telestial is a prerequisite to protecting ourselves from its destructive capacity. Understanding the celestial is a prerequisite to our successful progression toward that outcome, as "where there is no vision, the people perish" (Proverbs 29:18). In this chapter, we will consider the terrestrial realm, focusing on two main ideas: first, the terrestrial realm is good, but not good enough for those who seek celestial glory; and second, there will be good people—including some members of the Church[1]—in the terrestrial kingdom.

A terrestrial life is a good life. Those who harness the natural man and leave the telestial realm behind are no longer "enem[ies] to God" (Mosiah 3:19). Those who live terrestrially will not be destroyed when Christ comes again to the earth, but are "Christ's at his coming" (D&C 88:99) and will thereby qualify to continue on earth into the millennial era.[2] Understanding the goodness and strength of a terrestrial life should also, however, serve to caution us that some of us, even as members of the Church, which is the kingdom of God on earth, may be living mostly at a terrestrial level.

Just as the terrestrial realm is a good realm, though not good enough for those who seek the celestial kingdom, so, too, individuals who inherit the terrestrial glory will be good people, though not good enough for the celestial glory.[3] Section 76 of the Doctrine and Covenants says of those who inherit terrestrial glory:

---

1. President Joseph Fielding Smith taught: "Church members may go to any kingdom. We have our agency and many, very, very many members of this Church, when they come to the judgment and are judged according to their works, are going to be consigned to the telestial kingdom; others to the terrestrial kingdom; because that is the law that they have willed to obey; and we are going to get our reward according to the law that we obey. Bruce R. McConkie, ed., Doctrines of Salvation, (Salt Lake City: Bookcraft, 1954-1956), 2:28.

2. See also Bruce R. McConkie, "Millennium," in *Mormon Doctrine* (Salt Lake City: Bookcraft, 1958), 5.

3. I am aware of how politically incorrect that sounds, but although the value of every soul is the same, the goodness of a soul is the product of each individual's agency.

> These are they who are honorable men of the earth . . .
>
> These are they who are not valiant in the testimony of Jesus; wherefore, they obtain not the crown over the kingdom of our God (D&C 76:75, 79).[4]

The terrestrial, or middle, kingdom is for good people who were neither rebellious sinners nor perfected saints. They were good, honorable men and women who were not particularly disobedient, but neither were they especially valiant in their testimonies. Lest we be deceived into thinking that membership in the Church exempts us from the possibility of inheriting terrestrial glory, many scriptures, along with the teachings of our latter-day prophets, include warnings that we, as Church members, sometimes settle for less than our potential.

President Brigham Young warned the members of the Church that too often "we live far beneath our privileges."[5] An especially plain warning is found in the parable of the ten virgins, which teaches us that not all who wait for the Bridegroom, or Jesus Christ, will enter into the wedding feast, or the kingdom of God. Elder Dallin H. Oaks observed:

> The arithmetic of this parable is chilling. The ten virgins obviously represent members of Christ's Church, for all were invited to the wedding feast and all knew what was required to be admitted

---

[4]. The demands of justice are satisfied through either Christ's aAtonement and the plan of mercy, or through suffering the torments of hell; see Joseph Smith, *Teachings of the Prophet Joseph Smith,* comp. Joseph Fielding Smith (Salt Lake City: Shadow Mountain, 1977), 358; see also Alma 42; D&C 88; 1 Nephi 15:30-35; Jacob 6:9-10; D&C 76:32-49; D&C 29:27-30; Hebrews 6:4-8; 2 Peter 2:20-22; 2 Nephi 9:14-16; Revelations 20:13; 2 Nephi 9:10-12; D&C 76.

[5]. Brigham Young, *Discourses of Brigham Young,* ed. John A. Widtsoe, (Salt Lake City: Shadow Mountain, 1954), 32.

when the bridegroom came. But only half were ready when he came.[6]

As quoted in an earlier chapter, Elder Oaks went on to suggest some of the questions we, as members of the Church, should ask ourselves in order to evaluate if we are as the five wise virgins who were prepared and valiant:

What is the state of our personal preparation for eternal life? The people of God have always been people of covenant. What is *the measure of our compliance* with covenants, including the sacred promises we made in the waters of baptism, in receiving the holy priesthood, and in the temples of God? Are we promisers who do not fulfill and believers who do not perform?[7]

Thus, simple compliance with our covenants may not qualify us for the kingdom. We must consider the "measure of our compliance." Are we sufficiently valiant, or are we casual in our obedience? Are we committed to obey all the commandments, or do we tend to be selective about which commandments are "the important ones?" I suspect that we each have our "favorite" commandments, usually the ones that are easiest for us to obey. Other commandments may not be as convenient for us, and perhaps we have become skilled at deflecting admonitions and reminders concerning them. For instance, we may develop a number of "ox in the mire"[8] circumstances to justify Sunday purchases or labor. The Savior taught that some situations *do* warrant a reasonable flexibility in that observance (see Luke 14:1-6). Over the years, however, I have become keenly aware of the difference between an ox that stumbles by himself into

---

6. Dallin H. Oaks, "Preparation for the Second Coming," *Ensign,* May 2004, 7–10.

7. Oaks, "Preparation for the Second Coming," 2004, emphasis added.

8. When the Pharisees criticized Christ for healing on the Sabbath day, He responded with the question: "Which of you shall have an ass or an ox fallen into a pit, and will not straightway pull him out on the sabbath day?" (Luke 14:5).

the mire on a Sunday and should not have to await rescue until Monday morning, as opposed to the ox that was driven into the mire on Saturday night because of the inconvenience of making one more trip to the gas station or the grocery store, or because it seemed easier to compromise the Sabbath than to adjust plans, expectations, or comfort level. Perhaps we're scrupulous about Sabbath observance but casual about the way we wear the temple garment or quick to find excuses (e.g. beauty pageants or Halloween) to dress immodestly. Perhaps we are sticklers for modest dressing but sloppy in our selection of books, movies, or music. It is always a good exercise to review the "measure of our compliance" with the commandments.

Elder James E. Talmage, in *Jesus the Christ*, wrote:

> The virgins typify those who profess a belief in Christ, and who, therefore, confidently expect to be included among the blessed participants at the feast. The lighted lamp, which each of the maidens carried, is the outward profession of Christian belief and practice; and in the oil reserves of the wiser ones we may see the spiritual strength and abundance which diligence and devotion in God's service alone can insure.[9]

Honest self-examination can reveal where we may need to increase our "diligence and devotion."

Elder Bruce R. McConkie also made it clear that all ten virgins in this parable "represent those Church members who are looking for the Bridegroom to come."[10] He emphasized that the key distinction that divided this group was—

---

9. James E. Talmage, *Jesus the Christ* (Salt Lake City: Deseret Book Co., 1982), 578-579, emphasis added.

10. Bruce R. McConkie, *Doctrinal New Testament Commentary*, (Salt Lake City: Deseret Book Co., 2002), 1:684.

> —not good and bad, not righteous and wicked, but wise and foolish. That is, all of them have accepted the invitation to meet the Bridegroom; all are members of the Church; the contrast is not between the wicked and the worthy. Instead, five are zealous and devoted. . . . [T]en have the testimony of Jesus, but only five are valiant therein, Hence, five shall enter into the house where Jesus is and five shall remain without—all of which raises the question: What portion of the Church shall be saved? . . . this parable . . . does teach, pointedly and plainly, that there are foolish saints who shall fail to gain the promised rewards.[11]

President Ezra Taft Benson warned us, as members of the Church, that even a temple recommend does not guarantee that we are on the path to the celestial kingdom:

> Concerning those who will receive the terrestrial, or lesser, kingdom, the Lord said, "These are they who are not valiant in the testimony of Jesus; wherefore, they obtain not the crown over the kingdom of our God." (D&C 76:79; italics added.) Not to be valiant in one's testimony is a tragedy of eternal consequence. These are members who know this latter-day work is true, but who fail to endure to the end. Some may even hold temple recommends, but do not magnify their callings in the Church. Without valor, they do not take an affirmative stand for the kingdom of God. Some seek the praise, adulation, and honors of men; others attempt to conceal their sins; and a few criticize those who preside over them.[12]

---

11. McConkie, *Doctrinal New Testament Commentary,* 1:685, emphasis in the original.

12. Ezra Taft Benson, "Valiant in the Testimony of Jesus," *Ensign,* May 1982, 62, emphasis in the original.

In 1972, Elder Thomas S. Monson cautioned that it is not "only the gross sins of life [which] cause us to falter."[13] We can be obedient to basic commandments and still fail to qualify for the kingdom of God. To illustrate, Elder Monson recounted the New Testament story of the rich young man who asked the Savior what he needed to do to have eternal life.

Jesus answered him: "If thou wilt enter into life, keep the commandments.

"He saith unto him, Which?"

To Jesus' enumeration of the commandments, "The young man saith . . . All these things have I kept from my youth up: what lack I yet?

"Jesus said unto him, If thou wilt be perfect, go and sell that thou hast, and give to the poor . . . and come and follow me.

> "But when the young man heard that saying, he went away sorrowful: for he had great possessions." (Matthew 19:16–18, 20–22.)
>
> He preferred the comforts of earth to the treasures of heaven. He would not purchase the things of eternity by abandoning those of time. He faltered. He failed to finish.[14]

What a sad story this is. The story, however, is almost certainly not as much intended to generate compassion, as to motivate increased consecration. Many of us could declare, along with the rich young ruler, that we have been obedient from our early youth. We may even be wise enough to ask the question, "What lack I yet?" But it is *our response* to divine invitations to stretch our service, to lengthen our stride, and to stand taller

---

13. Thomas S. Monson, "'Finishers Wanted'," *Ensign*, Jul 1972, 68.
14. Monson, "'Finishers Wanted'," 1972.

that determines whether our own story ends with tragedy or triumph.

Again, it can be easy to fall into the trap of terrestrial complacency because a terrestrial life is a good life. Because those who live terrestrial law have harnessed the natural man and bridled their passions, they live with a generous measure of peace and safety. They are not subject to the same level of pain, violence, and destruction that typically—eventually—accompany telestial lifestyles. Missionaries, on occasion, express frustration that individuals or families that "would make great members" are not interested in joining the Church. It may be that some of those people are sufficiently happy and content with their good terrestrial lives and don't really feel the need for anything more. Similarly, Church members may become comfortable with their good, but still not celestial-bound, lives. Elder Neal A. Maxwell addressed this concern by comparing members of the Church who are honorable with other members who *valiantly strive to consecrate their lives to the will of the Father.* Elder Maxwell taught that members striving for a consecrated life go beyond an obedient life to give "obedience to the unenforceable."[15] They seek the Spirit to guide their efforts to give everything, to submit to trials more joyfully, to lose themselves in service and sacrifice that they might find themselves as children of Christ. Elder Maxwell contrasts this group of consecrating individuals with—

IT CAN BE EASY TO FALL INTO THE TRAP OF TERRESTRIAL COMPLACENCY BECAUSE A TERRESTRIAL LIFE IS A GOOD LIFE.

> A second group of members [who] are "honorable" but not "valiant." They are not really aware of the

---

15. "Lord Moulton coined a perceptive phrase, 'obedience to the unenforceable,' describing 'obedience of a man to that which he cannot be forced to obey' ("Law And Manners," *Atlantic Monthly,* July 1924, p. 1)." (From Neal A. Maxwell, "'Swallowed Up in the Will of the Father'," *Ensign,* Nov 1995, 22).

gap nor of the importance of closing it (see D&C 76:75, 79). These "honorable" individuals are certainly not miserable nor wicked, nor are they unrighteous and unhappy. It is not what they have done but what they have left undone that is amiss. For example, if valiant, they could touch others deeply instead of merely being remembered pleasantly. . . . Once the telestial sins are left behind and henceforth avoided, the focus falls ever more on the sins of omission. These omissions signify a lack of qualifying fully for the celestial kingdom. Only greater consecration can correct these omissions, which have consequences just as real as do the sins of commission. Many of us thus have sufficient faith to avoid the major sins of commission, but not enough faith to sacrifice our distracting obsessions or to focus on our omissions.[16]

We must recognize and remember, then, that we may be good people, we may be happy people, and we may be members of the Lord's true Church, but still not be sufficiently *valiant, devoted, diligent,* and *wise* to qualify for celestial glory. This is undoubtedly why, as President Harold B. Lee so eloquently put it, the gospel of Jesus Christ is "to comfort the afflicted and afflict the comfortable."[17]

This awareness is not intended to invite criticism or condemnation of ourselves or others. There is much good in the terrestrial, and the world is a nicer place to live in when it is generally more terrestrial. However, our potential is vastly greater. No wonder President Gordon B. Hinckley, addressing the students of

---

16. Neal A. Maxwell, "'Swallowed Up in the Will of the Father'," *Ensign,* Nov 1995, 22, emphasis added.

17. As quoted in Joseph Fielding Smith, "The Message My Dear Young Fellow Workers:," *New Era,* Jan 1971, 4.

Brigham Young University at a university devotional in 1998, admonished:

> I want to urge you to stand a little taller, to rise a little higher, to be a little better. . . . I am grateful for all of you, but I know that a few of you could do much better than you are doing.[18]

In order to reach our divine potential, we must recognize that the path to the kingdom of God—the celestial glory—is usually a two-fold process: turning away from sin (leaving the telestial realm for the safety of the terrestrial) and then becoming valiant in our testimonies of Christ (moving diligently toward the celestial realm). King Benjamin taught:

> For the natural man is an enemy to God, and has been from the fall of Adam, and will be, forever and ever, unless he yields to the enticings of the Holy Spirit, and putteth off the natural man and becometh a saint through the atonement of Christ the Lord (Mosiah 3:19).

Careful consideration of King Benjamin's inspired statement reveals this two-fold process, the two steps necessary for us to be redeemed from the Fall: first, putting off the natural man, and second, becoming a saint through the Atonement of Christ. In plain and simple terms, this is the same two-step progression found in the statement by President Brigham Young, often quoted by President David O. McKay, and many other latter-

---

18. Gordon B. Hinckley, "The Quest for Excellence," (devotional address, Brigham Young University, Provo, UT, November 10, 1998).

day leaders, that the gospel of Jesus Christ can "make bad men good and good men better."[19]

Elder Neal Maxwell taught that complete repentance requires not only turning away from evil, but also turning toward God. He explained,

> Initially, this turning reflects progress from telestial to terrestrial behavior, and later on to celestial behavior.[20]

More recently, Elder David A. Bednar reminded us that

> Prophets throughout the ages have emphasized the dual requirements of [first] avoiding and overcoming bad and [second] doing good and becoming better.[21]

Elder Bednar included a warning that some only accomplish the first task, saying, "It is possible for us to have clean hands but not have a pure heart."[22]

Better acquaintance with the terrestrial realm can help us fully appreciate the blessings of a terrestrial life, a terrestrial environment, and terrestrial relationships. The terrestrial is good, and good people live this law and enjoy the blessings that come with it. But for those of us who desire to inherit a greater glory, familiarity with and appreciation for the terrestrial can

---

19. Teachings of Presidents of the Church: Brigham Young (Melchizedek Priesthood and Relief Society course of study, 1997), 21. Thomas S. Monson, in "The Message: Never Give Up," *New Era,* Sep 1994, mentions that President David O. McKay "consistently taught" the same thing, as does Gordon B. Hinckley, in "Words of the Prophet: You Can Be Forgiven," *New Era,* Oct 2001.

20. Neal A. Maxwell, "Repentance," *Ensign,* Nov 1991, 30.

21. David A. Bednar, "Clean Hands and a Pure Heart," *Ensign,* Nov 2007, 80-83.

22. Bednar, "Clean Hands and a Pure Heart," 2007.

increase our diligence and devotion as we work to become more valiant and more consecrated servants.

CHAPTER ELEVEN

CHOOSING OUR GLORY

PROGRESSION THROUGH THE REALMS

We live on a telestial planet in an increasingly telestial society that constantly invites us to feed our appetites. Born with bodies endowed with strong appetites, we are highly susceptible to telestial behavior. We struggle with and sometimes give in to the natural man. As Paul wrote: "For all have sinned, and come short of the glory of God" (Romans 3:23). Is it realistic to suppose that we sinners can overcome our appetites and live solid terrestrial and perhaps even celestial lives? Of course it is. Even a basic understanding of God's plan of salvation tells us the whole purpose of the plan and its central act, the Atonement, is to make that possible. Again, "The purpose of the gospel is . . . to make bad men good and good men better, and to change human nature."[1]

---

1. From the film Every Member a Missionary, as acknowledged by Franklin D. Richards, *Conference Report,* October 1965, 136–37; see also Brigham Young, 22 July 1860, in *Journal of Discourses,* 8:130.

So what motivates us to make real and lasting life changes? Obviously, human motivation is a complex subject. Factors contributing to motivation may include new information, encouragement, attitude, awareness of possible consequences and available rewards, desire, access to supportive resources, previous success, and the example of others. Of course, the Light of Christ in each of us invites us to look heavenward, and the Holy Ghost can be a voice of conscience, motivating and supporting positive change. Many other things may also be involved in helping us become good, and then better, men and women. This chapter does not pretend to treat the subject of human progression in a comprehensive way but invites the consideration of a few elements that seem generally to contribute to our progression from telestial to terrestrial and then celestial lives.

From Telestial to Terrestrial

To come fully to Christ we must first eliminate sin—willful rebellion against God—from our lives. Moving from the telestial realm to the terrestrial realm requires repentance and consistent obedience, the spirit harnessing the flesh, so that our lives are not governed by the desires, appetites, and passions of the natural man. Again acknowledging that it's not possible to know what motivates each individual, it seems that *fear* and *misery* may often contribute to successful advancement from the telestial to the terrestrial realm.

It may seem remedial—perhaps even unpleasant—to speak in terms of fear. I suppose it might sound better to say that love, devotion, and a desire for celestial life are always what move us toward God. But consider the story told of a man who was teaching his donkey to follow directions using a carrot and a stick. An observer asked, "I understand that the carrot is to reward the donkey when he does what you want, but what is the stick for?" The man answered, "First, I have to get his attention." When we are living in a mostly telestial manner, making little attempt to harness the natural man, the fear of consequences may be the stick that gets our attention.

The scriptures are full of warnings concerning the judgments to come against the wicked. Surely the frequent repetition of these warnings is, at least in part, to motivate repentance. Alma explains:

Now, repentance could not come unto men except there were a punishment. . . .

Now, if there was no law given—if a man murdered he should die—would he be afraid he would die if he should murder?

And also, *if there was no law given against sin men would not be afraid to sin* (Alma 42:16, 19-20, emphasis added).

In other words, Alma is teaching that fear of consequences can be a healthy motivator in turning away from sin. In section 19 of the Doctrine and Covenants, the Lord goes to some length to describe how terrible the suffering for sin will be.

> Therefore I command you to repent—repent, lest I smite you by the rod of my mouth, and by my wrath, and by my anger, and your sufferings be sore—how sore you know not, how exquisite you know not, yea, how hard to bear you know not.
>
> For behold, I, God, have suffered these things for all, that they might not suffer if they would repent;
>
> But if they would not repent they must suffer even as I (D&C 19:15-17).

The Lord's counsel to us here is that the cost of sin is so great, the suffering so terrible, that it would be best for us to do what is necessary—repent—to access Christ's Atonement and avoid paying that awful debt ourselves. The Lord, with perfect knowledge of human nature, is utilizing our fear of suffering to motivate us to change from telestial behavior to at least terrestrial obedience.

One of the more vivid scriptural examples of changing realms is Alma the Younger, the rebellious son of a prophet father. Alma the Younger was living a telestial life and is described as "the vilest of sinners" (Mosiah 28:4). He was in deep rebellion with the four sons of King Mosiah when an angel was sent to confront them. Alma the Younger fell into a coma for three days and awoke a completely changed man. When he recounted his life-changing experience to his son Helaman, Alma told of the angel who spoke in a voice that shook the earth and warned, "If thou wilt of thyself be destroyed, seek no more to destroy the church of God" (Alma 36:9). Alma told his son:

> And the angel spake more things unto me, which were heard by my brethren, but I did not hear them; for when I heard the words—If thou wilt be destroyed of thyself, seek no more to destroy the church of God—*I was struck with such great fear and amazement lest perhaps I should be destroyed*, that I fell to the earth and I did hear no more (Alma 36:11, emphasis added).

It seems that at least part of what motivated Alma's dramatic conversion was fear of his own destruction. It's interesting that this was apparently the first time Alma seriously considered the negative consequences of his actions. He must have heard warnings before; after all, he grew up in a prophet's home. But somehow, Alma the Younger had successfully dismissed previous warnings. I suppose it's harder to ignore such warnings when delivered by an angel. As Alma recounted these events to his son, he recalled, "The very thought of coming into the presence of my God did rack my soul with inexpressible horror" (Alma 36:14). When Alma faced up to his personal accountability and the price he would pay for his sins, he seems to have felt intense motivation to change.

The same idea is expressed in the book of Enos. As Enos closed his record, he made an interesting comment about the approach he found most successful in keeping his people focused, more or less, on correct living. He said:

> And there was nothing save it was exceeding harshness, preaching and prophesying of wars, and contentions, and destructions, and continually reminding them of death, and the duration of eternity, and the judgments and the power of God, and all these things—stirring them up continually to keep them in the fear of the Lord. I say there was nothing short of these things, and exceedingly great plainness of speech, would keep them from going down speedily to destruction (Enos 1:23, emphasis added).
>
> Again, it seems that a healthy dose of fear is involved in motivating some people to renounce sin and move from a telestial realm to a more terrestrial realm.

Several years ago, I remember noticing teenagers wearing T-shirts that had intriguing slogans printed on the back to motivate outstanding athletic achievement; all of the shirts ended with the brand name, No Fear. Frankly, I enjoyed reading the slogans,[2] but I also took the opportunity to discuss with my children that, as a society, we are rearing a generation who might be fearless in the wrong ways. The scriptures speak consistently of fearing God as a safeguard and a mark of righteousness, and they warn against those who tell us not to fear. The teachings of Nehor, a man who helped introduce the destructive practice of priestcraft to the Nephites, included the following:

---

2. I no longer remember exactly what was on the T-shirts, but they included things like: "Time expired, one point behind, at the foul line, shooting two, No Fear."

> And he also testified unto the people that all mankind should be saved at the last day, and that *they need not fear nor tremble*, but that they might lift up their heads and rejoice; for the Lord had created all men, and had also redeemed all men; and, in the end, all men should have eternal life (Alma 1:4, emphasis added).

Of course, we don't want our children, or ourselves for that matter, to live *in* fear or to be terrified of God; nevertheless, we should teach our children to *fear to offend* God and to fear the destructive consequences of sin. I worry that we may not always be as successful as we should be with our youth when I observe a lack of reverence for sacred things or immodest dress, speech, behavior, and the like. While fear is neither the ultimate nor a sufficient motivator for those who seek the kingdom of God, it didn't work for Enos' people to live completely without fear, and I don't think it works for us or our children either.

Another powerful motivator that prompts progression may be misery. I suspect that most full-time missionaries could give examples of converts who embraced the gospel and Church membership—a more terrestrial life—because their lives were stressful or unhappy, often the result of telestial behaviors, relationships, or a telestial environment. Ironically, some of the solidly terrestrial non-members who so obviously would make great members of the Church aren't as interested in the message of the restored gospel precisely because they're not miserable enough. People who are hurting are often looking for a change. They want to escape telestial trouble and find greater happiness. Non-members who are already enjoying terrestrial peace, safety, and prosperity may not feel as strong a need to investigate a new set of values.

Misery can motivate people to do the difficult work of change in order to bring greater happiness into their lives. I have explained the three realms perspective to many non-members, using secular rather than religious terms. It's almost surprising how quickly some individuals will point to the telestial realm description and say, "That's where I am." They recognize that their choices are mostly guided by appetites and a desire for immediate gratification, and they are familiar with the pain, violence, and destruction that result. Whether it's spending money foolishly, not holding down jobs, indulging a temper that ruins relationships, or any number of other telestial problems, some people are finally miserable enough to not only long for a change, but to do whatever it takes to make that change happen in their lives.

Sue and Brent were a married couple with layers and layers of problems. Brent was in his second marriage, Sue in her third. They had yours, mine, and ours children and there were many struggles with blending the families. Some of the older children were seriously deviant and in trouble with the law. The couple's relationship was a nightmare. They had occasional moments of peace, but the vast majority of the time they were at each other's throats. They were both lifetime members of the Church but for years had disregarded basic standards, so, separately and together, they had a long history of drinking, abusing drugs, and extramarital sexual involvements. Their marriage relationship was characterized by physical, emotional, and verbal abuse. The death of a child had brought them back to Church activity, but they were still in a really bad place. I explained that their behaviors and choices were trapping them in a telestial realm, and they would never truly be free of the pain, violence, and destruction they were suffering unless they lived terrestrial law—self-control and deferred gratification. There was little discussion about it. Sue and Brent saw clearly what their choices were, and both indicated they where exhausted and miserable with the life they were living and ready to change.

Of course, the desire for a different life is only the beginning. Our daily choices demonstrate how sincere our desires are.

Whether the desire comes from fear or from misery or from some other place, if we are sincere, we make and follow commitments, such as: I will never again hit my spouse, I will always tell the truth, I will control my temper and my tongue, I will do whatever it takes to overcome my addiction (including the use of appropriate resources to support recovery), etc. Even committed change is not automatic, but the determined individual can leave a telestial life behind and build a new life. Sue determined to build a better, more terrestrial life and followed through with her commitments to curb her temper, to stop drinking and drugging. She terminated all extra-marital involvements. Sue began attending Church meetings regularly and met often with her bishop to go through the necessary repentance process. Her life began to stabilize. Sadly, Brent didn't follow through on the changes he said he wanted to make. He continued in his destructive and violent patterns and finally, after giving Brent several chances to make improvements, Sue divorced him and moved on. Ending the marriage was a painful choice, but Sue was grateful for the end of a life that included police responding regularly to domestic violence calls, children who were traumatized by the neglect and/or violence of substance-abusing parents, and the ugliness of infidelity. Sue realized there was still a road ahead for her to travel, but she was already feeling the relief and blessing of a safer day-to-day reality.

I don't know of a more vivid scriptural example of individuals determined to leave the telestial behind and build new lives than the people of Ammon. However, from my early youth in the Church, I was a little puzzled by their story in the Book of Mormon. This group of Lamanites, also called the Anti-Nephi-Lehis, was converted to the gospel through the missionary efforts of Ammon, one of the sons of Mosiah. After conversion and baptism, the people of Ammon buried their weapons of war as a symbol that their old, telestial life was over and they would never take up arms against anyone ever again.

Sometimes I wondered if it was really necessary for them to die rather than pick up weapons to defend themselves when they were later attacked by other murderous Lamanites. Would it really have jeopardized their salvation to engage in self-defense? After all, some of the great heroes of the Book of Mormon were military men. Captain Moroni, General Mormon, even the sons of the Anti-Nephi-Lehis, called the sons of Helaman, all went to war to defend family and country and were righteous, heroic figures. Wasn't it overzealous, then, for the people of Ammon to let themselves be slaughtered in the act of prayer, leaving widowed wives and fatherless children, rather than defending themselves (see Alma 24)?

Then, on another reading of the Book of Mormon, as I read again about the people of Ammon, a light went on in my mind, and I believe I finally understood. The people of Ammon had not merely repented of going to war and killing adversaries in battle, *they were recovering from an addiction.* Their warlike behavior had not been about defending freedoms or family, but had developed into full-blown bloodlust. I believe that when these men thrust a sword or ax into an opponent's body, they most likely experienced a type of sensual thrill or "buzz."

A RECOVERING ADDICT NEEDS TO BE MORE VIGILANT IN AVOIDING CONTACT WITH ANYTHING OR ANYONE THAT COMES CLOSE TO STIMULATING OLD APPETITES.

In my work with individuals repenting and recovering from addiction, I have learned that a necessary part of the process is to eradicate from one's life any element that continues to tie the individual to the behavior—to "bury their weapons of war" (Alma 25:14). This often requires a more rigorous standard of avoidance than would be required of one who has not ever been addicted. While no one is unaffected by exposure to inappropriate material or dangerous substances, a recovering addict needs to be more vigilant in avoiding contact with anything or anyone that comes close to stimulating old appetites. A recovering sex addict, for instance, may need to be quicker to leave a PG-13 or even a PG movie because the sexual jokes and innuendo stimulate an appetite that was too often and too heavily indulged, while the never-addicted individual may be less affected and more easily ignore those elements.

Not only was it necessary and right for the people of Ammon to bury their weapons, but it was necessary and right for their neighbor Nephites to defend them from the Lamanites who warred against them. Whatever the cost, whatever the effort required, whatever sacrifices must be made, *we must leave the telestial realm*. And as surely as the sun rises in the morning, progressing from a telestial to a terrestrial realm of life will bring us greater peace, safety, and prosperity.

From Terrestrial to Celestial

Moving from the terrestrial realm to the celestial realm requires more than changing behavior; it requires a change of heart, the death of the "old man of sin" and the birth of the new "child of Christ." This spiritual rebirth is not accomplished by sheer effort or restraint, but comes through the gentle tutorings of the Spirit, and as a result of offering the sacrifice of "a broken heart and a contrite spirit" (2 Nephi 2:7, D&C 59:8, D&C 97:8). The wilderness experiences discussed in Chapter Nine are so often a necessary part of our being able to offer a broken heart and to develop a contrite spirit. While fear and misery may be key motivators in moving from the telestial to the terrestrial, I believe the key motivators in moving from the terrestrial to the celestial are *love* and *humility*, or *love* and a *contrite spirit*.

As repeatedly discussed in this book, a terrestrial life is a good life. Peace, safety, and prosperity attend terrestrial life to such an extent that some good, terrestrial people may feel satisfied and not much interested in anything more. However, those of us who desire to fulfill our potential to become like Jesus Christ may instead be quite concerned that our good lives are, in fact, just terrestrial. Lest we become inordinately fearful that we're not yet celestial, let's review Alma 29:4.

> I ought not to harrow up in my desires, the firm decree of a just God, *for I know that he granteth unto men according to their desire, whether it be unto death or unto life;* yea, I know that he allotteth unto men, yea, decreeth unto them decrees which are unalterable, *according to their wills, whether they be unto salvation or unto destruction* (emphasis added).

Alma understood that when it comes to salvation, we get what we really want. Of course, the gospel teaches us that our desire must be strong enough to manifest itself in strict obedience and continued efforts to follow the path of the Savior. But we don't need to worry that we might have sufficient desire but nonetheless miss the boat somehow. Logically, it makes no sense that our Heavenly Father, who is well aware of how relatively few of his children are concerned about His opinion—"Strait is the gate and narrow is the way . . . and *few there be* that find it" (Matthew 7:14, emphasis added)—would sit back and watch with indifference if those children who *do* seek to please Him flounder out of ignorance. Knowing our hearts and our desires, the Lord will make sure His faithful Saints receive instruction and opportunity in keeping with their desires. After all, the plan of our loving Heavenly Father is not designed to keep people *out* of the kingdom, but to bring all who sincerely come unto Christ *in*to the kingdom. Nevertheless, it is useful to study what characterizes those who progress from good, terrestrial lives to a more celestial life. Let's consider how *love* and *humility* work to move us toward the celestial realm.

Several years ago, I asked one of our daughters, who was about seventeen years old at the time, why she thought she had never gone through a period of teenage rebellion. Her quick answer: "Fear." I was surprised and chagrined, particularly as

I was teaching a parenting class at BYU at the time and that wasn't exactly the point of the course. "Fear of what?" I asked. I was genuinely puzzled, since this daughter had always been cooperative and pleasant and her father and I had never felt the need to ground her or impose any other serious consequence or penalty. She thought for a moment and then responded, "I don't know. You guys never do anything." I like to think she meant we never did anything to generate fear in her. I pressed her a bit, and she came up with this: "I guess I'm afraid you'd be upset or disappointed with me." Well, that was an answer I could live with, and it also made more sense. Somewhere along that path of growing up, her fear of punishment had changed to a fear of damaging a relationship that she valued.

Perhaps in a similar way, we, who are the often foolish and sometimes rebellious children of God (see Helaman 12:4-7), begin progressing from the telestial realm to the terrestrial realm out of fear of the consequences of sin. Along the path of living a terrestrial life and enjoying the blessings that come with it, we may come to recognize and more deeply value our developing relationship with our Heavenly Father and our Savior, Jesus Christ. That is, as we more consistently live lives that are not offensive to the Father and the Son, we feel closer to Them and begin to feel that They are pleased with us. In addition, when we are no longer dabbling in the telestial realm, the Spirit is with us more consistently. Then, as happened with my daughter, fear of punishment gradually changes to the fear of jeopardizing the relationship we are building with each member of the Godhead.

The relationship we develop with each of these members of the Godhead is essential to our progression from the terrestrial to the celestial realm. In the great intercessory prayer that Christ offered for us to the Father, He said, "And this is life eternal, that they might know thee, the only true God, and Jesus Christ, whom thou hast sent" (John 17:4). It is the Father's generous plan for us that includes a celestial glory; it is the Savior's loving sacrifice for us that makes it possible for us to qualify for the great gift of exaltation in that glory; and the plan includes "the unspeakable gift of the Holy Ghost" (D&C 121:26), the actual reception of which provides the sanctified individual with a personal guide and tutor to help us learn what we must learn, do what we must do, and become what we must become, to be fit for the kingdom. We must come to know and love each of these Gods in order to embrace the gifts they offer us.

As we continue, line upon line, precept upon precept, and under the tutelage of the Spirit, toward a more celestial life, our love and appreciation for the goodness and generosity of the Father's plan grows. We also grow in our understanding, love, and gratitude for the Atonement of our Elder Brother, Jesus Christ. We accept His redemption as a personal rescue and gift. The sacrament hymns take on additional dimensions of meaning and may evoke tears as we sing of the One who "would rescue a soul so rebellious and proud as mine."[3] We come to a place where, like President James E. Faust, we are moved in grateful sorrow to wonder, "How many drops of blood were shed for me?"[4]

Our heightened awareness of the personal suffering that Jesus felt for each of us singly can work in us until we join in John's simple, but ever more profound, declaration: "We love him, because he first loved us" (1 John 4:19). And because we love Him, we are more motivated to keep His commandments (see John 14:15) and not add more to the burden of his suffering for sin. Yes, we know the Atonement is past, the price already paid, but nonetheless, we come to desire that by living obediently, by choosing good and rejecting evil, our "share" of the Savior's suffering is less. Fear may start us on the journey, but fear turns into love, and love pulls us along the path.

---

3. "I Stand All Amazed," *Hymns,* no. 193.

4. James E. Faust, "Opening the Windows of Heaven," *Ensign,* Nov 1998, 54.

When the law of Moses was fulfilled, there was an end to burnt offerings, and a new sacrifice was required of those who desire to qualify for the kingdom of God. This new offering was the personal sacrifice of "a broken heart and a contrite spirit" (2 Nephi 2:7). I heard this doctrine when I was quite young, but I remembered the phrase, and over the years I found I could say it quickly, in one breath, but with little understanding of its significance.

Years later, when my own life's journey included heartbreak, I remembered how glibly, almost antiseptically, I had repeated the phrase "a broken heart and a contrite spirit." I wondered how I could have failed to consider what it takes to break a heart. Hearts don't break easily. It takes serious failure, severe loss, deep hurt, or betrayal to break a heart. But I learned something else that I had not previously considered. I learned that, though we often combine the two in doctrinal discussions, a broken heart and a contrite spirit are two separate things. Our hearts may break in this life—perhaps more accurately, our hearts *will* break—but that doesn't guarantee a contrite spirit. The great plan of happiness includes "opposition in all things" (2 Nephi 2:15) as a necessary requirement for our earthly experience. We must know the bitter to know the sweet (see D&C 29:39). But when our turn(s) comes to experience the bitter and our hearts break, we have a choice; that choice ultimately comes down to whether or not we will have a contrite spirit.

It may seem that the contrite spirit would naturally follow when our hearts break, but that's not necessarily so. Suffering alone is not enough to make us true disciples. Anne Morrow Lindbergh, the wife of Charles "Lucky" Lindbergh, who was the first to fly non-stop over the Atlantic in *The Spirit of St. Louis*, wrote about suffering. The Lindberghs had experienced the tragedy of their first son being kidnapped and killed at age two. Much later in her life, Anne Lindbergh expressed great insight when she wrote:

> I do not believe that sheer suffering teaches. If suffering alone taught, all the world would be wise, since everyone suffers. To suffering must be added mourning, understanding, patience, love, openness and the willingness to remain vulnerable.[5]

We can see the truth of this on every side. Some who suffer become softer, more compassionate, more malleable, more understanding and insightful, kinder, more patient and tender. Others become harder, tougher, cynical, bitter, resentful, and less concerned with others. What makes such a dramatic difference? The answer seems to be those qualities of response that Anne Lindbergh would have us add to our suffering—"mourning, understanding, patience, love, openness and the willingness to remain vulnerable." All are encompassed in the contrite spirit.

Considering the three realms perspective again, we can better understand one of the serious impediments to having a contrite heart in times of heartbreak. Because terrestrial life brings external peace and safety, individuals may be reluctant to accept wilderness experiences that require abandoning terrestrial comfort for the internal upheaval involved in offering up a broken heart and a contrite spirit.

People at the telestial level, through their choices, sooner or later bring pain, violence, and destruction into their lives. Terrestrial individuals, through their choices, can enjoy peace, safety, and prosperity. However, the scriptures teach, "For whom the Lord loveth he chasteneth, and scourgeth every son whom he receiveth" (Hebrews 12:6). To be made fit for the kingdom of God, we must go through a refining process, and it's clear that the refining process is not painless. The Lord has said, "For,

---

5. Anne Morrow Lindbergh, *Hour of Gold, Hour of Lead: Diaries and Letter of Anne Morrow Lindbergh, 1929-1932* (New York: Harcourt Brace Jovanovich, 1973), 3.

behold, I have refined thee, I have chosen thee in *the furnace of affliction*" (1 Nephi 20:10, emphasis added).

The process by which we grow from terrestrial "honorable men of the earth" (D&C 76:75) to celestial "joint-heirs with Christ" (Romans 8:17) is not for sissies. Joseph Smith explained his personal journey of refinement:

> I am like a huge rough stone rolling down from a high mountain; and the only polishing I get is when some corner gets rubbed off by coming in contact with something else, striking with accelerated force against religious bigotry, priestcraft, lawyer-craft, doctor-craft, lying editors, suborned judges and jurors, and the authority of perjured executives, backed by mobs, blasphemers, licentious and corrupt men and women—all hell knocking off a corner here and a corner there. Thus will I become a smooth and polished shaft in the quiver of the Almighty.[6]
>
> Of the Savior, Himself, it is written, "Though he were a Son, yet learned he obedience by the things which he suffered," (Hebrews 5:8). In like manner, the Lord says of us, "And my people must needs be chastened until they learn obedience, if it must needs be, by the things which they suffer" (D&C 105:6).

A multitude of scriptures make it clear that some parts of the refining process are accomplished only through suffering. Elder Bruce C. Hafen tells of a poignant exchange with Elder Neal A. Maxwell, shortly after Elder Maxwell had been diagnosed with the leukemia that eventually took his life. Elder Maxwell, demonstrating his humble and contrite spirit, confided, "'I

---

6. Joseph Smith, Teachings of the Prophet Joseph Smith, comp. Joseph Fielding Smith (Salt Lake City: Shadow Mountain, 1977), 304, emphasis added.

should have seen it coming.' Why? Because ever since Okinawa, he had wanted to become a fully consecrated follower of Jesus, no matter what the price."[7]

There are many powerful examples before us of broken hearts *and* contrite spirits. Nevertheless, when our own hearts break, it is all too easy to feel betrayed and inclined to rebel against the unfairness of such deep pain. We protest, "But I've been good. Why is this happening to me?" At such times, we need to remember that even the best terrestrial life relies on "the arm of flesh," even if it is reliance on our own obedient arm. If we consistently live in the terrestrial realm, we often look for and find temporal safety in our own obedience and good works. Perhaps the most effective way our Heavenly Father can spur our movement to a more celestial level is by pulling the obedient-arm-of-flesh rug out from under our feet, allowing typical terrestrial rewards to fail. When we must face the fact that even diligent compliance with the commandments cannot guarantee temporal safety, *if our spirit is contrite*, we can grow to understand that our safety must not reside in our obedience and righteous works. Our safety must reside directly in the Father, in the Son, and in our hope of a glorious resurrection.

Letting go of our temporal hopes for peace and happiness here is not easy. Think of the prophet Joseph Smith in the spiritual wilderness of Liberty Jail: "O God, where art thou?" (D&C 121:1). He cried out against the injustice of such miserable circumstances for faithful disciples, doubtless wondering how long they would be in that terrible situation, suffering, while those who oppressed them seemed to live in comfort and ease. God answered Joseph:

> My son, peace be unto thy soul; thine adversity and thine afflictions shall be but a small moment [Joseph

---

7. Bruce C. Hafen, "A Disciple's Journey," (devotional address, Brigham Young University, Provo, UT, February 5, 2008).

was four and a half months in Liberty Jail, but relative to eternity, it was "but a small moment"];

And then, if thou endure it well, God shall exalt thee on high; thou shalt triumph over all thy foes (D&C 121:7-8).

And then God added: "Thou art not yet as Job" (D&C 121:10). I can almost hear the prophet Joseph asking, "Did I say I wanted to be? Is my name on a list somewhere?" Well yes, his name was on a list—and our names are on the same list. We signed up for the whole course in the pre-earth life, and again when we were baptized. If we want to become like our Heavenly Father, the only way to do so is to follow the Savior into a spiritual wilderness, where we will find Him. I remember once hearing it said, "There are some kinds of faith that can only grow in the dark." Our faith cannot be perfected when we see too clearly or are too comfortable, nor can we successfully acquire the attributes of the Savior when we are enfolded by the peace, safety and prosperity of the terrestrial realm. We must yield to the Refiner's fire. It is a demanding course.

When we yield our temporal safety to the process of discovering and embracing safety in the Lord Himself, we move toward celestial life. We come to share in Peter's rhetorical response to the Savior's query, "Will ye also leave?" with our own, "Lord, to whom shall we go?" (John 6:68). We begin to understand and approach Job's testimony, "Though he slay me, yet will I trust in him" (Job 13:15).

When Comes the Harvest?

Because becoming celestial is a refining process over time, our journey includes enduring to the end. Scriptural admonitions to endure are plentiful because many "faint in [their] minds" (Hebrews 12:3). Such "fainting" may be the result of wondering if the difficult refining wilderness experience is really worth it. While Christ can be found in the spiritual wilderness, there are times when He seems to withdraw from us, as His Father withdrew from Him during the performance of His great atoning trial (Matthew 27:46). Were it not for such withdrawal, the essential stretching and increase of our faith could not happen, as the Prophet Joseph learned in Liberty Jail. It is a painful irony, however, that we may feel most abandoned when we are most spiritually diligent.

The law of the harvest offers insight and motivation to help us endure: "*Be not deceived; God is not mocked*: for whatsoever a man soweth, that shall he also reap" (Galatians 6:7, emphasis added). Most of us are familiar with the law of the harvest, but we may not always remember that the law is prefaced by a warning to not be deceived. It may even seem an odd warning. After all, the law of the harvest seems so basic, so straightforward. "Plant a carrot, get a carrot."[8] It's not that complicated. Why then the strong warning against being deceived, punctuated by the stern reminder that "God will not be mocked?" Perhaps because it is so easy to be deceived.

When life doesn't seem to work out as we had hoped, we may protest in frustration, "Why did I waste my time trying to help? Why did I bother trying to do the right thing? Why did I care? Why did I make the effort?" Whenever such thoughts and feelings refer to our sincere efforts to do good, we are being deceived. We may not see any positive outcome or reward for our honest efforts, but *let us not be deceived*, the harvest has not yet come. As discussed in Chapter Nine, Alma explains, "There [is] a space granted unto man" (Alma 12:24). That space refers to the time between action and consequence, which allows for repentance—repentance that involves a true change of heart because it is not motivated by a jolt of lightning or some other

---

8. "Plant a Radish," *The Fantasticks,* music by Harvey Schmidt and lyrics by Tom Jones, 1960.

fierce and immediate threat but by the desire of the contrite heart to reconcile its will to the will of heaven.

This is no easy path. As we move forward in the path "the saints have trod,"[9] we gain new appreciation for the faith and endurance of those who have gone before us. Nevertheless, when life is especially difficult, we may struggle when it seems our prayers are not being heard or we are being tested beyond our personal capacity to endure. Elder Maxwell wrote concerning such times:

Inwardly and anxiously we may worry, too, that an omniscient and loving God sees more stretch in us than we feel we have. Hence, when God is actually lifting us up, we may feel He is letting us down.[10]

We must not be deceived. God does not abandon his people. A favorite hymn reminds us:

> The soul that on Jesus hath leaned for repose
> I will not, I cannot, desert to his foes;
> That soul, though all hell should endeavor to shake,
> I'll never, no never, no never forsake![11]

As the Apostle Paul admonishes, "And let us not be weary in well doing: for in due season we shall reap, if we faint not" (Galatians 6:9). It helps when we come to understand that "in due season" is a code phrase for "not as soon as you'd like it to be." But let us never doubt that the harvest will come. No, it is not an easy course. Indeed, it cannot be an easy course and successfully build a Zion people. But the promises are sure; the harvest is coming. As the Lord told Nephi:

---

9. "Onward Christian Soldiers," *Hymns*, no. 246, verse 3.

10. Neal A. Maxwell, *Lord Increase Our Faith,* (Salt Lake City: Bookcraft, 1994), 3.

11. "How Firm a Foundation," *Hymns*, no. 85, verse 7.

I will also be your light in the wilderness...wherefore, inasmuch as ye shall keep my commandments ye shall be led towards the promised land; and ye shall know that it is by me that ye are led (1 Nephi 17:13).

Choose Glory

One of the fundamental principles of the gospel is progression. The Lord explained that gospel progression is "line upon line, precept upon precept" (D&C 98:12). Even the Savior did not receive "of the fulness at first, but continued from grace to grace, until he received a fullness" (D&C 93:13). To follow in His path of progression, we must move forward, leaving behind us telestial life, securing the terrestrial, and adding to our terrestrial foundation line and precept until we can "abide the law of a celestial kingdom" so that we may "abide a celestial glory" (D&C 88:22). "Eye hath not seen, nor ear heard, neither have entered into the heart of man, the things which God hath prepared for them that love him" (1 Corinthians 2:9). There is much to learn and much to do so that we may fulfill the measure of our creation and partake of God's unspeakable gifts—the gifts He has prepared for us. As we take life a step at a time, always relying on the arm of Him who is "mighty to save" (2 Nephi 31:19), even the Lord Jesus Christ, our "bright and morning star" (Revelation 22:16), we can realize our potential. This is our purpose. We, like our Elder Brother, are born for glory.

Appendix A

Selected References with (Occasional) Annotation

Relevant to Telestial Law and Glory

- D&C 76:98-106, 109-112

    And the glory of the telestial is one, even as the glory of the stars is one; for as one star differs from another star in glory, even so differs one from another in glory in the telestial world;

    For these are they who are of Paul, and of Apollos, and of Cephas.

    These are they who say they are some of one and some of another—some of Christ and some of John, and some of Moses, and some of Elias, and some of Esaias, and some of Isaiah, and some of Enoch;

But received not the gospel, neither the testimony of Jesus, neither the prophets, neither the everlasting covenant.

Last of all, these all are they who will not be gathered with the saints, to be caught up unto the church of the Firstborn, and received into the cloud.

These are they who are liars, and sorcerers, and adulterers, and whoremongers, and whosoever loves and makes a lie.

These are they who suffer the wrath of God on earth.

These are they who suffer the vengeance of eternal fire.

These are they who are cast down to hell and suffer the wrath of Almighty god, until the fullness of times, when Christ shall have subdued all enemies under his feet, and shall have perfected his work;

But behold, and lo, we saw the glory and the inhabitants of the telestial world, that they were as innumerable as the stars in the firmament of heaven, or as the sand upon the seashore;

And heard the voice of the Lord saying: These all shall bow the knee, and every tongue shall confess to him who sits upon the throne forever and ever;

For they shall be judged according to their works, and every man shall receive according to his own works, his own dominion, in the mansions which are prepared;

And they shall be servants of the Most High; but where God and Christ dwell they cannot come, worlds without end.

- D&C 76:81, 88-89, 91, 98, 109

    And again, we saw the glory of the telestial, which glory is that of the lesser, even as the glory of the stars differs from that of the glory of the moon in the firmament.

    And also the telestial receive it of the administering of angels who are appointed to minister for them, or who are appointed to be ministering spirits for them; for they shall be heirs of salvation.

    And thus we saw, in the heavenly vision, the glory of the telestial, which surpasses all understanding;

    And thus we saw the glory of the terrestrial which excels in all things the glory of the telestial, even in glory, and in power, and in might, and in dominion.

    And the glory of the telestial is one, even as the glory of the stars is one; for as one star differs from another star in glory, even so differs one from another in glory in the telestial world;

    But behold, and lo, we saw the glory and the inhabitants of the telestial world, that they were as innumerable as the stars in the firmament of heaven, or as the sand upon the seashore;

- D&C 88:32-33

    And they who remain [after the resurrection of bodies celestial, terrestrial, and telestial] shall also be quickened; nevertheless, they shall return again

> to their own place, to enjoy that which they are willing to receive, because they were not willing to enjoy that which they might have received.
>
> For what doth it profit a man if a gift is bestowed upon him, and he receive not the gift? Behold, he rejoices not in that which is given unto him, neither rejoices in him who is the giver of the gift.

These verses refer to those who resurrect at the end of the Second Resurrection with no glory—the sons of perdition. But verse 33 states a principle that can be applied more broadly. That is, no matter how great the gifts that are available to us as children of God, if we do not actively receive the gifts, we do not profit from them, nor do we completely rejoice in and worship the Father and the Son.

- Proverbs 6:16-19

    > These six things doth the Lord hate: yea, seven are an abomination unto him:
    >
    > A proud look, a lying tongue, and hands that shed innocent blood,
    >
    > An heart that deviseth wicked imaginations, feet that be swift in running to make mischief,
    >
    > A false witness that speaketh lies, and he that soweth discord among brethren.

As these behaviors are described as "things . . . the Lord [doth] hate," we could include them in our understanding of telestial behaviors. The Catholic Church lists the "Seven Deadly Sins" as: anger, avarice (greed), envy, gluttony, lust, pride, and sloth.

- Exodus 20:3-17 [The Ten Commandments]

    > Thou shalt have no other gods before me.

Appendix A

Thou shalt not make unto thee any graven image, or any likeness of any thing that is in heaven above, or that is in the earth beneath, or that is in the water under the earth:

Thou shalt not bow down thyself to them, nor serve them: for I the Lord thy God am a jealous God, visiting the iniquity of the fathers upon the children unto the third and fourth generation of them that hate me;

And shewing mercy unto thousands of them that love me, and keep my commandments.

Thou shalt not take the name of the Lord thy God in vain; for the Lord will not hold him guiltless that taketh his name in vain.

Remember the sabbath day, to keep it holy.

Six days shalt thou labour, and do all thy work:

But the seventh day is the sabbath of the Lord thy God: in it thou shalt not do any work, thou, nor thy son, nor thy daughter, thy manservant, nor thy maidservant, nor thy cattle, nor thy stranger that is within thy gates:

For in six days the Lord made heaven and earth, the sea, and all that in them is, and rested the seventh day: wherefore the Lord blessed the sabbath day, and hallowed it.

Honour thy father and thy mother: that thy days may be long upon the land which the Lord thy God giveth thee.

Thou shalt not kill.

Thou shalt not commit adultery.

Thou shalt not steal.

Thou shalt not bear false witness against thy neighbour.

Thou shalt not covet thy neighbour's house, thou shalt not covet thy neighbour's wife, nor his manservant, nor his maidservant, nor his ox, nor his ass, nor any thing that is thy neighbour's.

The Ten Commandments might be seen—in some ways—as describing the dividing line between telestial and terrestrial realms. The first four admonish us not to offend God by worshipping other gods, worshipping graven images (which these days are sometimes carved in our own flesh), taking God's name in vain, and dishonoring the Sabbath. The fifth commandment admonishes us to honor our parents. Commandments six through ten admonish us to not offend our neighbors: don't kill, commit adultery, steal, lie, or covet. When we obey these commandments, we are not necessarily valiant, but we stop being offensive to God.

- 2 Timothy 3:1-5

    This know also, that in the last days perilous times shall come.

    For men shall be lovers of their own selves, covetous, boasters, proud, blasphemers, disobedient to parents, unthankful, unholy,

    Without natural affection, trucebreakers, false accusers, incontinent, fierce, despisers of those that are good,

    Traitors, heady, highminded, lovers of pleasures more than lovers of God;

Appendix A

> Having a form of godliness, but denying the power thereof; from such turn away.

It seems safe to categorize these behaviors as offensive to God.

- Bruce R. McConkie, "Telestial Law," in *Mormon Doctrine,* p. 778.

> Those who refuse to worship the true and living God, who are unclean and immoral, who are proud and rebellious, who walk in paths of wickedness, who are carnal and sensual, who do not maintain standards of decency uprightness, and integrity, are as a result conforming their lives to the provisions of telestial law.

- 2 Nephi 2:27-29, emphasis added

> Men . . . are free to choose liberty and eternal life, through the great Mediator of all men, or to choose captivity and death, according to the captivity and power of the devil
>
> . . . and now, my sons, I would that ye should . . . choose eternal life . . .
>
> And not choose eternal death, *according to the will of the flesh and the evil which is therein, which giveth the spirit of the devil power to captivate,* to bring you down to hell, that he may reign over you in his own kingdom.

Father Lehi, prior to his death, makes this plea to his descendants, explaining that what gives the devil power to ensnare us is "the will of the flesh." Thus, if we do not develop control over our appetites and passions, we are subject to the power of the devil and a telestial realm.

- 2 Nephi 10:24, emphasis added

    Reconcile yourselves to the will of God, and not to the will of the devil *and the flesh* . . .

- Proverbs 23:2

    And put a knife to thy throat, if thou be a man given to appetite.

This proverb is fairly self-explanatory.

- Matthew 26:41

    Watch and pray, that ye enter not into temptation: the spirit indeed is willing, but the flesh is weak.

- Mosiah 3:19

    For the natural man is an enemy to God, and has been from the fall of Adam, and will be, forever and ever, unless he yields to the enticings of the Holy Spirit, and putteth off the natural man and becometh a saint through the atonement of Christ the Lord, and becometh as a child, submissive, meek, humble, patient, full of love, willing to submit to all things which the Lord seeth fit to inflict upon him, even as a child doth submit to his father.

- Spencer W. Kimball, "An Eternal Hope in Christ," *Ensign*, Nov 1978, p. 71.

    Those who have lived after the manner of the world shall go to a telestial kingdom whose glory is as the stars.

Appendix A

Relevant to Terrestrial Law and Glory

- D&C 76:72-79

    Behold, these are they who died without law;

    And also they who are the spirits of men kept in prison, whom the Son visited, and preached the gospel unto them, that they might be judged according to men in the flesh;

    Who received not the testimony of Jesus in the flesh, but afterwards received it.

    These are they who are honorable men of the earth, who were blinded by the craftiness of men.

    These are they who receive of his glory, but not of his fullness.

    These are they who receive of the presence of the Son, but not of the fulness of the Father.

    Wherefore, they are bodies terrestrial, and not bodies celestial, and differ in glory as the moon differs from the sun.

    These are they who are not valiant in the testimony of Jesus; wherefore, they obtain not the crown over the kingdom of our God.

This description of the terrestrial kingdom is relatively brief but states significant descriptors of the inhabitants, the consistent theme being that they are good people but not good enough for the fullness of glory available in the celestial.

- Bruce R. McConkie, "Terrestrial Law," in *Mormon Doctrine,* p. 784.

> To attain a terrestrial kingdom it is necessary to abide a terrestrial law, which consists in living an upright, honorable life but one that does not conform to the standards whereby the human soul is sanctified by the Spirit.

Again, the inheritors of terrestrial glory are upright and honorable, but not sanctified by the Holy Ghost. Sanctification should be a goal for those seeking to rise above terrestrial life. The Lord instructs His people again and again to "sanctify yourselves"(Leviticus 11:44; Leviticus 20:7; Numbers 11:18; Joshua 3:5; Joshua 7:13; 1 Samuel 16:5; 1 Chronicles 15:12; 2 Chronicles 29:5; 2 Chronicles 35:6; D&C 43:11, 16; D&C 88:68, 74; D&C 133:4). Elder Bruce R. McConkie gives a very brief explanation of sanctification below, but the doctrine of sanctification warrants continued study and personal attention.

- Bruce R. McConkie, *Mormon Doctrine,* p. 675.

> Sanctification is a state or saintliness, a state attained only by conformity to the laws and ordinances of the gospel. . . . Sanctification is a basic doctrine of the gospel.

- D&C 88:21, 23, 30

> And they who are not sanctified through the law which I have given unto you, even the law of Christ, must inherit another kingdom, even that of a terrestrial kingdom, or that of a telestial kingdom.
>
> And he who cannot abide the law of a terrestrial kingdom cannot abide a terrestrial glory.
>
> And they who are quickened by a portion of the terrestrial glory shall then receive of the same, even a fulness.

APPENDIX A

- 1 Corinthians 15:40

   There are also celestial bodies, and bodies terrestrial: but the glory of the celestial is one, and the glory of the terrestrial is another.

- Spencer W. Kimball, "An Eternal Hope in Christ," *Ensign*, Nov 1978, p. 71.

   Those who have been decent and upright and who have lived respectable and good lives will go to a terrestrial kingdom whose glory is as the moon.

Relevant to Celestial Law and Glory

There is a great deal of information in the scriptures concerning celestial law and glory. This makes sense, of course, as the plan of salvation has as its ultimate aim to invite all to celestial life and glory. What follows is in no way a complete summary of references on this topic.

- D&C 76:51-70

   They are they who received the testimony of Jesus, and believed on his name and were baptized after the manner of his burial, being buried in the water in his name, and this according to the commandment which he has given—

   That by keeping the commandments they might be washed and cleansed from all their sins, and receive the Holy Spirit by the laying on of the hands of him who is ordained and sealed unto this power;

   And who overcome by faith, and are sealed by the Holy Spirit of promise, which the Father sheds forth upon all those who are just and true.

They are they who are the church of the Firstborn.

They are they into whose hands the Father has given all things—

They are they who are priests and kings, who have received of his fulness, and of his glory;

And are priests of the Most High, after the order of Melchizedek, which was after the order of Enoch, which was after the order of the Only Begotten Son.

Wherefore, as it is written, they are gods, even the sons of God—

Wherefore, all things are theirs, whether life or death, or things present, or things to come, all are theirs and they are Christ's, and Christ is God's.

And they shall overcome all things.

Wherefore, let no man glory in man, but rather let him glory in God, who shall subdue all enemies under his feet.

These shall dwell in the presence of God and his Christ forever and ever.

These are they whom he shall bring with him, when he shall come in the clouds of heaven to reign on the earth over his people.

These are they who shall have part in the first resurrection.

These are they who shall come forth in the resurrection of the just.

> These are they who are come unto Mount Zion, and unto the city of the living God, the heavenly place, the holiest of all.
>
> These are they who have come to an innumerable company of angels, to the general assembly and church of Enoch, and of the Firstborn.
>
> These are they whose names are written in heaven, where God and Christ are the judge of all.
>
> These are they who are just men made perfect through Jesus the mediator of the new covenant, who wrought out this perfect atonement through the shedding of his own blood.
>
> These are they whose bodies are celestial, whose glory is that of the sun, even the glory of God, the highest of all, whose glory the sun of the firmament is written of as being typical.

This description of those who obtain a celestial glory doesn't focus as much on the requirements or demands of obeying a celestial law as on some of the rewards, glory, and privileges to come. A few qualifications are mentioned. The celestial "received a testimony of Jesus Christ" and were baptized. Drawing upon what is said concerning the terrestrial, "they who are not valiant in the testimony of Jesus; wherefore, they obtain not the crown over the kingdom of our God" (D&C 76:79), it follows that the celestial are indeed valiant in their testimonies of Christ. Also, as opposed to others who likewise enter into covenants through receiving the ordinances of the gospel, the celestial are those whose ordinances "are sealed by the Holy Spirit of Promise, which the Father sheds forth upon all those who are just and true (D&C 76:53). As discussed in Chapter Five, only ordinances that are sealed by the Holy Spirit of Promise endure after this life.

- D&C 132:7, emphasis added

    And verily I say unto you, that the conditions of this law are these: *All covenants,* contracts, bonds, obligations, oaths, vows, performances, connections, associations, or expectations, *that are not made and entered into and sealed by the Holy Spirit of promise,* of him who is anointed, both as well for time and for all eternity, and that too most holy, by revelation and commandment through the medium of mine anointed, whom I have appointed on the earth to hold this power (and I have appointed unto my servant Joseph to hold this power in the last days, and there is never but one on the earth at a time on whom this power and the keys of this priesthood are conferred), *are of no efficacy, virtue, or force in and after the resurrection from the dead; for all contracts that are not made unto this end have an end when men are dead.*

Many souls may be baptized and receive all the other ordinances of the gospel, including those made in the temples, seeking to enter into the kingdom of God, but the celestial are those whose baptisms—as well as all other ordinances—are sealed up into eternity, securing legitimate entry into our Heavenly Father's kingdom, rather than expiring at death.

- Bruce R. McConkie, "Holy Spirit of Promise," in *Mormon Doctrine*, pp. 361-2.

    . . . the power given [the Holy Ghost] to ratify and approve the righteous acts of men so that those acts will be binding on earth and in heaven. . . . The ratifying seal of approval is put upon an act only if those entering the contract are worthy as a result of personal righteousness to receive the divine approbation. They 'are sealed by the Holy Spirit of promise, which the Father sheds forth upon all those who are *just* and *true*" (D&C 76:53). If we are not just and true and worthy, the ratifying seal is withheld.

- D&C 76:70, 92, 96

    These are they whose bodies are celestial, whose glory is that of the sun, even the glory of God, the highest of all, whose glory the sun of the firmament is written of as being typical.

    And thus we saw the glory of the celestial, which excels in all things—where God, even the Father, reigns upon his throne forever and ever;

    And the glory of the celestial is one, even as the glory of the sun is one.

- D&C 137:1, 7, 10

    The heavens were opened upon us, and I beheld the celestial kingdom of God, and the glory thereof, whether in the body or out I cannot tell.

    Thus came the voice of the Lord unto me, saying: All who have died without a knowledge of this gospel, who would have received it if they had been permitted to tarry, shall be heirs of the celestial kingdom of God;

    And I also beheld that all children who die before they arrive at the years of accountability are saved in the celestial kingdom of heaven.

- 1 Corinthians 15:40

    There are also celestial bodies, and bodies terrestrial: but the glory of the celestial is one, and the glory of the terrestrial is another.

- D&C 78:7

    For if you will that I give unto you a place in the celestial world, you must prepare yourselves by doing the things which I have commanded you and required of you.

- D&C 105:1-5, emphasis added

    Verily I say unto you who have assembled yourselves together that you may learn my will concerning the redemption of mine afflicted people—

    Behold, I say unto you, were it not for the transgressions of my people, speaking concerning the church and not individuals, they might have been redeemed even now.

    But behold, they have not learned to be obedient to the things which I required at their hands, but are full of all manner of evil, and do not impart of their substance, as becometh saints, to the poor and afflicted among them;

    And are not united according to the union required by the law of the celestial kingdom;

    And Zion cannot be built up unless it is by the principles of the law of the celestial kingdom; otherwise I cannot receive her unto myself.

- D&C 130:11

    And a white stone is given to each of those who come into the celestial kingdom, whereon is a new name written, which no man knoweth save he that receiveth it. The new name is the key word.

- D&C 101:65

    Therefore, I must gather together my people, according to the parable of the wheat and the tares, that the wheat may be secured in the garners to possess eternal life, and be crowned with celestial glory, when I shall come in the kingdom of my Father to reward every man according as his work shall be;

- D&C 131:1

    In the celestial glory there are three heavens or degrees . . .

The Beatitudes

Perhaps the best summary of celestial law can be found in Christ's Sermon on the Mount (Matthew 5 and, to the Nephites, 3 Nephi 12). He begins with a series of statements commonly referred to as the Beatitudes.

- Matthew 5:3-12

    Blessed are the poor in spirit: for theirs is the kingdom of heaven.

    Blessed are they that mourn: for they shall be comforted.

    Blessed are the meek: for they shall inherit the earth.

    Blessed are they which do hunger and thirst after righteousness: for they shall be filled.

    Blessed are the merciful: for they shall obtain mercy.

> Blessed are the pure in heart: for they shall see God.
>
> Blessed are the peacemakers: for they shall be called the children of God.
>
> Blessed are they which are persecuted for righteousness' sake: for theirs is the kingdom of heaven.
>
> Blessed are ye, when men shall revile you, and persecute you, and shall say all manner of evil against you falsely, for my sake.
>
> Rejoice, and be exceeding glad: for great is your reward in heaven: for so persecuted they the prophets which were before you.

While at first this group of declarations may seem like no more than a statement that men and women who seek to do good will be recognized of God, a more careful examination of the promises reveals that the individuals described in the Beatitudes will inherit celestial glory. As Elder McConkie wrote, "Truly his teachings were the gospel of the kingdom, not just ethical principles!"[1]

Those promised the kingdom of heaven will ultimately be the celestial glory; the comfort promised comes through sanctification by the first comforter or Holy Ghost and by the second comforter, Jesus Christ Himself. Those who receive the Second Comforter have their calling and election made sure and are sealed up for the celestial glory.[2] Since this earth will be glorified and take upon it celestial glory, those who inherit

---

1. Bruce R. McConkie, *Doctrinal New Testament Commentary*, (Salt Lake City: Deseret Book Co., 2002), 1:215.

2. For summaries of the doctrines of sanctification, the Second Comforter, and calling and election made sure, see *Mormon Doctrine* by Bruce R. McConkie.

Appendix A

the earth will inhabit the celestial kingdom. The promise in verse 6 was corrected by Joseph Smith to read, "filled with the Holy Ghost," another reference to sanctification. Verse 7 promises that mercy, forgiveness of sins, will be extended to the merciful. Verse 8 promises that "every living soul who is pure in heart shall see God, literally and personally, in this life, to say nothing of the fact that he shall dwell with and see him frequently in the celestial world hereafter."[3]

These verses, then, describe those who obtain the celestial kingdom as being:

— The poor in spirit (3 Nephi 12:3 clarifies "the poor in spirit who come unto me")

— They that mourn

— The meek

— They who do hunger and thirst after righteousness

— The merciful

— The pure in heart

— The peacemakers

— Those persecuted for Christ's sake

It has been suggested that the Beatitudes may describe a specific order of progression to the celestial state. First, we must recognize that we are in need of what the gospel and the Savior makes available to us, and we must come unto Jesus Christ, seeking salvation. We must mourn for our sins and weaknesses.

---

3. Bruce R. McConkie, *Doctrinal New Testament Commentary*, (Salt Lake City: Deseret Book Co., 2002), 1:216. See also Ether 3:19-20, 26; D&C 67:10-14; Joseph Smith, *Teachings of the Prophet Joseph Smith*, comp. Joseph Fielding Smith (Salt Lake City: Shadow Mountain, 1977), 9, 149-151. And to be called the "Children of God" refers to those who become heirs of God and joint-heirs with Jesus Christ (see Romans 8:14-18; Galatians 3:26-29, 4:1-7).

We must become meek as the Savior is meek. Meekness, I believe, means appropriately controlled power, requiring the conquering of the appetites and passions. After gaining mastery over the natural man, we must hunger and thirst after righteousness. The story is told of a young man who asked the great philosopher, Socrates, to teach him. Apparently Socrates led the young man to a nearby body of water and held the young man's head underwater until the he was straining every muscle to lift his head from the water. When Socrates released him, the young man gasped for air, and the philosopher told him that when he desired to learn as much as he had desired air, nothing could prevent him from acquiring knowledge and wisdom. It must be this kind of "hunger and thirst" of which the Lord is speaking. Then, as all our energy is focused on living righteously, we can qualify for the constant companionship of the Holy Ghost, being filled and sanctified by this member of the Godhead. Enos, when forgiven, cleansed from all his sins and filled with the Holy Ghost, felt an outpouring of concern for his brethren, the Nephites, and even his enemies, the Lamanites. As we are sanctified, we will be desirous of extending mercy to and sharing the gospel of peace with all those around us, truly becoming the peacemakers of whom it is written, "How beautiful upon the mountains are the feet of them that bringeth good tidings, that publisheth peace" (Isaiah 52:7).

The Master closes the Beatitudes with a final promise and warning: "Blessed are all they who are persecuted for my name's sake, for theirs is the kingdom of heaven" (Matthew 5:12). As recorded in 3 Nephi, in His sermon to those on the American continent, Jesus continued, "And blessed are ye when men shall revile you and persecute, and shall say all manner of evil against you falsely, for my sake . . . for so persecuted they the prophets" (3 Nephi 12:11–12). In other words, the strait and narrow path that leads to the kingdom of God is not for the weak. Determined disciples will be tested and proven.

APPENDIX A

- Joseph Smith, *Teachings of the Prophet Joseph Smith*, pp. 149-151.

  > After a person has faith in Christ, repents of his sins, and is baptized for the remission of his sins and receives the Holy Ghost (by the laying on of hands), which is the first Comforter, then let him continue to humble himself before God, hungering and thirsting after righteousness, and living by every word of God, and the Lord will soon say unto him, *Son, thou shall be exalted.* When the Lord has thoroughly proved him, and finds that the man is determined to serve him at all hazards, then the man will find his calling and election made sure, then it will be his privilege to receive the other Comforter.

The other Comforter, or the Second Comforter, is Jesus Christ Himself, who will personally minister to the individual who has had his calling and election made sure.[4]

THE SERMON ON THE MOUNT

In the Sermon on the Mount, Jesus Christ went on teach much more about the law of Christ, showing us the way to come unto Him and be saved in the celestial kingdom. He explained that He had come not to destroy the law of Moses, but to fulfill it. He contrasted some of the commonly held standards of behavior with the expectations of a higher law, inviting us not only to control our behavior, but to purify our hearts from improper desires and attitudes. Some particular admonitions to all who would follow the Savior include:

—To be the salt of the earth, and a light to others

---

4. See also Bruce R. McConkie, "Second Comforter," in *Mormon Doctrine* (Salt Lake City: Bookcraft, 1958).

— To have a broken heart and a contrite spirit

— Not to be angry with our brother

— To reconcile with others before approaching the Lord

— To moderate our language and not make oaths

— Not to be combative, even when mistreated

— To love our enemies

— Not to do good, pray, or fast to be seen of men, but to make those offerings in secret

— Not to set our hearts on earthly treasure, but to seek treasures in heaven

— Not to try to serve two masters, God and Mammon, or the world

— Not to judge unrighteously

— Not to criticize or try to correct our brother, but to address our own faults

— To treat others as we would be treated

— To build on rock by not only hearing the gospel, but by doing it

- Matthew 5:21-22, 27-28

    Ye have heard that it was said by them of old time, Thou shalt not kill; and whosoever shall kill shall be in danger of the judgment:

    But I say unto you, That whosoever is angry with his brother without a cause shall be in danger of the judgment: and whosoever shall say to his brother, Raca, shall be in danger of the council: but

Appendix A

whosoever shall say, Thou fool, shall be in danger of hell fire.

Ye have heard that it was said by them of old time, Thou shalt not commit adultery:

But I say unto you, That whosoever looketh on a woman to lust after her hath committed adultery with her already in his heart.

- Matthew 5:48

    Be ye therefore perfect, even as your Father which is in heaven is perfect.

- 3 Nephi 12:48

    Therefore I would that ye should be perfect even as I, or your Father who is in heaven is perfect.

- 3 Nephi 27:27

    Therefore, what manner of men ought ye to be? Verily I say unto you, even as I am.

- John Taylor, in *Journal of Discourses*, Vol. 26, p. 342b.

    One thing we do know; one thing is clearly told us, and that is if we are not governed by the celestial law and cannot abide a celestial law, we cannot inherit a celestial kingdom. What is it to obey a celestial law? Where does the celestial law come from to begin with? From the heavens.[5]

---

5. John Taylor, "Nature of the Gospel, and of Our Position and Calling—Responsibilities of the Latter-Day Saints—The Right of All Men to Religious Freedom—Honorable Men of the Earth—We Aim at a Higher Exaltation Than the Rest of the World." (address delivered in Tabernacle, Ogden, UT, 20 July 1884), in *Journal of Discourses*, 26:324b.

- Bruce R. McConkie, "Celestial Law," in *Mormon Doctrine*, p. 117.

  > That law by obedience to which men gain an inheritance in the kingdom of God in eternity is called *celestial law*. It is the law of the gospel, the law of Christ, and it qualifies men for admission to the celestial kingdom because in and through it men are "sanctified by the reception of the Holy Ghost, " thus becoming clean, pure, and spotless (3 Ne. 27:19-21). . . . Those who have the companionship of the Holy Ghost and are guided thereby in their lives are "able to abide the law of a celestial kingdom," including the law of consecration or anything else the Lord might ask of them. They are the ones who—"united according to the union required by the law of the celestial kingdom" (D&C 105:1-5)—will build up Zion in the last days.

- D&C 88:28-29

  > They who are of a celestial spirit shall receive the same body which was a natural body; even ye shall receive your bodies, and your glory shall be that glory by which your bodies are quickened.

  > Ye who are quickened by a portion of the celestial glory shall then receive of the same, even a fulness.

- L. Tom Perry, "The Role of the Stake Bishops Council in Welfare Services," *Ensign,* May 1977, 88.

  > Love and service, work and self-reliance, stewardship and consecration, the provident living that comes from personal and family preparedness, caring for the poor and the needy—these are principles members must learn and practice if they would live celestial lives in a telestial world.

Appendix A

- Spencer W. Kimball, "An Eternal Hope in Christ," *Ensign*, Nov 1978, 71.

  > Those who have believed in Christ, who have forsaken the world, who have taken the Holy Spirit for their guide and been willing to lay their all on the altar, those who have kept the commandments of God—they shall go to a celestial kingdom whose glory is as the sun.

A Few Other Statements Concerning Three Degrees of Law and Glory

- John Taylor, priesthood meeting address given October 6, 1883.

  > We are told that if we cannot abide the law of the celestial kingdom we cannot inherit a celestial glory. Is not that doctrine? Yes. "But," says one, "Are not we all going into the celestial kingdom?" I think not, unless we turn round and mend our ways very materially. It is only those who can abide a celestial glory and obey a celestial law that will be prepared to enter a celestial kingdom. "Well," says another, "are the others going to be burned up, etc.?" No. Do you expect everybody to walk according to this higher law? No, I do not. And do I expect those that do not, are going into the celestial kingdom? No, I do not. Well, where will they go? If they are tolerably good men and do not do anything very bad, they will get into a terrestrial kingdom, and if there are some that cannot abide a terrestrial law, they may get into a telestial kingdom, or otherwise, as the case may be, etc., etc. Did you ever read in your Bibles that "Strait is the gate, and narrow is

the way, which leadeth unto life, and few there be that find it."[6]

- Heber C. Kimball, address given October 6, 1865

    All who profess to be Latter-day Saints will not be saved in the celestial world, for they cannot abide the celestial law, but all will attain to the glory which they can abide. Every righteous thing that we do in this mortality is a rudimental lesson in the celestial law of our God. Let us go to with our might, mind, and strength to abide the celestial law, as it shall be revealed to us from time to time, until we can abide its fulness, that we may ultimately be introduced into the presence of our heavenly Father to dwell with him for evermore.[7]

- Joseph Fielding Smith, *Take Heed to Yourselves,* p. 347.

    Paul speaks of our being joint heirs with Jesus Christ. And as heirs of God we will be entitled to inherit. To inherit what? Not that he is going to step down from his throne that we may ascend. Not that, but we will inherit the same blessings and privileges, opportunities of advancement that he possesses, so that in course, I was going to say of

---

6. John Taylor, "Privilege of Meeting Together—We Are Here to Do Our Father's Will—All Dependent Upon God for Assistance, Guidance and Direction—The Lord Revealed to Adam the Purpose of Sacrifice—Adam, Before His Death, Called His Family Together and Blessed Them and Prophesied—Many Spirits Have Been Destined to Hold Certain Positions Among Men—Why We Are Gathered—We Must Follow the Teachings of the Spirit, and Honor the Priesthood in All Its Callings—Prepare Ourselves to Enter Holy Places—The Priesthood Must not Tolerate Iniquity—The Church Must Be Purified—Concluding Exhortations" (priesthood meeting address, Salt Lake Assembly Hall, Salt Lake City, UT, October 6, 1883), reported by John Irvine.

7. Heber C. Kimball, "Others' Sins No Justification of Ours," (address delivered in the Bowery, Salt Lake City, UT, October 6, 1865), reported by G. D. Watt.

APPENDIX A

time, but I will say of eternity, we may become like him, having ourselves kingdoms and thrones. If any of you who are here present prefer, when you get on the other side, to be a servant and perhaps go into the terrestrial kingdom, you will have that privilege. You do not have to keep other commandments. You do not need to pay your tithing if you want to go into those other kingdoms. You do not need to pray to your Father in heaven, and you can go into one of those other kingdoms. You do not even have to be baptized for the remission of your sins to go into those other kingdoms. And as you have been baptized and are members of the Church, you do not have to keep all the commandments the Lord has given—you will have to keep some of them, but you will not have to keep them all—and you can go into the telestial kingdom or into the terrestrial kingdom. But if you want to go into the presence of God and dwell in the celestial kingdom and see the glories of exaltation, then you must live by every word that proceeds forth from the mouth of God.[8]

- Joseph Fielding Smith, *Doctrines of Salvation*, Vol. 2, p. 28.

    Church members may go to any kingdom. We have our agency and many, very, very many members of this Church, when they come to the judgment and are judged according to their works, are going to be consigned to the telestial kingdom; others to the terrestrial kingdom; because that is the law that they have willed to obey; and we are going to get our reward according to the law that we obey.

---

8. Joseph Fielding Smith, *Take Heed to Yourselves,* (Salt Lake City: Deseret Book Co., 1966), 347.

> A man who has accepted the testimony of Jesus in the flesh may inherit any of the three kingdoms, according to the degree of faithfulness he has shown in keeping the commandments of the Lord. If he keeps the full law, he shall be entitled to enter the celestial kingdom. If he is willing to abide by only a portion of the law, and rejects the covenants which govern in the celestial kingdom, notwithstanding he is honest, virtuous, and truthful, he shall be assigned to the terrestrial kingdom where other honorable men shall be found. If he enters into the Church, but rejects the light, and lives a life of disobedience and corruption, he may be assigned to the telestial kingdom and obtain such blessings as he is willing to receive, because he was not willing to enjoy that which he might have received.[9]

- Joseph Fielding Smith, *Church History and Modern Revelation*, Vol. 2, pp. 58-59.

> Into the terrestrial kingdom will go all those who are honorable and who have lived clean virtuous lives, but who would not receive the Gospel, but in the spirit world repented and accepted it as far as it can be given unto them. Many of these have been blinded by tradition and the love [of] the world, and have not been able to see the beauties of the Gospel. Into this kingdom, or glory, will also go these who are without law, and therefore redeemed through the blood of Jesus Christ. (See Mosiah 3:11; 15:24; Moroni 8:22; D&C 29:50.) Another class is those who are not valiant in the testimony of Jesus. All who enter this glory "receive not the crown over the kingdom of our God" which is reserved for the

---

9 Joseph Fielding Smith, *Doctrines of Salvation*, 3 vols., edited by Bruce R. McConkie [Salt Lake city: Bookcraft, 1954-1956], 2:28.

faithful in the celestial kingdom. Jesus Christ, the Son, will visit them but not the Father and they receive blessings by ministrations of those from the celestial. Their glory is far greater than the glories in the telestial (v. 91). The Lord will make them as happy, and will bless them as far as he can but their blessings are restricted while those of the celestial are unlimited.

President John Taylor has said of these: "As eternal beings we all have to stand before Him to be judged; and he has provided different degrees of glory—the celestial, the terrestrial, and the telestial glories—which are provided according to certain unchangeable laws which cannot be controverted. What will he do with them? For those who are ready to listen to him and be brought under the influence of the Spirit of God and be led by the principles of revelation and the light of heaven, and who are willing to yield obedience to his commands at all times and carry out his purposes upon the earth, and who are willing to abide a celestial law, he has prepared for them a celestial law, he has prepared for them a celestial glory, that they may be with him for ever and ever. And what about the others? They are not prepared to go there anymore than lead is prepared to stand the same test as gold or silver; and there they cannot go. And there is a great gulf between them. But he will do with them just as well as he can. A great many of these people in the world, thousands and hundreds of millions of them, will be a great deal better off through the interposition of the Almighty than they have any idea of, but they cannot enter into the celestial kingdom of God; where God and Christ are they cannot come." (Salt Lake Stake Conf., Jan. 6, 1879.)[10]

- Harold B. Lee, "On Earning Salvation," *Improvement Era,* 1947 Annual General Conference.

    > As I pondered those scriptures . . . these conclusions seemed clear to my mind. In the first place, we are our own judges of the place we shall have in the eternal world. Here and now in mortality, each one of us is having the opportunity of choosing the kind of laws we elect to obey. We are now living and obeying celestial laws that will make us candidates for celestial glory, or we are living terrestrial laws that will make us candidates for either terrestrial glory, or telestial law. The place we shall occupy in the eternal worlds will be determined by the obedience we yield to the laws of these various kingdoms during the time we have here in mortality upon the earth.

---

10. Joseph Fielding Smith, *Church History and Modern Revelation*, 4 vols. (Salt Lake City: The Church of Jesus Christ of Latter-day Saints, 1946-1949), 2:58-59.

APPENDIX B

JUDGMENT WITHOUT CONDEMNATION

WHY AND HOW WE MUST LEARN AND USE RIGHTEOUS JUDGMENT

The Lord requires his people to judge righteous judgment (see JST, Matthew 7:1) and explains how to do so in the seventh chapter of Moroni:

> It is given unto [us] to judge, that [we] may know good from evil . . . that [we] may know with a perfect knowledge, as the daylight is from the dark night.
>
> For behold, the Spirit of Christ is given to every man, that he may know good from evil; wherefore, I show unto you to the way to judge; for every thing which inviteth to do good, and to persuade to believe in Christ, is sent forth by the power and gift of Christ . . .

> But whatsoever thing persuadeth men to do evil, and believe not in Christ, and deny him, and serve not God, then ye may know with a perfect knowledge it is of the devil (Moroni 7:15-17).

Elder Dallin H. Oaks explained that what the Lord prohibits is *final judgment*.

> ... final judgment is the Lord's and ... mortals must refrain from judging any human being in the final sense of concluding or proclaiming that he or she is irretrievably bound for hell or have lost all hope of exaltation.[1]

However, Elder Oaks goes on to explain:

> In contrast to forbidding mortals to make final judgments, the scriptures require mortals to make what I will call "intermediate judgments." These judgments are essential to the exercise of personal moral agency. ... The Savior ... commanded individuals to be judges, both of circumstances and of other people.[2]

Elder Oaks gives guidance on how to righteously exercise intermediate judgment, including the following: we should seek guidance from the Spirit of the Lord; we should not be motivated by anger, revenge, jealousy, or self-interest; we should judge within our stewardships, not outside of our personal responsibilities; we should, as much as possible, only

---

1. Dallin H. Oaks, "Judge Not and Judging" (devotional address, Brigham Young University, Provo, UT, March 1, 1998).

2. Oaks, "Judge Not and Judging," 1998.

judge when we have an adequate knowledge of the facts;[3] where possible, we should judge situations not people; we should always apply righteous standards; and we should remember the commandment to forgive.[4]

If we don't learn to make righteous judgments, we cannot make effective use of our agency. How are we to choose the good and shun the bad if we do not determine which is which? And in tragic irony, if we are not willing to label some things as evil and instead consider it wrong, or even evil, to judge, we may fall into the trap Isaiah warned of when he said,

> Woe unto them that call evil good, and good evil;
> that put darkness for light, and light for darkness;
> that put bitter for sweet, and sweet for bitter! (Isaiah 5:20).

At the very least, we risk falling into the more subtle trap of moral relativity.

Moral or ethical relativism, a widely accepted philosophy, suggests that morality—what is right and wrong—is relative to its context. In other words, what may be right for one person may not be right for another given different circumstances, cultural background, experience, beliefs, and so forth. Moral relativism promotes tolerance of pretty much any behavioral or lifestyle choice made by consenting adults. Advocates of this philosophy reject the idea of absolute truth and often consider strongly held beliefs to be intolerant, bigoted, and narrow-minded. The gospel of Jesus Christ, however, teaches many absolute truths, including clear condemnations of many specific behaviors. And while we can, and should, respect and tolerate

---

3. This should be done with the exception of situations that may not provide us with total information but that, nevertheless, require a judgment in order to keep people safe, e.g. someone arrested for child sexual abuse, but whose guilt is not proven and is free on bail, is not a good choice to tend your children.

4. See Oaks, 1998, for explanations of each of these ideas.

people with vastly different beliefs, respect and tolerance does not require that we respect the beliefs themselves or that we tolerate actions that grow out of those beliefs.

To give an extreme example, we may respect an individual who believes in human sacrifice and respect his right to believe as he chooses. Nevertheless, we do not have to respect the idea of human sacrifice, neither must we accept its practice in our community. To use an example closer to home, we should respect individuals who promote same-sex marriage but—as our prophets clearly teach and admonish—we should join with other like-minded citizens to work against the adoption of this practice in our society.[5] The Lord's commandment to hate evil (see Psalm 97:10)[6]—and to protect our communities from the destructive impact of sinful behaviors—neither mandates nor excuses hating sinners.

Freedom and Agency

Some worry that restricting the right for individuals to practice their beliefs in our community limits that person's agency. This is an unnecessary concern. To return to our extreme example, restricting the practice of human sacrifice *does* infringe on the freedom of one who believes in it, but *does not* limit the believer's agency. To repeat the point made in Chapter Seven, *freedom and agency are not the same thing*. Freedoms can be restricted, legally or illegally. While we should never promote illegal restrictions of freedom, we should recognize that the cost of membership in any group is the relinquishment of some freedoms. For instance, if we want to be in good standing in the kingdom

---

5. Dallin H. Oaks and Lance B. Wickman, interview by the Public Affairs Department of The Church of Jesus Christ of Latter-day Saints, http://www.newsroom.lds.org/ldsnewsroom/eng/public-issues/same-gender-attraction (accessed July 9, 2009).

6. See also Amos 5:15, 2 Nephi 4:31.

Appendix B

of God on earth, we relinquish the freedom to smoke, drink, behave immorally, and so on. If we want to be free citizens of our country, we relinquish the freedom to drive through intersections when the light is red, or to drive over the posted speed limit, or to behave in any way that violates the country's laws. In the case of Church membership, the restrictions are set by God. In the case of citizenship, the restrictions are set by the governing body, whether a monarch or a representative government. Of course, we can choose to break those laws, but we would be subject to penalties for doing so and, if we continued to ignore the requirements of membership, we might ultimately lose our membership in that group.

Sadly, some members of the Church worry overmuch about limiting freedom, wrongly confusing the limitation of freedom for the restriction of agency. Thus, they may hesitate to vote for legislation that limits certain unrighteous or dangerous behaviors in our communities, fearing that any legislation limiting freedoms must be contrary to our belief in agency. Not so.

Our latter-day leaders have offered the following clarifying counsel:

> Those who consider freedom of choice as a goal can easily slip into the position of trying to justify any choice that is made. . . . in today's world we are not true to our teachings if we are merely pro-choice. We must stand up for the right choice.[7]
>
> Interesting how one virtue, when given exaggerated or fanatical emphasis, can be used to batter down another, with freedom, a virtue, invoked to protect vice. . . . People who are otherwise sensible say, "I do not intend to indulge, but I vote for freedom

---

7. Dallin H. Oaks, "Weightier Matters," (devotional address, Brigham Young University, Provo, Utah, Feb 9, 1999).

of choice for those who do." The phrase "free agency" does not appear in scriptures. The only agency spoken of there is moral agency, "which," the Lord said, "I have given unto him, that every man may be accountable for his own sins in the day of judgment" (D&C 101:78).[8]

The confusion over agency and freedom is typical of what can happen when philosophies of the world mingle with gospel beliefs. It can sound correct to say we shouldn't limit others' agency. The fact is, however, that we *can't* limit others' agency. It is not possible. When we decline to limit freedom to participate in activities we know to be wrong or harmful to society, we move right past appropriate tolerance for others' beliefs, arriving instead at tolerance of sinful behaviors based on those beliefs. We end up joining the ranks of the politically correct, rather than demonstrating that we, like Paul, are "not ashamed of the gospel of Jesus Christ" (Romans 1:16). If we don't understand the difference between freedom and agency in today's politically correct climate, we may find ourselves trying to "serv[e] the Lord in such a way as to not offend the devil."[9]

The world contains both good and evil, darkness and light, the bitter and the sweet. We must learn—and be willing—to identify the bitter, the dark, and the evil before we can protect ourselves from their destructive powers. As we learn how to make righteous intermediate judgments, we more clearly see the connection between what we choose and the eternal direction our choices take us.

---

8. Boyd K. Packer, "Our Moral Environment," *Ensign*, May 1992, 66.

9. Marion G. Romney, "The Prince of Peace," (devotional address, Brigham Young University, Provo, Utah, March 11, 1955).

Index

A

Abrahamic Covenant, 63
abusive relationships: accepting victim role in, 62-63; blaming the victim in, 75-76; confronting offenders in violent, 74; establishing terrestrial boundary lines to end, 64-74; long-lasting emotional effects of, 113; passive acceptance role in, 70-74; protecting children from family, 112-14; telestial behaviors creating, 61-62; temple marriage and, 74-75. See also telestial partner (or roommate)
Adam, 70-71, 136
addiction: pornography, 120, 122, 124, 125; recovering from, 183-84; war as, 183. See also appetites
adultery: blaming the spouse for, 126-27; emotional affair form of, 66-67; forgiveness and healing from, 132-33; making amends for, 131-32; as "the sin next to murder," 119, 132; victimization leading to, 69
affliction: God's answer on, 191-92; Job's, 192; refining process of suffering and, 189-91; responses to suffering and, 188-89
agency: consequences of, 137-39; definition of, 111; our children's, 111-12, 115; parent and child's unrighteous, 115-18. See also life choices
Alma the Younger, 178, 193
Ammon, 182
Analisa, 106
The Andy Griffith Show (TV show), 17-18
Ann, 112-13
Anna Karenina (Tolstoy), 78
Anti-Nephi-Lehis (people of Ammon), 182-84
apologies: power of sincere, 130-31; repentance as including, 131-32
appetites: exiting telestial realm by controlling, 25-27; recognizing the attractiveness of some, 55-56; teaching children to control their, 101-6; telestial law governing gratification of, 7-8, 175; terrestrial law governing delayed gratification of, 8-10, 53-54. See also addiction
The Atonement: emotional healing possible through, 113; gaining understanding and gratitude for, 187-88; power to change lives through, 58-59; salvation through obedience and, 57-58, 63, 175. See also Jesus Christ

B

Ballard, M. Russell, 144, 145
Beck, Julie, 154, 155-56
Bednar, David A., 173
Benjamin, King, 115, 172
Benson, Ezra Taft, 23, 168
Bill, 66-67, 112-13
Black, Margaret B., 141
blaming: spouse for problems, 120-27; the victim, 75-76
Book of Mormon: on conversion of Alma the Younger, 178; on destructive priestcraft practices, 179-80; on people of Ammon, 182-83. See also Nephites
Boy Scout program, 39-41, 42
Brent, 181, 182
Brittany, 106
broken heart, 189, 191
Bryan, 88-90

C

"Can't Skip" principle: avoiding parental trap of, 103-4; description of, 21; forgiveness and the, 64-65; importance of understanding the, 44-45; Old Testament Israelites illustration of, 22; stages of, 22-23; trenchwork of the terrestrial component of, 24-28, 64-65

233

Carl, 85-86
celestial behavior: marriage choices based on mimicry of, 51-52; slow progression toward, 52-53; terrestrial foundation of, 52-54
celestial kingdom of glory: choosing, 195; the gospel as path leading to, 16; law of the harvest and, 192-94; life choices as determining future in, 1-2; pre-earth choice setting path to, 1; refining process of path to, 189-92; scripture description of, 4; terrestrial realm as bridge to the, 163-74, 184-92; two-fold process of path to, 172-73; valiant life preparing for the, 6. See also three realms perspective
celestial marriage: blessings of the patriarchal order in, 84-86; built on foundation of terrestrial behavior, 80; covenant of, 74-75, 90; The Family: A Proclamation to the World on, 80; Holy Spirit of Promise sealing, 74, 78, 94; putting God first in, 90-91; role of persuasion in, 87-95. See also marriage; temple marriage
celestial realm: being like Jesus Christ characteristic of, 11; "Can't Skip" principle of progression to, 21-28, 44-45, 64-65, 103-4; divine designation of, 77n.1; Holy Spirit as guiding behavior in, 12; outcomes of living in the, 11-13; parenting by using laws of terrestrial and, 100-103; past societies which have embraced principles of, 2; summarizing characteristics of the, 13; telestial imitation of the, 30-47; terrestrial life as bridge to, 163-74, 184-92; visualizing specific behaviors of, 12-13
celestial stress: choosing, 161; "wilderness experience," 157-59, 184
change of heart: consistent obedience required for, 34-35; consistent pattern of behavior demonstrating, 57-59; contrite spirit and, 130-32, 188, 190-91; as gospel purpose, 173, 175; motivations for, 176; by the people of Ammon, 182-84; repentance and, 193-94; true conversion accompanied by, 35-36. See also conversion; testimonies
charity: definition of, 62; difference between victimhood and, 67-73; understand Christ manifests his, 62-63. See also love
children: agency of, 111-12, 115; balancing charity and victimhood with adult-aged, 67-68; communicating which behaviors are destructive to, 128-29; developing concrete terrestrial behaviors in, 103-6; disrespect to parents by, 98-99; enforcing terrestrial behavior costs and payoffs, 107-11; facilitating agency of our, 111-12; "The Marshmallow Experiment" predicting future behavior of, 9-10; parental help in mastering natural man by, 27-28; parent responsibility for unrighteous, 115-18; protecting from telestial parenting, 112-14; supporting safety in relationships by, 70-71, 76; teaching them to control their appetites, 101-6. See also parents
Chris, 91-92, 136, 142, 153-54
Christofferson, D. Todd, 35-36
Church of Jesus Christ of Latter-day Saints: consolidated Church schedule of, 146-49; conversion to the, 23-25, 35-36, 53; The Family: A Proclamation to the World of the, 80, 90; the Lord on persecution suffered by, 71-73; revision of the budget program by the, 149-54. See also gospel principles
Church service: barriers to simplifying our, 153-56; blessings and responsibilities of, 144-45; budget program revision to simplify, 149-54; burnout from, 150; consolidated Church schedule to simplify, 146-49; wise counsel regarding, 145-46, 148-49

City of Enoch, 2
communication: characteristics of loving, 94; telestial problems excused as poor, 125, 127-28
communism, 32
complacency risk, 4
consequences: of agency, 137-39; fear of, 176-84; parental enforcement of, 107-11; sin and deferred, 137-39; of tolerating telestial behaviors, 62-63. See also punishment
contrite spirit, 130-32, 188, 190-91
conversion: of Alma the Younger, 178; change of heart accompanying true, 35-36; as miraculous event, 23; more typical process of, 23-24; transition from childhood testimonies to personal, 53. See also change of heart
converts: misery motivation of, 180; trenchwork of the terrestrial required of, 24-25
covenants: celestial marriage, 74-75, 90; Holy Spirit of Promise sealing, 74; measuring our compliance with the, 166-67; on nature of stewardships, 38; reflecting on our compliance with, 46; salvation promised by the Abrahamic, 63

D

dating. See safe dating/marriage choices
delayed gratification: "The Marshmallow Experiment" on, 9-10; teaching children, 101-6; as terrestrial law characteristic, 8-9, 53-54
desire: daily choices demonstrating our, 181-82; for obedience, 185. See also motivation
Diagnostic and Statistical Manual, 123
divorce: good choices as protection from, 50; increasing rate of, 49-50
Don, 100
Dunn, Paul H., 142
Dustin, 131

Index

E

"Eagle Mill," 39
Eagle Scout program, 39-41, 42
earthly theocracies, 30
Eli, 115-17
Ellen, 69
emotional affairs, 66-67
Enos, 179
Equal Rights Amendment, 91
"Essay on Man" (Pope), 18-19

F

faith: development of personal testimonies and, 53; Job's testimony of, 192; in a loving God, 194; refining process and increase of, 189-92
The Family: A Proclamation to the World, 80, 90
Faust, James E., 187
fear: of damaging valued relationships, 186; as motivation, 176-80, 185-86; to offend God, 180; repentance motivated by, 177-78
forgiveness: the "Can't Skip" principle and, 64-65; problem-solving and role of, 132-33; time required for, 132-33; tolerating evil versus, 63-65; victimhood versus charity and, 67-73
"foyer time," 107-8

G

gentleness, 87
"Girls' Camp syndrome," 34-35
glory. See celestial kingdom of glory
God: on adversity, 191-92; behaviors that are abominations to, 200; counsel to Joseph Smith on persecution by, 71-72; faith in a loving, 194; on making righteous judgment, 14; mercy and love shown by, 15; natural man as enemy to, 172; our relationship with, 186-87; putting Him first in the marriage, 90-91; what He requires of parents, 114-18; zero tolerance policy concerning sin by, 67. See also Jesus Christ

"golden" investigators, 24
gospel principles: emotional healing possible through the, 113; leading us to the kingdom of God, 16; to make good men better, 173, 175; on persecution and victimization, 71-73; resisting temptation to browbeat using, 81-82; safety in telestial world through the, 3-4; translated into concrete life tools, 3-4. See also Church of Jesus Christ of Latter-day Saints
government: communism mimicry of United Order, 32; earthly theocracy, 30; Nephite elected judges system of, 31-32; Nephite prophet-kings form of, 30-31
Graydon, 91, 92
guile, 88

H

Hafen, Bruce C., 190
Heather, 34
Helaman, 178
Hinckley, Gordon B., 3, 171-72
Holland, Jeffrey R., 153-54
Holly, 66-67
Holy Ghost: celestial behavior guided by the, 12, 25; conversion tutored by, 23-24; obedience for feeling Spirit of, 154; our relationship with, 186-87; reproving with sharpness when moved by, 92-94; role in marriage choices by, 50; spiritually charged moments through the, 35-36; as voice for positive change, 176
Holy Spirit of Promise, 74, 78, 94
hypocrisy, 88

I

integrity: definition and meaning of, 27n.6; progression from disobedience to, 27
Israelites, 22

J

Jackson, 40-41
Jared, 70-71

Jesus Christ: answer to the rich young man, 169; divine mission of, 15; how He defines His own stewardship, 63; as leading us to the kingdom of God, 16; our relationship with, 186-87; story of Martha and Mary with, 139-40; understanding charity of, 62-63; withdrawal from us by, 193. See also The Atonement; God
Jesus the Christ (Talmage), 167
Job, 192
Joe, 65-66
Josh, 117
Joy, 131
Judeo-Christian beliefs, 17-18
judgment: making righteous, 14-16; moral relativism demanding lack of, 122; unrighteous, 14

K

Kara, 131-32
Katrina, 127
Kent, 132
Keri, 54-55
Kimball, J. Golden, 153
kindness, 88

L

Laman, 158
Lamanites, 183-84
Laura, 132
law of Moses, 188
law of the harvest, 192-94
Lee, Harold B., 171
Lemuel, 158
life choices: future glory determined by, 1-2; safe dating/marriage, 49-59; translating gospel principles into tools for, 3-4. See also agency; motivation
Light of Christ, 176
Lindbergh, Anne, 188-89
Lindbergh, Charles "Lucky," 188
Lisa, 84-86
long-suffering, 87
love: developing Christlike, 138; as part of loving communication, 94; reproving with sharpness and increase in, 92-94. See also charity
"Love at Home" (hymn), 103
love unfeigned, 87-88

lying: as abomination to God, 200; as child's response to parents' anger, 128-29; as telestial behavior, 11, 33, 34, 120

M

Madsen, Truman, 45-46
Marie, 67-68
Marissa, 58-59
marriage: accepting victim role in, 62-63; blaming spouse for problems in, 120-27; equal partnership in, 84-86; establishing terrestrial boundaries in abusive, 64-74; persuasion stewardship in, 86-95; Proclamation on the Family on, 80, 90; putting God first in the, 90-91; telestial, 74-75, 77-78; terrestrial, 79-80, 84-86; victimization taking place in, 61-62. See also celestial marriage
marriage choices: celestial characteristics versus telestial mimicry in, 51-52; identifying patterns of behavior for, 54-59; importance of making good, 49-50; increasing challenges for making good, 51; questions distinguishing terrestrial from telestial, 53-54; recognizing red flags when making, 55-56; role of the Spirit in, 50; solid terrestrial foundation of good, 52-54; taking the time to make good, 56; "unequally yoked" issue of making, 57
"The Marshmallow Experiment," 9-10
"Martha syndrome" stress: description of, 139-40; slipping into the, 146; women, Patti Perfect, and, 140-43
Mary, 109
Matt, 69
Maxwell, Neal A., 21, 111, 170-71, 173, 190-91, 194
McConkie, Bruce R., 22-23, 167-68
McKay, David O., 172
"measure of our compliance," 166-67
meekness, 87
Melchizedek's Salem, 2
men: stewardship designations for, 80-83; terrestrial kingdom inherited by honorable, 5, 164-65, 168, 190; terrestrial marriage and equal partnership of, 84-86; terrestrial stress experienced by, 143-56; worthiness for the priesthood, 117-18. See also patriarchal order; women
Mike, 57
mimicry. See telestial counterfeits (or mimicry)
Mischel, Walter, 9
misery, 180-81
Mitch, 55
Monson, Thomas S., 149, 169
moral relativism, 122
Moses, 22
Mosiah II, King, 30, 31-32
Mosiah I, King, 30, 178, 182
motivation: factors contributing to, 176; fear as, 176-80, 185-86; law of the harvest, 192-94; misery as, 180-84. See also desire; life choices

N

narcissism, 123
natural man: as enemy to God, 172; harnessing the, 164; "on a good day," 51, 56; parental help for children's mastering of, 27-28; teaching children to control the, 101-3. See also telestial behaviors
Nauvoo, 105-6
Nehor, 179-80
Nephi, 157-58, 194
Nephites: destructive priestcraft practiced by, 179-80; elected judges government system of, 31-32; prophet-kings governing the, 30-31. See also Book of Mormon; people of Ammon
Nielsen, Midge W., 141

O

Oaks, Dallin H., 14, 46, 50, 149, 151, 165-66
obedience: as central to plan of salvation, 57-58, 63, 175; change through consistent practice of, 33-35; desire for, 185; feeling the Spirit through, 154; as first law of heaven, 25; measuring our compliance with, 166-67; required to correct telestial behaviors, 25-28; self-control required for, 8-9; to the unenforceable, 170n.15. See also willful disobedience
ox in the mire, 166-67

P

Packer, Boyd K., 3, 97-98, 114, 137, 146-47, 156
parable of the sower, 24
parable of the ten virgins, 45, 165-68
parenting: using both celestial and terrestrial laws in, 100-103; challenges in a telestial world, 97-99; enforcing terrestrial behavior rewards/penalties, 107-11; facilitating our children's agency, 111-12; focusing on concrete terrestrial behaviors, 103-6; permissiveness style of, 110-11; protecting children from telestial, 112-14
parents: balancing charity/victimhood with adult children, 67-68; disrespect of children to, 98-99; duty to protect children, 112-14; helping children to master the natural man, 27-28; responsibility for unrighteous children, 115-18; supporting safe relationships of children by, 70-71, 76; teaching children to control their appetites, 101-3; what God requires of us as, 114-18. See also children
patriarchal order: characteristics of the true, 80; equal marriage partnership under the, 84-86; telestial mimicry of the, 80, 81-82; understanding great blessings of the, 84-86. See also men; priesthood
"Patti Perfect" (Black and Nielsen), 141-43
Paul, Apostle, 23, 82, 83, 175, 194
people of Ammon, 182-84. See also Nephites
permissive parenting, 110-11
persecution, 71-72
persuasion: characteristics of, 87-88; cultivating qualities

Index

of, 94-95; example of what it is, 91-92; example of what it is not, 88-90; reproving with sharpness role in, 92-94; resolving disagreements through, 86-87
Pete, 58, 117
Peter, Apostle, 192
plan of salvation: counterfeit alternative offered by Satan, 29-30; obedience as central premise of the, 57-58, 63, 175; three kingdoms of

glory taught as part of, 4-6. See also The Atonement
Pope, Alexander, 18-19
pornography: addiction to, 120, 122, 124, 125; pain caused by, 78, 97, 100, 117, 123. See also sexual sin
premarital sexual activity, 129
priesthood: disrespect of Eli's sons for, 115-17; unrighteous dominion of the, 38-44, 80-81, 113; worthiness for the, 117-18. See also patriarchal order
problems: blaming the spouse for, 120-27; exaggerating terrestrial/minimizing telestial, 120-26; focusing on eliminating destructive, 126-30; ranking in order to address, 119, 120-26, 128-30. See also sin
problem-solving: forgiveness and, 132-33; identifying destructive behaviors for, 126-30; true contrition and remorse as part of, 130-32
Proclamation to the World, 80, 90
Psalm of Nephi, 157-58
punishment: fear of, 186; "time out," 108-9. See also consequences
pure knowledge, 88

R

Rachel, 123-26
Rebecca, 57
refining process, 189-92
relationships: accepting victim role in, 62-63; Doctrine & Covenants 121 advice on, 92-94; establishing terrestrial boundary lines to end abusive, 64-74; fear of damaging valued, 186; with Godhead members, 186-87; persuasion role in, 86-95; protecting children from abusive family, 112-14; telestial behaviors creating victimization in, 61-62
remorse, 130-32
repentance: apologies as part of, 131-32; change of heart and, 193-94; daily choices demonstrating, 181-82; fear motivating, 177-78
"reproving with sharpness," 92-94
responsibility: blaming spouse instead of taking, 120-27; of parents for unrighteous children, 115-18; for telestial behavior, 26
righteous judgments: Joseph Smith on making, 14; making intermediate, 14-16
Riley, 40

S

Sabbath observance, 166-67
safe dating/marriage choices: identifying patterns of behavior for, 54-59; importance of making, 49-50; questions to ask for determining, 53-54; recognizing red flags when making, 55-56; solid terrestrial foundation of, 52-54; taking the time necessary to make, 56; "unequally yoked" issue of making, 57
safety: from complacency, 4; establishing terrestrial boundary lines to create, 64-74; forgiveness following, 132-33; parental duty to ensure child's, 112-14; provided through the gospel, 3-4; from victimization in relationships, 61-76
Salem (Melchizedek's), 2
Sally, 65-66
Samuel, 115, 116-17
Satan: counterfeit plan offered by, 29-30; unrighteous dominion temptation of, 38-43
Scott, Richard G., 133
self-control: required for obedience, 8-9; teaching children, 101-6; terrestrial law characterized by, 8-10, 53-54; trenchwork of the terrestrial requiring, 24-25
"7 Deadly Days" (Time magazine), 139
sexual sin: adultery as, 66-67, 69, 119, 126-27, 131-33; premarital sexual activity as, 129. See also pornography
siblings: controlling contention between, 103-5; providing consequences to fighting, 109-10; sincere apologies between, 130-31
sin: deferred consequences of, 137-39; differences in degree of, 119, 120-26, 128-30; forgiveness versus tolerating, 63-65; God's zero tolerance policy concerning, 67; importance of not tolerating, 66-67; messages to children about degrees of, 128-29; moral relativism philosophy about, 122-23; need to eliminate from our lives, 176-84; sexual, 66-67, 69, 119, 126-27, 129, 131-33. See also problems; telestial behaviors
Smith, Joseph: crying out to God against injustice, 191-92, 193; on governing with correct principles, 105-6; on his personal journey of refinement, 190; the Lord's counsel on persecution to, 71-72; on making righteous judgments, 14; on the mercy of God, 15
Smith, Joseph Fielding, 90
"soap opera syndrome" stress: choices leading to, 137-39; description of, 136-37
societies: living celestial principles, 2; post-World War II terrestrial, 17-19
sons of Helaman, 183
sons of perdition, 200
Sorensen, David E., 64
stewardships: covenants on nature of, 38; designations for husbands and wives, 80-83; Doctrine & Covenants 121 on, 38, 41, 43-44; how Christ defined His own, 63; learning celestial pattern of, 43-44; marriage and persuasion, 86-95; of telestial counterfeit of unrighteous

dominion, 39-44
stresses: learning to evaluate and manage, 135-36; "Martha syndrome," 139-43, 146; our choices related to, 160-62; "soap opera syndrome," 136-39; terrestrial, 136-56, 160-62; "wilderness experience" of celestial, 157-59, 184
Sue, 181, 182
suffering: God's answer to Joseph Smith on, 191-92; Job's, 192; refining process and, 189-91; responses to, 188-89

T

Talmage, James E., 167
Tate, 67-68
telestial behaviors: abominations to God, 200; avoid subsidizing self-destructive, 68-69; consequences of tolerating, 62-63; description of, 33; establishing terrestrial boundary lines to end, 64-74; hierarchy for addressing problems of, 120-33; identifying consistent patterns of, 54-59; lying as, 11, 33, 34, 120, 128-29, 200; mistake of minimizing, 120-26; obedience required to correct, 25-28; pain caused by, 6-8; parental enforcement of consequences for child's, 107-11; people of Ammon abandonment of, 182-84; protecting children from parent's, 112-14; "soap opera syndrome" stress and, 136-39; struggling to effect lasting change from, 34-36; taking responsibility for, 26; victimization resulting from, 61-62. See also natural man; sin
telestial counterfeits (or mimicry): being fooled by people practicing, 36-38; change of heart required to reject, 35-36; distortion of patriarchal authority as, 80, 81-82; forms of government as, 30-32; good people deceived or victimized by, 32-33, 36-45; marriage choice based on celestial characteristics versus, 51-52; Satan's proposed plan as, 29-30; understanding pattern of deception of, 44; unrighteous dominion as, 38-43
telestial kingdom of glory, 4, 5. See also three realms perspective
telestial marriage: characteristics of a, 78; patriarchal authority distorted in, 80, 81-82; suffering misery of a, 77-78; temple covenant and an abusive, 74-75
telestial partner (or roommate): accepting victim role by tolerating, 62-63; blaming the victim for abuse by, 75-76; confronting violent, 74; description of, 6; establishing terrestrial boundary lines with, 64-74; pain caused by, 7-8; responses to terrestrial boundaries by, 73-74; victimization by, 61-62. See also abusive relationships
telestial realm: defining designation of, 77n.1; immediate gratification as driving, 7-8, 175; pain caused by living law of the, 6-8; summarizing characteristics of, 13
telestial world: barriers to making a temple marriage in a, 100; challenges of parenting in a, 97-99; differences between terrestrial and, 5-6; finding safety in our, 3-4, 6; growing dangers of the, 2-3, 16-17; societies living celestial principles in, 2
temple marriage: abusive relationship in, 74-75; telestial challenges to making a, 100. See also celestial marriage
temple recommends: basic interview questions for, 45; Truman Madsen's story on renewing his, 45-46
ten virgins parable, 45, 165-68
Teresa, 103
terrestrial behaviors: celestial traits built on foundation of, 52-54; ending abusive relationships through, 64-74; enforcing costs and payoffs of, 107-11; identifying consistent patterns of, 54-59; parenting to develop children's, 103-6; self-control or delayed gratification as, 8-10, 24-25, 53-54, 101-6; trenchwork of the terrestrial aspect of, 24-28, 64-65
terrestrial boundary lines: establishing safety through, 64-74; responses from offender to, 73-74; turning victims into agents through, 69-73
terrestrial kingdom of glory: avoiding trap of complacency, 2, 170-74, 184-85; honorable men who will inherit the, 5, 164-65, 168, 190. See also three realms perspective
terrestrial marriage: celestial marriage built on foundation of solid, 80; characteristics of a, 79-80; equal partnership in, 84-86
terrestrial realm: avoiding trap of settling for, 2, 170-74, 184-85; as bridge to the celestial life, 163-74, 184-92; defining designation of, 77n.1; distinguishing between good versus valiant life in, 6; parenting by using laws of celestial and, 100-103; self-control or delayed gratification law of the, 8-10, 53-54; trenchwork of the, 24-28
terrestrial societies: differences between telestial and, 5-6; post-World War II, 17-19
terrestrial stresses: avoiding the trap of, 160-62; Church program changes to reduce, 146-50; Church service callings and related, 144-46, 150-51; "Martha syndrome" and "Patti Perfect," 139-43, 146; potential traps related to, 143-44; simplifying Church service to reduce, 151-56
testimonies: development of personal, 53; Job's, 192; "testimony bonfire," 34-35. See also change of heart
theocracy government, 30
three realms perspective: on dealing with stress, 135-62; defining designations of the, 77n.1; hierarchy for addressing problems using, 120-33; overview of the,

4-6; parenting application of the, 97-118; to select companions wisely, 49-59; summarizing the individual realms of the, 13. *See also* celestial kingdom of glory; telestial kingdom of glory; terrestrial kingdom of glory

Three's Company (TV show), 19

Time magazine, 139

"time out" punishment, 108-9

Tolstoy, Leo, 78

Tom, 131-32

trenchwork of the terrestrial: "Can't Skip" principle applied through, 24-28, 64-65, 103-4; Tyler's growing understanding of, 26-27

Trent, 123-26

Trent family, 37-38

TV shows: Judeo-Christian beliefs of post-World War II, 17-18; moral decay evidenced in prime time, 18-19

Tyler's story, 25-27

U

Uchtdorf, Dieter F., 151

United Order, 32

unrighteous dominion: avoiding the telestial counterfeit of, 38-43; distortion of patriarchal authority as, 80-81; Doctrine & Covenants 121 on, 44, 113

unrighteous judgment, 14

V

victimization: blaming the victim for, 75-76; Doctrine & Covenants principle on, 71-73; establishing terrestrial boundaries to end, 64-74; forgiveness versus tolerating, 63-65; marriage and, 61-62; passive acceptance role in, 70-74; telestial behaviors that result in, 61-62; temple marriages and, 74-75; understanding difference between charity and, 67-73

victims: confronting violent offenders, 74; establishing terrestrial boundaries, 64-74; never blame the, 75-76; passive acceptance by, 70-74; terrestrial boundaries creating agents out of, 69-74; tolerating evil versus forgiveness by, 63-65; turning to inappropriate behavior themselves, 69

violent offenders, 74

W

war: as addiction, 183; people of Ammon rejection of, 182-84

wedding dress cover-ups, 44

Wendy, 88-90

"wilderness experience" stress, 157-59, 184

willful disobedience, 33. *See also* obedience

without guile, 88

without hypocrisy, 88

women: Martha syndrome, Patti Perfect, and, 140-43; patriarchal order and, 80-82; stewardship designations for, 80, 83; terrestrial kingdom inherited by honorable, 5, 164-65, 168, 190; terrestrial marriage and equal partnership of, 84-86. *See also* men

Y

Young, Brigham, 83, 165, 172-73

Z

Zion societies, 2

Scripture Index

Old Testament

1 Samuel 2:12 116
1 Samuel 2:29 116
1 Samuel 3:13, 18 ... 116
1 Samuel 8:2-3 116
1 Samuel 15:22 154
Job 13:15 192
Psalms 24:4 11
Proverbs 6:16-17 34
Proverbs 29:18 164
Isaiah 5:20 123
Isaiah 28:10-13 53
Isaiah 55:2, 1 161
Jeremiah 31:33 11
Ezekiel 36:26 100
Hosea 8:7 .... 7, 137,160

New Testament

Matthew 5:16 12
Matthew 5:46 138
Matthew 5:48 11
Matthew 6:33 11
Matthew 7:1 .... 12, 14
Matthew 7:14 185
Matthew 7:15 52
Matthew 7:15 37
Matthew 10:16 37
Matthew 10:34-37 .. 159
Matthew 11:21 130
Matthew 13:18-23 .. 24
Matthew 18:22 64
Matthew 19:6 90
Matthew 19:16-18 .. 169
Matthew 19:20 158
Matthew 19:20-22 .. 169
Matthew 23:24 122

Matthew 25:14-30 .. 38n.9
Matthew 27:46 193
Luke 10:41, 42 139-40
Luke 14:1-6 166
John 3:16-17 15
John 6:68 192
John 14:15 187
John 17:4 186
John 17:11-19 161
Acts 10:34 116
Acts 20:29 52
Romans 2:14 13
Romans 3:23 175
1 Corinthians 2:9 195
2 Corinthians 5:17 .. 11
2 Corinthians 6:14 .. 57
2 Corinthians 6:17 .. 157
2 Corinthians 12:9 .. 15
Galatians 3:24 22
Galatians 6:7 193

Galatians 6:9 194
Ephesians 5:22 82
Ephesians 5:22-33 ... 81
Philippians 4:7 11
1 Timothy 5:8 .... 38n.10, 78
Hebrews 12:3 192
Hebrews 12:6 189
James 4:4 157
1 Peter 2:9 100
1 John 4:19 187
Revelation 22:16 195

Book of Mormon

1 Nephi 17:13 .... 161, 195
1 Nephi 20:10 190
2 Nephi 2:2 159
2 Nephi 2:7 .... 184, 188
2 Nephi 2:15 188
2 Nephi 2:27 111
2 Nephi 4:17-19 157-58
2 Nephi 4:27 158
2 Nephi 4:31 46
2 Nephi 4:32 12
2 Nephi 9:6 14
2 Nephi 25:23 15,26,158
2 Nephi 26:24 63
2 Nephi 27:23 3
2 Nephi 28:7 160
2 Nephi 31:19 195
Jacob 4:14 155
Enos 1:23 179
Mosiah 2:36 25
Mosiah 3:19 .... 8, 25, 33, 45, 159, 164, 172
Mosiah 4:14 115
Mosiah 4:27 .... 85, 143
Mosiah 5:2 12
Mosiah 7:29 63
Mosiah 7:30 137
Mosiah 11:25 130
Mosiah 13:20-30 22
Mosiah 16:3, 5 25
Mosiah 27:26 11
Mosiah 28:4 178
Mosiah 29:13 32
Mosiah 29:16-18 32
Mosiah 29:17 30
Mosiah 29:25-27 32
Alma 1:30 12
Alma 5:12-14 35

Alma 5:14 .... 12, 158
Alma 12:12 138
Alma 12:24 193
Alma 13:12 11
Alma 24 183
Alma 25:14 183
Alma 26:31 13
Alma 36:9 178
Alma 36:11 178
Alma 36:14 178
Alma 39:5 .... 119, 129
Alma 41:10 137
Alma 42:10 106
Alma 42:15 14
Alma 42:16 177
Alma 42:19-20 177
Alma 42:25 14
Alma 45:16 .... 15, 122
Alma 57:21 12
Helaman 12:4-7 186
Helaman 11:23 12
3 Nephi 13:33 11
3 Nephi 18:29 118
3 Nephi 27:20 11
3 Nephi 27:27 67
Mormon 9:9 3
Ether 12:12 27
Ether 12:26-27 15
Moroni 7:17 30
Moroni 7:47 13
Moroni 7:48 158
Moroni 7:74 62
Moroni 10:32 15

Doctrine and Covenants

Section 1:31 .... 15, 67
Section 1:35 116
Section 4:2 145
Section 6:17 157
Section 9:7-8 50
Section 17:8 15
Section 18:31 15
Section 19:15-17 177
Section 29:39 188
Section 38:16 116
Section 42:42 .... 38n.8
Section 45:57 12
Section 50:27 136

Section 58:32 156
Section 58:32-33 150
Section 59:8 184
Section 59:23 13
Section 64:10 132
Section 75:29 .... 38n.8
Section 76:75 .... 160, 190
Section 76:75, 79 .... 165, 171
Section 76:79 168
Section 76:103 34
Section 82:10 .... 41, 63
Section 82:18 86
Section 84:25 22
Section 88:22 195
Section 88:22-24 4-5
Section 88:36,38-39 4-5
Section 88:99 164
Section 93:13 195
Section 93:36 2
Section 97:8 184
Section 98:12 195
Section 98:23-32 71-72
Section 104:16 145
Section 121 .... 41, 43-44, 81, 83
Section 121:1 191
Section 121:7-8 191-92
Section 121:10 192
Section 121:26 187
Section 121:34 38
Section 121:34-45 ... 81
Section 121:37 82
Section 121:39 .... 38, 83
Section 121:41 .... 81, 86, 87, 89
Section 121:41-42 ... 44
Section 121:43-44 ... 92
Section 132:7 75
Section 132:19 78

The Pearl of Great Price

Moses 1:1 80
Moses 1:39 63
Moses 5:1 143
Moses 5:10-12 80
Moses 5:13 106
Moses 6:49 106
Abraham 3:26 1

About the Author

Lili De Hoyos Anderson is a first generation American. Her mother is French and her father is Mexican. She grew up in the Midwest, moving to Utah with her family when her parents began teaching at Brigham Young University. She met Christian Anderson in high school and later married him when both attended BYU. She graduated with a bachelor's degree in Sociology just before the birth of their first child.

Dr. Anderson spent the next two decades as a full-time wife and mother of eight children. Having become converted as a teenager to the importance of her role as an at-home mother, she was surprised to feel a strong direction to return to school to obtain a master's degree in Social Work from the University of Nevada, Las Vegas (UNLV) and then to become a licensed clinical social worker. She later completed a doctorate in Marriage, Family, and Human Development from BYU, where she taught part-time for the School of Family Life for several years.

Dr. Anderson is an avid reader. She also enjoys sewing, music, quilting, making stained glass windows, and photography—none of which she currently has time for. She has published in the *Ensign* and various books and journals. She wrote her first book, Family Foundations, at the request of the BYU students taking her class on "The Family: A Proclamation to the World." *Choosing Glory* was also written in response to many requests to put these ideas on paper.

The Andersons have eight children. While growing up, they were affectionately referred to as the "Alphabet Kids" because their names are Adam, Bethany, Caitlin, Dominic, Eden, Faith, Graydon, and Harper. The family has lived in Oklahoma, Chicago, and, for fifteen years, in Las Vegas, where the Andersons mostly raised their family. In Las Vegas, Dr. Anderson taught both early morning seminary and two adult religion classes for several years. Her greatest love, after the gospel and her family, is teaching.

Dr. Anderson presents often at professional conferences and Church groups around the country. Favorite opportunities to speak include a devotional address at BYU-Idaho and pinch-hitting for the injured Glenn Beck at an internationally broadcast LDS Family Services Addiction Recovery Program Conference. She especially enjoys presenting with her husband, Chris, who is also a licensed clinical social worker.

The Andersons currently live in Draper, Utah where Dr. Anderson has a full-time private practice in individual, marriage, and family counseling. The Andersons are now collecting grandchildren and have sixteen, so far.

Dr. Anderson welcomes comments. She can be contacted through her website: lilianderson.com.